Emotional
TRIALS

Emotional
TRIALS

THE MORAL DILEMMAS OF WOMEN CRIMINAL DEFENSE ATTORNEYS

CYNTHIA SIEMSEN

NORTHEASTERN UNIVERSITY PRESS ■ *Boston*

Northeastern University Press 2004

Library of Congress Cataloging-in-Publication Data
Siemsen, Cynthia, 1953–
    Emotional trials : the moral dilemmas of women criminal defense attorneys / Cynthia Siemsen.
        p.   cm.
Includes bibliographical references and index.
        ISBN 1–55553–615–8 (cloth : alk. paper)—ISBN 1–55553-614-X (pbk. : alk. paper)
    1. Women lawyers—United States. 2. Defense (Criminal procedure)—United States—Psychological aspects. 3. Violent crimes—United States. I. Title.
        KF299.C7 S55   2004
        345.75'05044'0922—dc22   2003023139

Designed by Gary Gore

Composed in Electra by Coghill Composition Company in Richmond, Virginia. Printed and bound by Maple Press in York, Pennsylvania. The paper is Sebago Antique, an acid-free sheet.

MANUFACTURED IN THE UNITED STATES OF AMERICA
08 07 06 05 04   5 4 3 2 1

To my ballast, Dwight Francis Frey

Contents

Acknowledgments

The first place I turn to when opening a book is the acknowledgments section. I never cease to be amazed by the number and variety of people whose inspirations and labor stand silently behind a book's pages. I, too, owe much to a host of people.

Foremost, I am gratefully indebted to all the women criminal defense attorneys and the men of color district attorneys that most generously contributed their time to this research. I cannot identify you by name, but I acknowledge my respect for the vigilance with which you perform your job duties, and your thoughtfulness in reflecting upon your professions. I thank the twenty-seven of you for your patience in allowing me a view into your hectic work lives.

Then there are my criminal defense attorney friends whose names I can mention. Stephen G. Wright, thank you for our many years of friendship on and off the job, for your advice, and for your encouragement. How can I ever thank you for opening the doors to all of those jail cells? And to Samara Marion, the first attorney to encourage me to seek a university education back in our days at the "appellate annex" of the public defender's office and my first gatekeeper, thank you.

I am grateful for the mentoring I received from Marcia Millman. For the last two years of my doctoral work, Marcia insisted that I was writing a book, not a thesis. I thank her for changing my mind-set and for her faith in my ability as an ethnographer, writer, and sociologist. She is in every sense of the word my mentor, a wise and trusted teacher.

Another woman whom I admire greatly played a significant role. It was my fortune to be taught by Candace West. Anyone who has been lucky enough to work with Candace on a project knows that her standards of scholarship are high and that those same standards are matched by her generous engagement with the research process.

Several other professors from the University of California, Santa Cruz, inspired this research. This book was born in a sociological methods course. Dane Archer's enthusiastic response to a paper I wrote on the conflicts of being a woman working in the criminal justice system turned my graduate studies in the direction of social psychology, gender, and law. I thank Craig Haney for sharing his perspectives on feminist jurisprudence and the everyday work lives of women criminal defense attorneys. Craig Reinarman was influential in the conceptualization of this project. And John Kitsuse acted as a soundboard for my ideas.

I am extraordinarily grateful to Sarah Rowley, my editor at Northeastern University Press, for her continual good cheer and painstaking efforts to bring this book into production, as I am to my meticulous production editor, Emily McKeigue. And special thanks to Claire Renzetti of Saint Joseph's University for her detailed review of the full manuscript and accompanying suggestions, and to an anonymous reviewer who offered many helpful insights.

I appreciate the willingness of my colleagues at my new academic home—the California State University, Chico—to engage in dialogue on this project. In particular I express my gratitude for friendship, trust, and solidarity to Janja Lalich and Laurie Wermuth for wading through several chapters while they were writing their own books. Tony Waters also read and gave valuable comments on the theory chapter. And of course there is the Gumption Collective!

I thank Soroptimist International, Sierra Pacific Region; Jeanne Thomas, Dean of Behavioral and Social Sciences at CSU Chico; Kathy Kaiser and Tony Waters, Chairs of the Sociology Department at CSU Chico; Martin Chemers, Dean of Social Sciences at the University of California, Santa Cruz; and the Sociology Department at UC Santa Cruz for funding my research.

I also appreciate the support I received from the staff of Chico's Sociology Department, in particular Alison Dutro and Maureen Knowlton.

More than this, there are those loved ones who make life worthwhile. I want to thank my parents, Henry and Myrtle Siemsen, for their longevity genes, generosity, and pride. To my children, who have grown up thinking that it is normal to have a mother writing a book, Clark Jared Kaunis Maki and Ian Patrick Kaunis Maki: We did it! And to my husband, Dwight Frey, whose unflinching faith in me, inspired me to persevere in the final stretch, thank you from the bottom of my heart. I dedicate this book to you.

PART **I**

INTRODUCTION

1

Opening Remarks

There are occasions when we must wait until things are almost over before discovering what has been occurring.
—Erving Goffman,
   Frame Analysis

THIS book explores the work lives of women criminal defense attorneys who routinely handle cases that would grossly offend the sensibilities of the ordinary woman or man. Their work lives offer an intriguing opportunity to examine the social processes involved in an unexplored relationship between emotion and ideology. This book is about how women defense attorneys manage conflict, how they use ideologies in defense of their work, and how they deal with their emotional stress.

From years of work in a public defender's office, I knew that criminal defense work is rife with emotional and ideological dilemmas for all lawyers, and especially for women defense attorneys, whose number is growing. In 1980 women made up 26 percent of attorneys employed as legal-aid and public defense attorneys;[1] corresponding figures show that number grew to 45 percent by 2000.[2] These dilemmas may be intensified when women attorneys defend men accused of violent crimes against women to symbolically strengthen the defense. As defense lawyers, they are expected to represent their clients in the justice system. As women in the courtroom setting, often they are expected to defend publicly men's acts of violence against women. Still, the conflicts these women experience may not be the ones we as outsiders to their profession expect.

It is common sense to most people, and a fundamental tenet of the
social sciences, that social processes become most apparent in their extreme
forms. Extremity is also fascinating. For the sake of science—I am by train-
ing a sociologist—and that of personal interest, I began this study after
reading an extreme example of such moral conflict in a legal context:

> Last year I defended a man charged with assault and rape. He and the
> complainant were dance partners in a club featuring provocative "live
> dancing." She testified that the defendant appeared at her door late
> one night, forced his way inside, then dragged her into the basement
> where he viciously raped and beat her. The client said that he had been
> invited into the house for sex which was interrupted when the com-
> plainant's husband came home; it was her husband who beat her, not him.
>
> After more than a week of trial where emotions ran high for every-
> one the jury acquitted him. Afterwards, I met with jurors. One woman
> juror told me that she believed in his innocence because she was certain
> that I could not have fought for him in the way that I did had he
> committed that crime. . . . I later learned that he was arrested and
> convicted in two new rape/assault cases similar to the one I had tried.
> . . . [T]hat trial and that complainant still haunt me. I think of the
> horror described from the witness stand and I believe now that it is
> true. I think about the fact that the defendant left the courthouse a
> free man and returned to a community that pitied him as a victim and
> despised her as the victimizer. I think about the two women that were
> beaten and raped by him just a few months later. Finally, I think about
> my role in that.[3]

I began with the question, How can a woman attorney defend a man
who has raped another woman, especially if the attorney has feminist sensibilities? The women attorneys I interviewed were wary of the pejorative
question I posed initially and the negative assumptions behind it. By asking,
"How can a woman defend a rapist?" I implied an underdeveloped sense of
sisterhood. I kept hearing from the women that they hated that question
and that they heard it all of the time. For as novel as a sociologist or a
layperson might think the question, the women often heard it when they
first met a person or when they gathered for holidays with friends and fam-

ily. According to them, the question misses the point, as I too am coming to believe.

Here, examples of some of the women's reactions to my initial interviews and evolving questions will be helpful to explain why the emphasis of my approach changed. One of my first interviews took place in midsummer 1997 with a woman I call Pat Hardy. She is a twenty-year-plus veteran of a large urban public defender's office—someone I would call a seasoned woman defender. I was introduced to her by a well-known psychologist, who often gives expert testimony during the penalty phase of capital murder trials. As someone staunchly opposed to the death penalty, he tells the jury the life history of the defendant and all the reasons why this person is not the worst possible kind of human being, deserving society's ultimate punishment. The criminal justice system is a world divided by sides. Based on who introduced us Pat certainly considered me on her side—the defense.

When we first set up the interview, I told her only that I was writing a book on women criminal defense attorneys. When I asked her, "Have you ever struggled with defending a particular client because you're a woman?" she replied, "From my point of view do you mean, or from his?" I replied, "From yours," and Pat said, "No." Our conversation continued in the same laconic vein, leaving me frustrated:

> CS: How about the crime? [Have you ever struggled defending] a particular type of crime because you're a woman?
>
> PH: No.
>
> CS: Okay, do you consider yourself a feminist?
>
> PH: Yes.
>
> CS: And do you think that when a person, a generic person, becomes a public defender they need somehow to adopt a view that isn't consistent with being a feminist?
>
> PH: No.
>
> CS: Okay. Tell me about defending a case where there's been an act of male violence against a woman. What kind of stress does it add to your life? Is it any different?
>
> PH: I don't think so. No.
>
> CS: And so you aren't more anxious when those cases go to trial than other cases?
>
> PH: No.

What is interesting about this limited exchange is how different it was from the rest of the interview. Up to this point, Pat had been expansive in her answers. The subject seemed to irritate her as much as it frustrated me.

After the interview was over I asked her, "What kinds of questions were you expecting me to ask?" Her response was, "Well, I guess I didn't realize it was going to be quite so feminist slanted, how-do-you-represent-those-rapists kind of thing." Clearly Pat was defensive of her work role and annoyed by questions that seemed at odds with what she felt was the heart of her profession.

I found the women in future interviews more responsive if I asked, "How do you respond to people who question your work by asking, 'How can you defend that guy'?" The women opened up as the conversation steered away from the feminist ideological problem of a woman defending a man who is violent against women, and toward other ideologies, particularly those at the heart of the legal profession—such as the fundamental right to a fair defense.

A month and a half later I interviewed Annette Petroff, a young woman in the early stages of her career. When Annette distinguished between giving voice to her client and defending his crime, she gave an example of the interplay between ideology—in this case her views on feminism—and emotion:

> CS: Do you think that when you become a public defender, you adopt a view that's inconsistent with being a feminist?
>
> AP: No. I just think that it's separate. Defending people who commit crimes against women, or who are accused of committing crimes against women, I don't think it damages in any way feminism or its goals, or anything else. I think if anything it's supportive of it. Because if everyone doesn't get treated with the same constitutional protections, then it's defeating the role of feminism. It's to make it so that everyone's on equal footing. And along those same lines I think that everybody, no matter how guilty they may look, needs to get the best defense they may get no matter what the allegations are.
>
> CS: Do you think that when you worked on those cases [where a man had committed a violent crime against a woman] you ever had to compartmentalize your own personal beliefs and your public role to be able to do your work?

AP: Not my personal beliefs. If anything you have to compartmentalize to some extent maybe your own emotional reaction to the crimes because they can just be so horrendous, and there are victims out there, and it's just a very painful process for a lot of people. So I think that sometimes you have to compartmentalize your personal, maybe emotional, reaction to the crime in order to be able to focus on your job, but not beliefs really.

Not even a week later, I interviewed another woman in the early stages of her career, Darla Wilson. I was now asking the same questions, but indirectly:

CS: How do you respond to people who question your work representing criminals, especially if there's a sexual-assault case or a rape case, when somebody says to you, "How could you defend that guy?"

DW: God, you know, I hate those questions coming up. And they come up once a week. I'm at a party, I'm at a dinner or something . . . it's kind of too bad that I feel that way because I think that it's helpful—it's educational—if I can relax and explain. But I feel a lot of times like—and this is going to sound really snotty—but I feel like I'm dealing with people who haven't given any thought to the question. It's like they've had six beers and they go, "Ha, ha, you represent those people." I've got to pull myself out of my being relaxed at a dinner, go back to fundamentals, and it takes a long time. And then I feel like I'm giving some speech.

But I will engage in the subject, and I do explain what I've been saying today. I think everyone's entitled to representation, and it's a good system, and it's necessary. And I have to put my emotional response to the situation somewhere else. And that's what everybody really has to do about these things.

I think you have asked the question that I sort of find more engaging and more interesting, which is not "How do you represent those people?" but "Given that you're representing those people, is it difficult for you?"

I was making progress. The women were opening up to me more as the conversations steered away from the supposed feminist ideological conflict inherent in their work. Other ideologies (e.g., the right to representation) were at play in connection with emotional responses to their work. Six months later, in an interview with Gina Rossi, a woman in the middle of her career, the generic version of my original question emerged without my prompting. Again I closed the interview by asking if there were any questions Gina thought I would ask:

> GR: No, I'm just glad you didn't ask me that question that everybody asks: "How can you defend those people?" That is a question that just drives me absolutely insane! I hate the question. I just hate it. And do you know what? I don't have the patience for it anymore when I'm at home. I even get it at home sometimes! I get it a lot of places, even among people who are sophisticated, well-educated people, even lawyers. And I'm thinking, "You don't even have a clue." It just strikes me as odd, as how a lawyer could ask a lawyer that.

Even though I was not a lawyer, I realized I did not want to ask that question. As Pat Hardy's short yes or no answers in my first interview illustrate, it would never get me anywhere. I wanted to ask the more interesting question.

My question did not take long to change, but some people who have followed my project like to hold on to the intrigue of the original line of inquiry, no matter how much I tell them (and myself) that it is different. My choice to study women whose work by its very nature may put them in the public position of "betraying" their gender—and my own role in defending their voices—has sometimes led to negative responses from feminist scholars. They point fingers and raise analogies: somehow these women are to their gender in the late twentieth and early twenty-first centuries what Uncle Toms were to their race in the nineteenth century.[4] Perhaps I, too, am delving into an arena that turns our assumption of what women *should* do in the workplace—something that advances women—on its head. Like the woman quoted previously, I would be asked to think and rethink my position in telling their stories to the point that after reading my work a former sociological colleague accused me of suffering from my own "ideological blindspots." But as I asked her, what would we see if we looked at women defenders' work from their view? So, for the sake again of social science, personal interest, and now of self-protection, I chose to rephrase my question.

I should have seen my colleague's rebuke coming. A long tradition in the sociological study of work and occupations traced back to Everett Hughes concerns the attitudes and social relations of "good people" toward those who perform society's "dirty work" on behalf of the rest of us.[5] Within occupational hierarchies jobs at the bottom of the ladder get the dirty work. There is also a "moral division of labor" that reflects how moral functions differ for various members of society. Work tasks vary not only along lines of "knowledge and skill required, but in the social relations and social roles involved."[6] This frame of reference would have worked well had I emphasized society's negative view of the defense attorney's work role. In this instance, however, she might also be described as performing good work, noble work, or social work—even "the Lord's work." The moral division of labor for lawyers is indeed hierarchically arranged in the way Hughes identified. However, it is the good-works attorney who finds herself at the bottom of the heap. Looking from the standpoint of the person who might be described as performing dirty work reveals a theoretical contradiction.

Cynthia Fuchs Epstein established that a large proportion of women attorneys provide legal service for indigent clients, often choosing careers in government "because the expectation [is] that they ought to do 'good works.'"[7] Furthermore she found that women's trial work takes place primarily in criminal law because "the profession ranks criminal law as the lowest form of courtroom work."[8] I would argue that, for the woman defense attorney, it is her gender that makes others see her work as "dirty." Instead of asking how society looks at women who perform criminal defense work, I would rather ask, "What does the emotion work, in terms of ideological adjustment, demanded of women defenders tell us about the society in which we live?"

From the perspective of a social scientist, who is a woman, this question places me in the intriguing landscape of the emotion work of women willing to defend a man who has committed a sexual crime against a woman. Given that they are in this line of work, how do they do it? What they share is a willingness to defend their defendant, not the crime. The distinction between actually defending the man who perpetrates violence against women and willingness to defend him is situational. The similarity between willingness and situation is ideology. For me, the ideological-emotional makeup of the situation is the interesting domain of the woman who would, if asked, sit at the defense table with such a man.

As stated earlier, this book aims to address the understudied intersection of emotion and ideology. I do not expect that the majority of you reading this book are sociologists or sociologists in the making. In fact I hope that many of you practice criminal law or simply find the topic of professional stress relevant to your lives. At the same time, I strongly believe certain sociological theories and concepts illuminate the social processes involved in day-to-day criminal lawyering. In a very pragmatic way, then, the same tradition that informs my research and method serves as a lens through which to view this stressful career.

Ideologies are intimately connected to several social institutions with which we self-identify—for example, the family, religion, law, and work. My study focuses on women defense attorneys' emotion work that happens to occur in their world of work. The same processes of emotion work through idea adjustment and transformations in identity that we will see in the women defenders' stories can also be observed in other social contexts—for example, when someone marries into a family or converts to a new religion. In this sense the book's theory goes beyond the work setting and comprises both the work of a woman defender's job and the work of her managing emotions. We see two very different conceptions and levels of the word "work." At the structural level we have the work world of the criminal justice system, with its fortified systems of stratification—the sociology of work. At the psycho-social level we have the emotion work performed by participants negotiating life within that social world—social psychology. My theoretical concentration is on the latter to help explain the social processes of idea revision.

Certain foundational theories inform my research: Bennett Berger's concept of ideological work,[9] Arlie Russell Hochschild's notion of emotion work,[10] and Erving Goffman's understanding of moral careers.[11]

For the purposes of this book, ideological work is the activity of working through tensions that arise when our ways of viewing the world are challenged by competing values that come up in the course of our everyday lives. An example would be the woman defender who finds her profession conflicts with her feminism.

Emotion work refers to the conscious efforts of individuals to bring their feelings in line with the demands of a particular social context. For example, in court lawyers must convey competence through feeling rules that set limits on their emotions. When they behave according to the feeling rules established by their profession, their courtroom performances should go smoothly. But there is a "gendered" aspect of trial work; legal culture does not encourage the same range of emotional display for the woman defender as society at large. The difference between how she feels and how she is supposed to feel produces conflict.[12] I will argue that the disparity can be minimized or resolved through a combination of ideological work and emotion work that becomes increasingly sophisticated the longer she stays in her career.

A moral career comprises the common sequence of identity transformations individual members of a group undergo, such as those described by women defenders. I draw on these specific perspectives to help conceptualize the overlap between ideological work and emotion work in what I call "moral work." Ultimately, the woman defender's evolving use of group ideology as a strategy against the emotional content of her work reflects the lines of development that mark the progress of her moral career.

This theoretical foundation amounts to sociological *stare decisis*, my profession's version of legal precedence. The theoretically fainthearted or sociologically averse may wish to forego the following methodological and theoretical discussions and go directly to the core of these women's stories, in part two.

My interest in the rationalizations people rely on when the reality of day-to-day existence butts contradictorily into the wall of guiding beliefs began long before I was aware of the terms academics use to describe them. In 1978, when I was the lead legal secretary at a public defender's office, I was typing a letter for one of the attorneys—this was back in the days we were still using typewriters. The circumstances behind the letter were as follows. An emergency-room doctor had been subpoenaed to testify in a child abuse trial. The facts of the case were gruesome enough for me to remember more than twenty years later. The defendant had plunged his young child's hands into boiling water. The doctor's job had been to treat the nasty burns on the child's hands. His job became telling the jury just how awful those burns were. The attorney's job was to represent the father, whose actions were unconscionable.

By criminal trial standards, the defense attorney won. The jury found the father's actions to be the result of spontaneous anger rather than the willful intent to cause great bodily harm—the difference between a misdemeanor and a felony. The doctor wrote a letter to the attorney questioning the morality of a person who would defend such a monster. The response I typed was an eloquent statement of the duty of the criminal defense attorney to defend even the monsters in our society, a duty that the attorney found all the more difficult, since he had three small children at home. The attorney said the responsibility of a criminal defense attorney is as sacred as the healing of the child's hands. My memory of the letter is as vivid as if I had typed it yesterday.

My own dilemma began soon after the birth of my first child. By this time, I already had several years behind me at the public defender's office, working routinely on cases that, like the child abuse case, were far from victimless, including murders, rapes, and child molestations. My friends asked, how could the lawyers in the office defend some of their clients, and how—since my responsibilities were increasing—could I be a part of the process of defending them? A superficial answer came easily to me, the same maxim American children learn in grade school when studying the Constitution: People are innocent until they're proved guilty.

The problem began when I started to think of myself as a mother. I found it increasingly difficult to work on some cases, especially those involving children. Before, there was excitement, even intrigue, in the work. Each day when I went to work I was exposed to the stuff of mystery novels, crime dramas, and social deviance. But now I was asking the questions my friends asked me. I remember becoming more and more upset. I was at work, and my baby was in childcare, outside of my protection. For some reason, it seemed all the cases I was working on had child victims. One day I was transcribing a taped interview between a psychologist and a little girl who was an obvious victim of sexual molestation. Their conversation centered on her dramatization of the molestation with a set of dolls. The way this child spoke so matter-of-factly about what the defendant had done to her, where he had put his fingers on her body, and what sexual acts he asked her to perform on his—as if she had been describing how to tie her shoes— tore at my heart. The attorney on the case, recognizing how the tape affected me, offered to send it out of the office for transcription. Soon thereafter I avoided conflict by accepting a job working almost solely on the legal technicalities of cases on appeal, rather than continuing my earlier work, which focused more on pretrial discovery.

Still, I wondered how the women attorneys in the office could defend men accused of rape, considering that their appointments on such cases were consciously based on the impact their gender would have upon the jury. The incongruity of it all did not escape me, yet I rarely, if ever, gave a passing thought to the ways in which these women managed the contradiction between what I imagined to be their values as women and their interests as practicing defense attorneys.

Thus my decision to study women defense attorneys was an intellectual challenge and a pragmatic advantage resulting from my lived experience. My research question did not emerge miraculously: presenting this part of the research process in such a light would deny my subjectivity and standpoint. For nearly a decade I was a working member of the criminal defense world. I left to pursue my doctorate and came back as a researcher and, eventually, as a participant in that world again.

To present the research process as if it were outside of my experience would also deny my access to the gates and gatekeepers of women defenders.[13] The world of women defenders is a world not easily entered.[14] These women are skeptical of the questions people ask about their jobs. Going into the field able to say that I had a background in criminal defense work helped. I also had contacts with many defense attorneys who were willing to introduce me to their women colleagues. I began by interviewing the women my contacts introduced me to and then asked them to introduce me to others. Thus I utilized a "snowball" sample of one particular group. I would not limit the interviews to women who regularly represented men accused of violent crimes against women, because one thing I wanted to find out was what led them into their line of work. That question also implied an inverse one: What prevented them from taking on certain work?

Some might see the ideal study as a comparison of at least two combinations of gender and social category,[15] such as women defenders to their male colleagues. Certainly the public defender mentioned above who was the father of three young children had ideological and emotional conflicts in representing the client who put his toddler's hands in boiling water. Others might see the ideal study as requiring my total immersion in the community I wanted to study. Neither of these ideals was feasible: a broad study was beyond my individual means, and a larger comparison was at odds with my intention of an in-depth project; and I would never be the attorney representing men in sex cases. To offer a comparative perspective, I conducted interviews with men of color who are prosecutors (see the appendix). To inform my analysis, I again sought employment in criminal defense work, observed trials, and attended conferences for women defense attorneys.

I began by reflecting on my work, which increasingly diverged from my personal politics or identity as a new mother, and on my change in job duties to narrow the gap between the two.[16] This does not mean that I believe my personal politics are "correct," or that I am critical of the work women defenders do. I have much respect for both defense attorneys in general and for the women defenders I have come in contact with and their professional and personal convictions. I do not want this book to be interpreted as a negative judgment of their work. As someone who has spent a great deal of time assisting in such cases, I am sympathetic to the work they perform and the dilemmas they face. My subjectivity thus "ties into the integration of rational with emotional. Agendas are about goals and goals imply values. We do not simply choose a standpoint—we make a commitment to a group of people, we own a relationship with them. We let our anger and theirs lead us toward our priorities."[17]

My initial goal was to conduct interviews with thirty women defense attorneys. I also wanted to gather an ethnically diverse sample. However, well into the interviewing process I realized the lack of diversity in the women I was interviewing. As is common in the field of women defense attorneys, most of the women I was referred to were white.[18] Time also limited the number of interviews. To meet my interviewees face to face I had to travel considerable distances across several counties in central and northern California, the site of the study. Interviews usually took place in the women's offices, at restaurants, or sometimes both. The interviews lasted from one and a half to four hours. After I had conducted face-to-face interviews with eighteen women, I decided to use a phone interview accompanied by one attorney's videotaped reflection on her criminal defense work as my nineteenth and final interview. By this time several patterns were apparent in the interviews. I interviewed until the point of "theoretical saturation":[19] I found several themes and patterns that repeated themselves in these women's stories, and relatively few new categories were emerging in the data.

For close to two years I examined the work lives of women defenders. I use the term "women defenders" because this is the way the members of an association for women criminal defense attorneys in California, where my study took place, self-identify. The work lives of fourteen of these women are explored through each of their narratives in the book. Darla Wilson, Becky McBride, Emily Locatelli, Annette Petroff, Fran Jones, Meg Lowe, Kay Owens, Gina Rossi, Holly Porter, Rose Carr, Olivia George, Sally

Tan, Trudy Kaufman, and Vivian Gold took me into their worlds, and this book relates their everyday work lives to readers. (For each of these women I use a pseudonym to protect her identity.)

The women in my study ranged in age from thirty-three to sixty-one years (their median age was forty-three). Ten were married (of the specific women highlighted, these include Meg, Kay, Holly, Rose, Olivia, and Sally); four were in domestic partnerships (including Darla, Emily, Fran, and Vivian); five were single (including Becky, Annette, Gina, and Trudy); three self-identified as lesbians (including Darla, Emily, and Fran); fourteen self-identified as heterosexual (including Becky, Meg, Gina, Kay, Holly, Rose, Olivia, and Sally); and two chose not to reveal their sexual orientation (including Trudy and Vivian). Of the twelve mothers, two were single parents (including Trudy), and two were lesbians in domestic partnerships (Darla and Emily). The other mothers highlighted in the study include Meg, Kay, Holly, Rose, Olivia, and Sally. As noted before, most of the interviewees were white. One was African American (Holly), one was Asian American (Sally), and one identified herself as Native American (Olivia). Prior to the interviews, these women had practiced criminal law from six to thirty-five years, and averaging fifteen years. On average, each had taken thirty-eight felony cases to trial. All had been deputy public defenders at one time or another. Three had since gone into private practice (including Holly and Sally), two became law school professors (Emily and Trudy), and the rest remained deputy public defenders, although a few specialized in one area of public criminal defense. All but the two law professors were still actively engaged in criminal litigation. All of the interviews occurred during a single twenty-month period that ended during the winter of 2000.

My reputation in the community as someone who knew the various facets of criminal defense work, combined with my new status as a soon-to-be Ph.D. in sociology and my desire to reenter the legal field, led to consulting work on various high-stakes criminal cases. These ranged from a rape case where, if convicted, the defendant was facing a sentence of 300-plus years, to a case of vehicular hit-and-run where the defendant eventually pled guilty to maiming an Olympic bicyclist at the height of her career. In each case a male attorney needed a "woman's perspective" to aid in constructing a defense or a woman investigator to interview participants who were more likely to open up and give their version of events to another woman.

I was also appointed by the superior court to work for the defense as an investigator–social historian in a high-profile case where a young woman was facing the death penalty. Even though I observed several trials and attended conferences, those aspects of my research were secondary to the work I secured. My sixteen months in the field ended in 2000. Even though I did not work as an attorney, my background, observations, and self-reflections were advantageous in posing questions and analyzing the data for this project.

While I entered the study sympathetic to the work of women defenders, I still strove toward a detached and interpretive ethnography. Because of the need for honest responses, I went into my research promising confidentiality—all names have been changed—and intending to remain as unassuming as possible. Even so, I was worried about interpretations of my work as overreaching or even betrayal.

The glaring irony was that I was beginning a study on the resolution of gaps between personal beliefs and professional roles while I was keenly aware of my own. As a researcher studying women defense attorneys, I felt committed to presenting the meanings behind their voices in such a way that readers would not automatically assume that these women's standpoints were distorted.[20] I was especially sensitive to taking this approach considering the work defenders do. In the court system, the defense attorney is the defendant's voice. In this book I give voice to women defense attorneys. My conviction is to remain honest to their stories and meanings in the following discussion. At times I write that a woman "feels" a certain way or that she is "bothered" by something. In those instances the interviewee told me what she feels or what she is bothered by, though I may not present a direct quote. In other words, I make no claims to be clairvoyant.

My point of departure in this book is social interactionist, with a focus on culture:[21] women criminal defense attorneys construct a commonsense justification for the possible contradictions between their personal beliefs and their professional roles, and culture in interaction with their selves and others. This is a "theoretical assertion"—a term I choose carefully. While this book is not conceived as a project in hypothesis testing, I am also not a tabula rasa. My professional and personal experience in the criminal justice system and the theories mentioned earlier are the sources of my "theoretical sensitivity."[22] Aware of these sensitivities, I went about examining the interviews and my fieldnotes for themes. Using the logic of grounded theory, I constantly compared emerging categories.[23] A reader might conclude that I was involved solely in deductive, rather than inductive, analysis. The theoretical background in the second chapter was written, and its structure fully conceived, long after my last interview was completed. The emphasis on the criminal defense culture as a subsidiary of the criminal justice system is an important one. To quote Norm Denzin, "Culture, in its meaning-making and interactional forms, becomes a site of political struggle."[24] I would add that the criminal defense culture also becomes a site of social change.

A note on gendered dualisms in social science research: One of the first lessons I learned in studying sociological research methods was that the underlying assumptions a sociologist brings to her subject has an impact on her methodology. I will make my primary assumption explicit: I have a profound skepticism of dualisms (e.g., emotion/reason). How we theorize these gendered divisions constructs and transforms reality.[25] How we research them might also legitimate reality. Not wanting my research to merely legitimate reality, I based the framework for my research on the claim that the separation of emotional and ideological is artificial and useful in maintaining patriarchal relations.[26] Women's emotion, if thought of as belonging to the domestic realm or as part of a nurturing role, ultimately supports gender inequality. The type of study that glorifies or upholds women's emotionality or intuition over reason supports the dominant ideology, which serves gender inequality. In other words, our choices in studying women may in fact legitimate the system that oppresses women.

When sociologists study emotion work, they tend to study women. Likewise, men are the primary subjects when the focus is on ideological work. I have argued elsewhere that these tendencies reproduce gender inequities within the field of sociology and the wider social worlds it reaches.[27] My skepticism of dualisms, which helped me recognize the power of categories we apply to women and men in our research (i.e., how we research), reveals more than the assumption and theoretical assertion that I began my study with. Throughout this book, and in the appendix, I will focus on the interplay between the ideological and emotional components of both women's and men's thought processes. My purpose is to move outside the dualistic research box of studying women as performing emotion work, and men ideological work. Women and men, as I will demonstrate, perform both—and ultimately in combination, as moral work.

In retrospect, the extreme question I posed in my initial interviews was as good as any to launch my project. Even though I was a participant-observer in the criminal justice system, my connection to the social world of women attorneys was only by association, and my departing assumptions were off target. Yes, the women you will read about in the following pages have strong feminist sensibilities, though those sensibilities vary. At times they may rationalize their work in light of their particular feminism. But what emerged from the interviews is a picture of emotional stress, which was for the most part not about feminist ideologies in conflict with career ideologies. Rather, the stress arose from being a woman in a line of work that has been dominated by men until recently.[28] The longer a woman criminal defense attorney stays in this line of work, the better she gets at managing her emotions through ideological justifications.

A sexual-assault case is not necessarily the most difficult case for a woman defender to take on. She may for example find cases where her client is mentally ill to be more difficult. Sitting next to a man at the defense table who is a serial rapist may not disturb her any more than sitting next to someone who has committed an armed robbery. She may find delivering the "bad news" of a plea bargain for twenty-five years to life to that serial rapist the more disturbing aspect of his case. The phrase "twenty-five years to life" reverberates throughout these women's stories, most often in conjunction with California's three-strikes law (TSL).

March 7, 1994, is a meaningful date to all of the women I interviewed. All except two—both criminal law professors—were actively practicing defense attorneys in California when then Governor Pete Wilson signed into law California's version of a "three time loser" statute. America's growing resentment toward habitual criminals was evident in three-strikes-and-you're-out laws that were implemented throughout the United States in the mid-1990s. Washington State was the first state to pass a TSL in 1993. Since then the federal government and about half the other states have passed similar legislation. However, implementation in other jurisdictions has not brought about the same magnitude of sentiment and change as it has in California. California alone accounts for over 90 percent of all three-strikes sentences in the United States.[29]

Hostility toward repeat felons exploded in California after the Polly Klaas murder. In October 1993, twelve-year-old Polly was abducted at night from her bedroom in Petaluma, California, just north of San Francisco. For a month the girl's disappearance was the topic of nightly news, and her family's widely publicized search for the girl captured an outpouring of public sympathy. After weeks of search and dwindling hope, Richard Allen Davis was arrested in the case. Davis, a twice-convicted violent felon, confessed to sexually assaulting and murdering the young girl. He then directed authorities to her body. California was ripe for the three-strikes legislation signed by Governor Wilson five months later. The following November, 72 percent of California voters favored the complementary citizen's initiative Proposition 184, backed by the National Rifle Association and a California prison guards' union.

California has the largest prison system in the United States. The full impact of the TSL will not be realized on California's prisons until 2010 or 2015. However, the effect on defense attorneys is apparent in the case studies in this book. Some, like Lily Tate (who has practiced law for fifteen years), now see parallels between medical oncology and felony defense work. Like an oncologist delivering a fatal prognosis, she finds informing clients of their long sentences as the most unsettling aspect of her job:

LT: I view myself in a lot of ways as a doctor, in the sense that I'm presenting options to people who lots of times don't have very good options. And so we talk about what's the best way to go. "Should you try your case? Should you settle your case? If you settle your case, you'll get out some day." I've had conversations with people where I've had to explain, you'd better take life without the possibility of parole. Lawyers aren't comfortable having those conversations, and a lot of doctors aren't either. But sensitive lawyers and sensitive doctors can learn how to do that in a compassionate way. I learned a lot from [my oncologist friend] about how to talk to people about those kinds of things. People come to an acceptance of their situation at different times, and some people never accept it. Some people want no information, and some people want lots of information. Some people act out as a way to try to control what's a horrible situation for them, and some become completely passive and give up. Seeing the similarities between the two helps me step back when [clients] get angry at me. You know if you're a doctor treating a patient who's been given serious news, and they get angry with you, if you're any kind of professional at all, you can step back and say, "This is their reaction to the disease and not the messenger; I did not give this person cancer." Somehow as public defenders we have a hard time with that. We get ourselves involved in the message and the news, and they involve us in it. Clients treat lawyers really bad. And I really feel that over time I've become very effective at learning to work with people in a compassionate way so that I can still have a relationship with them when they're angry. But that takes a lot of time to get to that point.

California's defense attorneys find themselves in a unique position in delivering awful news to second- as well as third-strikers. Unlike other TSLs, California's allows sentencing enhancements for second felony convictions as well as for third strikes. A person is considered for a second strike if he or she has a prior violent or "serious" felony (e.g., residential burglary). Second-strike convictions result in minimum sentences of twice the standard sentence for the current crime, and, depending on the defendant's record, the sentence may be tripled. Persons with two or more "special-category" convictions qualify for third-strike sentencing enhancements. Unlike second-strike convictions, third-strike sentences are not determined by standard sentences for the third felony. Whatever the felony, the sentence is twenty-five years to life, with a minimum time served of twenty years.

In their study of California's TSL, Zimring, Hawkins, and Kaming see lawyers—defense lawyers in particular—as intermediaries between their clients and what may be regarded as extreme public sentiment that has resulted in excessive punishments.[30] Examples include the cases of a man who received a twenty-five-year sentence for stealing a piece of pizza; Leandro Andrade, who got fifty years for stealing nine videos from a Kmart; and Gary Ewing, who stole three golf clubs from a golf course and is now serving twenty-five years to life.[31]

None of this says that a woman defender does not grapple with conflict between her feminist ideologies and her work. But those conflicts are compounded by the changing political climate they find themselves working in. The years that women have been entering criminal defense work in California roughly coincide with the implementation of mandatory sentencing and the victims' rights movement, which drew heavily from both conservative and liberal politics. Women defense attorneys were caught somewhere in between.

I argue that a fundamental task of the woman defender is to narrow the gaps between her ideologies of identity, emotions, and role. I will explore the ways in which many women defenders use their views of feminism as an ideology that is not in conflict with the demands of their work. For them, feminism is a bridge, a justification for their role in a system that may seem to outsiders—especially women outsiders—at odds with their values as women. I will further assert that the woman defender develops a work ethic laced with professional ideology that enables her to negotiate her way through the emotional minefields of her job. Transformations in identity signal this development, which occurs over a long period of time. Ultimately, ideological work becomes part of emotion work. Ideological work may, in fact, be the most effective emotion work for a woman in this profession. The recognizable differences between emotion work and ideological work and their conceptual overlap in moral work are the subject of the next chapter.

In chapters three, four, and five I introduce the women and present their stories, through which I show how, in the early stages of their careers, these women are often driven by the notion that they can give voice to the underdog, who does not have a voice in society. However, as chapter three illustrates, they do not necessarily start work with those ideals. The emotional and physical toll their work takes becomes apparent. A clear pattern of emerging identities and evolving ideologies begins to appear. They come to use various ideals and emotion work strategies to defend against the emotional content of their work as the result of a developing moral career, beginning early in a period of identity formation.

As I proceed through the narratives, I find distinctive patterns of connections between emotions and ideology that occur at different times and stages in women defenders' careers. The implication is that a pattern—a longitudinal trajectory—is emerging. I argue that midcareer, as represented in chapter four, is a period of transformation. Using striking illustrations from their own stories, I show how the woman defense attorney undergoes the shift in identity that occurs with the transition to seasoned defender, normally accompanied by the challenge of handling a particularly repugnant case. Midcareer transitions and transformations result from situations in which usual emotion work strategies are no longer sufficient—these turning points hold the key to their career progression.

Women who have experienced midcareer transformations consciously drape themselves in the ideological mantle of their profession. When they realize that they can take on the challenge, their professional ideals are fortified, as are their abilities to manage emotions through those same ideals. In chapter five I show how seasoned women defenders came into criminal defense work keenly aware of the constitutional ideal of equality and the everyday reality of social inequality in the criminal justice system. These women see social change occurring at the level of ideas. They also recognize their public roles as key to the protection of individual rights. Driven by many of the same ideals they entered legal practice with, these women and their ideals have grown stronger over time. Their identities as women defense attorneys and their rigid adherence to the dominant ideology of their profession have been reinforced.

My goal remains to stay true to the voices of these criminal attorneys. In the long run, however, I own and am responsible for the analysis in chapter six.

Emotional energy generated in one context can become displaced and symbolically linked to other . . . contexts.
—Francis X. Sutton,
  The American Business
  Creed

2

The Reintegration of Emotion in Ideology

EARLY on in my project, I discussed my work with a colleague. I mentioned the connection between ideology and emotion that I noticed in one woman's reflections on her work. To that point, our discussions had centered on ideological work and its applications to my findings. The emotional content of my subject's "work" led me to ask, "Is this ideological work or emotion work?" My friend responded, "What are the differences between the two? I'm not so sure there are many, if any." I remember thinking, "Come on, one's emotion work and one's ideological work—they're different." Looking back, I appreciate the wisdom of that simple question and the direction it took me. Although the differences between the two are few, their nuances make those differences meaningful.

Much of my argument is based on the realization that the theorizing of ideological work overlooks emotions and that the literature on emotion work minimizes the role of ideology in resolving emotional clashes. Thirty years ago Clifford Geertz called for a conceptualization of ideology as the "symbolic outlet" for emotional conflict. Bennett Berger, whose idea of ideological work was influenced by Geertz, did not incorporate emotions. Arlie Russell Hochschild made the major advance in this direction by addressing ideology's relationship to emotion work. Limiting the theoretical background to these theorists would ignore significant recent contributions on ambivalent identities, ideological work in law, and gender and emotions in the justice system. A discussion of authors who have contributed to this field and of Erving Goffman on moral careers will complete this brief theoretical chapter.

IDEOLOGY AND IDEOLOGICAL WORK

The popular definition of ideology is associated with groups on the political spectrum. People are referred to as Marxist ideologues, or as left- or right-wing ideologues, even as feminist ideologues—meaning that their response to an issue is believed to be predictable and consistent with their political perspective. To say that someone is "ideological" is to imply that their immediate emotional responses to a situation are filtered through their political beliefs. The current implied meaning of being ideological is, then, to be removed from one's senses or one's direct experiences. This connotation is vastly different from the original definition of ideology. The purpose of this section is not to trace the intellectual lineage of ideology as a concept.[1] I will instead concentrate on theorists who explore the conflictual nature of ideology.

In *Ideology and Utopia* Karl Mannheim exposed two distinct meanings of ideology—the "particular" and the "total." The particular conception of ideology is connected to an individual's self-interests and thoughts; the total conception is the thought system of the whole group, which goes beyond particular individuals' experiences. All thought is grounded in social and life circumstances: "The ideological element in human thought . . . is always bound up with the existing life situation of the thinker. . . . We need not regard it as a source of error that all thought is so rooted."[2] To study ideology is, then, to explore the interplay of the particular view of the individual with the total social process. This implies a potential for conflict due to individuals' real life circumstances and how they would wish them to be otherwise, based on the ideas of groups they identify with.

Clifford Geertz pointed out that social scientists have failed to look at ideology as anything more than the total thought system. In his essays *The Interpretation of Cultures*, Geertz suggested that to study ideology as a separate, total entity apart from the individual thought process risks a pejorative view of the person who is deluded by the ideas of the powerful—not unlike the popular connotation of the term. To account for individual motives we should look to ideology as a "'symbolic outlet' for emotional disturbances" because "ideology bridges the emotional gap between things as they are and as one would have them be."[3] The problem, however, lies in how social scientists approach the ideological-emotional connection:

> How . . . ideologies transform sentiment into significance and so make it socially available is short-circuited by the crude device of placing particular symbols and particular strains *side by side* in such a way that the fact that the first are derivatives of the second seems mere common sense [and there is] very little idea of how the trick is really done.[4]

In effect, Geertz calls for a conceptualization of ideological work with an emotional component. The "trick" may not be identified without uncovering how people resolve clashes between ideologies and subsequent emotions.[5]

Bennett Berger's ethnography on the relationship between hippie ideals and communal life was influenced by both Mannheim and Geertz.[6] In *The Survival of a Counterculture*, Berger also looks to the relationship of ideas to the social context. Like Geertz, he wishes to explore how a "trick is done." In Berger's case, however, the trick is how people resolve, cope with, or reduce tensions when their beliefs contradict their interests or when the requirements of their everyday lives are at odds with their beliefs. Resolution, coping, or reduction occurs when ideas or contexts are changed or rethought. Thus Berger emphasizes the rational component of ideological thought. Still, he suggests that the reified nature of ideology in the form of cultural rules does not explain the ambiguities that arise in day-to-day life. Rigid ideological notions are never so neat when put side by side with the unanticipated situations we find ourselves in. Examples Berger gives come straight from the Judeo-Christian tradition: "'Thou shalt not kill' requires interpretation to be applied in war or self-defense or defense of others— although the authoritative source of that particular commandment does not state it contingently."[7] Not everyone is a Talmudic scholar or a theologian, and not everyone can perform the trick of taking a fixed idea and interpreting it to meet the requirements of an ambiguous situation: but ideological work requires just that. However, ideologies are rarely so fixed as a commandment. Berger describes the need for manipulation of ideology in everyday life, in which beliefs become "workable":

> The empirical study of interaction in real communities enables a re-
> searcher to see in microcosm the ways in which the practical pressures
> of daily life do or do not affect the beliefs that groups bring with them
> to that life . . . either by sustaining them and strengthening them or by
> modifying or undermining them through experience that "tests" their
> workability; that tests, in effect, the meaning of what people believe
> they believe they believe . . .[8]

In short, people come to understand their beliefs while working through
tensions between the ideas they bring to a situation and the pressures of
that situation. If tensions remain, either the ideas require adjusting, or the
circumstances need to be changed.

Despite the emotional demands Berger's communards faced while living out their communal vision (e.g., coping with group marriage, dealing
with drug use by children), he sees "feeling work," as analogous to ideological work.[9] In feeling work, as he describes it, there is a discrepancy between
feelings and beliefs. Inappropriate feelings are consciously or unconsciously
controlled through feeling rules. Feeling rules are as potentially abstract and
reified as moral dictums. Following Berger's propensity for citing biblical
injunctions, what is "love your neighbor as yourself" if not a feeling rule?
As beliefs need adjustment in ideological work, so do feeling rules in emotion work. Included are the beliefs and feeling rules of particular professions.

While Berger's sociological analysis is of groups, in his reflexivity on his
role as researcher he offers an example of the ideological work of a professional. The professional ethic of sociologists includes an approach to research that has taken the forms of objectivity, value neutrality, subjective
reflexivity, and "analytic detachment." Berger found the need to protect
himself from the passionate arguments of the communards in favor of a
utopian existence that called into question much of what larger society held
near and dear with respect to marriage, family, and child-rearing practices.
Even as I was worried about future interpretations of my own work as betrayal, it was disconcerting to read Berger's statement on the ideological
dilemmas of his own fieldwork:

> The ethnographer neither sees nor interprets the same ways that parti-
> cipants do, even when phenomenological Theory and Method constrain
> the ethnographer to try; and adherence to the validity of my own per-

ceptions, I imagine, could be maintained only at the probable cost of discounting theirs.[10]

At the same time, it was reassuring to know I was not alone in my fear or in the practical understanding of the utility of ideological work:

> The very concept of ideological work, which looks for the meanings of beliefs in the social situation of those who believe them, functioned as an ideology for me, lending legitimacy to my detachment and honoring my identity as a social scientist studying the meanings of culture.[11]

The relationship of ideology to individual subjectivity emerges in Berger's work, albeit through self-reflection, with the added dimension of identity reinforcement. Berger recognized the potential for conflict when his personal values were called into question and negotiated his way through it by embracing his professional identity and practice. Therein lies the connection to the group. Ideological contradictions are exacerbated by the different ways we identify ourselves, especially when our self-identities oppose one another.[12] We need to consider what happens when our conflicting identities draw us in opposing emotional directions.

Michael Billig bifurcates the term ideology in a manner similar to Mannheim's "particular" and "total" conceptions. "Lived ideology" is the common sense of everyday thinking—what we might think of as culture, or a society's way of life. "Intellectual ideology" is a formalized system of ideas, for example, the legal code. Ideological dilemmas occur when the informal and formal expressions conflict: "The head of the lived ideology and the heart of the [intellectual] ideology may pull in different directions."[13] We need to take into account the orientation of the subject—that is, what they value more, the lived or the intellectual. The more equal the value, the more emotion work that needs to be done. Though the source of ideological dilemmas is not limited to conflicts between the lived and the intellectual, the differences between the two suggest conflict for professionals.

So what is ideology? First, ideology is always grounded in the social and lived experiences of groups and individual members, whether they be hippie communards or women defense attorneys. As Raymond Williams puts it, "Our way of seeing things is literally our way of living."[14] To provide a definition of ideology that accounts for the emotional component it is necessary to recognize that there are two sides to the term. The first side of ideology is the patterned set of ideas that shapes the thoughts of members of a group. In its more concrete form, it is represented in the practices and modes of discourse of the group (hence, sociology's tendency to latch onto this side of the definition). The second side is less concrete. It is the medium through which members of a group reason, make sense of, and rationalize their lived experiences. In this sense, it is the symbolic outlet for emotional disturbances generated by conflicting ideas. The first side constitutes the lived experience of groups; the second is the nature of subjectivity. We live and act through ideology, pointing to its creative and emergent quality. While ideologies represented in more concrete forms may appear coherent, they are always being formed, contested, and reformed. As Williams says, "The offering, reception and comparison of new meanings [leads] to tensions and achievement of growth and change."[15] Whether at the level of the group or the level of the subject, the process suggests ideological work.

And what is ideological work? At the level of the individual, ideological work is belief and, I will argue, identity formation (in Berger's formulation, *how we come to believe what we believe we believe*). Ideological work may include various techniques of idea adjustment (including apology, reconciliation, justification, and rationalization); however, it is not solely about logic and argument. We need to consider what happens just when our conflicting identities pull us in opposite emotional directions: the legal setting is an ideal site for study.

LAW AS IDEOLOGY

When taken together, criminal cases that are filed, their pretrial dispositions, and trial outcomes represent politics practiced at the everyday level. How we got to this understanding of law is the stuff of critical legal studies (CLS) and feminist jurisprudence. These fields are not presented as an explanation for the actions of particular individuals in this book, but rather to show the importance of the legal site to a study of ideological conflict.

The American critical legal studies movement takes to heart the "idea that general concepts in legal doctrine do not determine [case] outcomes."[16] CLS writers view legal doctrine as a sort of mystification: case outcomes are not concrete because legal ideas are so malleable. There is not just one possible outcome in a case. The wide variety in possible outcomes is related to the number of ways possible interpretations can be rationalized and "by the political context in which the interpretations are being offered."[17]

Taking a clearly sociological approach, CLS writers argue that legal doctrine is closely tied to our social construction of reality; it helps to order our social life. Legal doctrine even gives us certain categories of thought (e.g., justice, property, and crime) and legitimates social relationships we think of as "natural" or somehow come to accept (e.g., family, employer/employee, corporate dominance, and uneven power relationships). Legitimization of these relationships occurs through the general acceptance of an "idealized" model of law.[18] In the Weberian sense, this is legitimate authority in its most effective form. Ultimately, power is based on the capacity to use violence, as is legal power, and works best through consent.[19] Through the acceptance of the idealized model of law, the many consent to their social position in a legal order dominated by the few. Part of the contradiction is that law can also be just and can serve the powerless. Law is not always determined by the powerful. According to CLS, the one constant to law is that it is politics practiced by humans in robes.[20] Law as politics is also a point of departure for feminist jurisprudence.

Catharine MacKinnon defines feminist jurisprudence as "an examination of the relationship between law and society from the viewpoint of all women."[21] Taking politics a step further than critical legal studies, feminist jurisprudence is theorizing as a political activity. MacKinnon's critique of a gendered legal system is that sexual inequality is universal. To understand how sexual inequality affects law, we must first define women's interests as their fates bound together.[22] If gender inequality is universal, then law is politics divided, but heavily in favor of men's power.

MacKinnon suggests that women who do not adopt the feminist view are "passing" for men.[23] I find that statement to be less interesting than MacKinnon's underlying argument, one that is not that different from the critical legal studies writers' or, for that matter, Weber's. If we accept MacKinnon's thesis that heterosexual sex implies possession of the woman by the man, consensual sex (i.e., "rape" not by force) is the most efficient way for men to maintain power. By using the extreme example of rape, MacKinnon illustrates that ultimate power is based on the capacity to use violence. By accepting the male model of law, women consent to their social position in a legal order dominated by men. Of course the majority of women in this book would disagree. They would, instead, say that their presence in the criminal justice system helps to unmask the reality of the legal order and its gendered politics. The failure to unmask the relations would be to consent to the male model.

Feminist justice requires change, not theorizing. If law is a reflection of norms that reflect man's dominant views, there needs to be a change in the relationship between gender and law. The traditional enterprise of legal doctrine is to make law neutral—to separate morality from politics and morality and politics from judicial decision making. But—in line with the critical legal studies writers' position that "existing law is not neutral,"[24]— "the demarcations between morals and politics, the personality of the judge, and the judicial role, bare coercion and the rule of law, tend to merge in women's experiences"—including those of women defense attorneys.[25]

If what CLS does best is to demystify, then the continued project of feminist jurisprudence is the demystification of the way law legitimates, maintains, and retains men's power in society. Unfortunately, discussions of law as ideology amount only to theorizing: they do not take us far enough.

Is law a social construction? More important, is a complete separation of law, morality, and justice for the common good? What the contemporary theories do not adequately address are the assumed inequalities built into the legal system. Critical legal studies and feminist jurisprudence move in the right direction through the recognition that law is political and gendered. But the notion of justice remains highly philosophical for a social science that seeks legitimacy through empirical study.

Perhaps society must retain some of its cultural myths about justice in order to reduce the gap between the logic of legal ideology and the feelings of experienced reality. That is what my study of women criminal defense attorneys is about.

IDEOLOGY AND EMOTION WORK

That feeling and logic are not at odds is explicit in Arlie Russell Hochschild's perspective on emotion management. Using Berger's formulation, the analogous relation of ideological work to emotion work lies in the comparison of what must be qualitatively dissimilar—*how people come to believe what they believe they believe* to *how people consciously try to feel*. My interest here is not in word games; I use the formulation only to get closer to a theory that accounts for how people alter their beliefs to make them consistent with what they try to feel in relation to their social context. Hochschild's perspective sets the theoretical course in that direction. The following is a roadmap to her theory.

> Emotion . . . can be and often is subject to acts of management. The individual often works on inducing or inhibiting feelings so as to render them "appropriate" to a situation. The emotion-management perspective draws on an interactive account of emotion. . . . it allows us to inspect . . . the relation among emotive experience, emotion management, feeling rules, and ideology. Feeling rules are seen as the side of ideology that deals with emotion and feeling. Emotion management is the type of work it takes to cope with feeling rules.[26]

For Hochschild, emotional life is not a completely passive experience; "to some degree" the individual deliberately manages his or her feelings. Emotional life is also not completely internal to the individual; through interaction with the self and with others a person sets up an "emotion-work system" that includes emotion work "done by the self upon the self, by the self upon others, and by others upon oneself."[27] Emotional life does not equate to nonconscious life, either; emotion work refers to the cognitive attempts of the individual to bring his or her feelings in line with the social context. There are two "broad" types of emotion work: "*evocation*, in which the cognitive focus is on a desired feeling which is initially absent, and *suppression*, in which the cognitive focus is on an undesired feeling which is initially present."[28]

To this point, we have examined the flexibility of emotion much like those who study the malleability of ideology—in relationship to the actor's appraisal of his or her feelings in a particular social situation. We can say that not only is "the ideological element in human thought" rooted in social circumstance,[29] but also the ideological element is rooted in emotional thought. Just as ideological thought is connected to class position, emotional reasoning is part of a general pattern presented by society to shape emotional thought in accordance with the individual's position in the social structure.[30] The connection is found in the hierarchical nature of emotion work and in feeling rules. While we are not necessarily concerned with the successful management of feeling, how well a person is able to manage his or her feelings is connected to knowledge of what is appropriate behavior in a given situation for his or her social group. Occupationally, knowledge translates into a reproduction of class and gender hierarchy.

Hochschild makes clear the ideological character of feeling rules for the group she studied (flight attendants). Knowledge of feeling rules and the appropriate accompanying expressions of emotions implies group membership and shapes and constrains the emotions of individual members. At the individual level, we are constantly involved in managing feelings through these rules. They limit the range of acceptable feelings in specific social situations by creating a zone of permissible emotions. But what about competing ideologies that result from multiple group memberships—for example, competition between the guidelines for feeling in one situation and the guidelines for feeling in another or the competing guidelines for feeling within a single situation?

Hochschild describes an individual's change in ideological stance as the dropping of "old rules" and assumption of "new ones."[31] But is changing an ideological stance as easy as dropping old rules for feeling and adopting new ones? A person's ideology is connected to his or her identity: emotion might alter ideology along with identity. What is more, there can be situations—such as those the woman defender finds herself in—in which multiple feeling rules will collide and multiple identities clash. We will go a long way in figuring out how "ideologies transform sentiment into significance" by examining the emotion work it takes for feeling rules, ideologies, or identities to become dominant.

Now I return to my friend's question: What is the difference between emotion work and ideological work? The former deals with the more concrete side of ideology, the latter with the more abstract side. In the concrete form, ideologies are formalized practices: social institutions and feeling rules can be thought of as expressions of ideology. At the individual level, we are constantly involved in managing feelings through feeling rules. That is what Hochschild's perspective explains—*how people try to feel*. At the individual and the group levels, we are continually involved in the logical process of constructing and reformulating ideologies, not only managing our emotions through feeling rules. The process is exacerbated when ideologies conflict or collide. The resolution of that conflict is Berger's notion of ideological work—*how people come to believe what they believe they believe*.

The theoretical juncture I explore in my study of women defense attorneys is where the abstract and concrete sides of ideology intersect—*how people adjust their beliefs to make them consistent with what they try to feel*. It is at this juncture that idea adjustment becomes the symbolic outlet for emotional conflict. The process is not independent of identity formation, transformation, and reinforcement of self as illustrated in the moral career of the woman defender.

IDEOLOGY, IDENTITIES, AND EMOTIONS
IN THE JUSTICE SYSTEM

Robert Granfield and Thomas Koenig use the paradigm of ideological work to explore the conflicts and ambivalence Harvard Law School students experience when their personal values conflict with those of their elite institution.[32] During the process of reconciling contrary values, forming new meanings with their selves and others, a coherent identity emerges, and there is an end to personal conflict. While these authors emphasize the total thought system of the group, the interactional quality of ideology is explicit. Ideology becomes the medium through which day-to-day life becomes meaningful. To put it another way, the ideological dilemmas inherent to law school are the subject of Granfield's and Koenig's studies—the conflict between an elite law school's goals and the personal values students bring to that organization. However, law school is not just about ideologies. Emotions connected with personal values also require resolution in order for one to redefine oneself as an elite lawyer.

Debra Meyerson and Maureen Scully argue that persons who do not adopt the dominant culture of their organizations face pushes and pulls between their personal and professional identities. The result is ambivalent identities for people who challenge the status quo of an organization "just by being who they are."[33] A problem arises when persons who manage multiple identities are suspected of hypocrisy.[34] Because their credibility is at stake they may be required to give up one group's position. A possible result is that they will hold emphatically to their profession's ideology. The implications for a woman defender could be damning. Her role might be interpreted as reproducing patriarchy.[35] Or by embracing the dominant ideology of her profession she might be selling out to its traditional masculine model.[36] Such interpretations are conducive to a framework that focuses primarily upon the gendered lines in the division of labor.

Everett Hughes's theory of the "straw boss"—akin to an Uncle Tom—offers one way to view the moral positioning of these women. As long as racial lines exist in the work world, the argument goes, Black middlemen perpetuate the system by acting as liaisons between management and workers. According to Hughes, "Like the straw boss, women can fill positions in the society which permit the stratification system to work more smoothly."[37] Such formulations do not get us very far in thinking about changing the system from within.

I will argue that the woman defender's role puts her in a unique position to produce institutional change. She might also be termed a "tempered radical,"[38] someone who identifies with her profession at the same time that she recognizes that the criminal justice system reproduces gender (and racial) inequalities. As an "outsider within"[39] her organization, the woman defense attorney may be a critic of the status quo and of radical change even while she advocates both. Still this participation with others' ideologies suggests the adjustment if not the forfeiture of an individual identity.

The goal of the tempered radical is consistent with the argument of Lani Guinier and her colleagues in their study of women law students: The University of Pennsylvania Law School, as a "formerly all-male educational [institution] cannot . . . take advantage of difference without changing from within."[40] The study suggests that the increasing presence of women in law school can result in the abandonment of a culture that embraces emotional detachment. Another reading is possible, one consistent with Jennifer Pierce's ethnography of the legal world. As part of larger institutional and social contexts, behavior and "gender-specific identity" must be analyzed in relation to structure. Gender in this reading is not limited to behavior that one does, it "is a principle of organization and an aspect of identity" that locates one within the organization.[41] In other words, lawyers are not only bound by their gender-specific identity, they are bound by their gender-specific location within the job.

Susan Martin and Nancy Jurik discuss the double bind of the woman attorney: when aggressive in court, she risks being labeled too adversarial; when kind, she may be considered incompetent.[42] "Doing gender" in this context can be considered appropriate or not.[43] The justice system is a reflection of the larger social structure that locates individuals along the lines of race, class, sexuality, and gender. The woman working in this system works in a professional climate that perpetuates the gendered division of labor, its gendered power relations, and the cultural rules concerning masculinity and femininity.[44]

This culture defines appropriate emotional displays for women differently than the larger society. In terms of psychological health, the downside of performing this emotional labor results from unresolved contradiction between her behaviors and her feelings.[45] The upside comes with "an estrangement between self and work role that comes at the expense of the work role"—this is especially the case when workers lack autonomy.[46] But what are the possible consequences of performing emotional labor when a woman's profession gives her some autonomy. Is it an estrangement between self and work role that comes at the expense of the self? Or is it possible that sustained performance of emotional labor that transforms self-identity and work role might be psychologically healthy for the woman defender—as well as for the larger criminal justice system?

MORAL CAREERS AND MORAL WORK

Erving Goffman describes moral careers as two-sided, connecting the individual self to his or her position in the larger structure.[47] They are "moral" in the sense that they represent the norms of a group at a particular time. Moral careers share natural history; over time members of a social group undergo similar developmental changes in their selves and their framework for judging themselves and others. Their sequence of development can be traced by examining those specific points when individuals change the way they view themselves and the world.

The term can describe both an individual woman's professional path and the course she shares with other women criminal defense attorneys. The defense attorney constructs her new identity by taking into account self-judgments and perceived judgments of others in her social group. She presents an image of self that is consistent with and defends the moral values of her profession. The woman defender's evolving use of group ideology as a strategy against the emotional content of her work reflects the lines of development that mark the sequence of her moral career. This is her moral work. Furthermore, because her corresponding self is expressed at any given time through those same ideologies, by identifying her current dominant ideology in comparison to other women defenders we can recognize also the stages of her identity formation, transformation, and reinforcement.

The narratives that follow explore the ways in which many women defenders adapt their feminist ideology to the demands of their work. They illustrate the development of a professional ideology that helps women defenders survive their emotionally stressful work. While the data are cross-sectional, they still indicate that the longer a woman stays in this line of work, the better she gets at managing her emotions through ideological justifications. Like other moral careers, those of women defenders are marked by a sequence of changes in identity. Three phases in the line of development that correspond to number of years in practice are identified strictly as a heuristic device to further understand their moral work: identity formation—early career (one to ten years); identity transformation—midcareer (eleven to fifteen years); and identity reinforcement—the seasoned woman defender (sixteen-plus years). I suggest that distinct strategies of emotion work are connected to these specific phases.

Career trajectories are never so neat that all women defenders will move through the same phases in the same way. A flaw in the moral-career framework is that it overlooks individual life histories and cohort effects. The women in the study are situated in their individual histories and distinct generations, and their ideologies are influenced by different political periods. The combination of these effects will be noted.

PART

THE NARRATIVES

Sometimes I feel like we're looking at sort of the underbelly of life, the most depressing part, so much ugliness, so much pain, screwed up lives, and nobody being a winner. It can be very depressing and sad, and heavy. Very heavy.
—Becky McBride

I have pretty strong feminist beliefs but I think more than that I take my duty to my client very seriously, and that's in part because in my mind what happens with criminal defendants is there's this huge well-financed machine that's grinding them down. It's the judges, it's the probation department, it's the district attorneys office, and in this county it's the taxpayers just all coming down on them at once. And it's that person and myself against this huge machine and it's important that I be there for them, and listen to them, and try to tell their side of the story, and that requires me to disregard my own individual beliefs about their treatment of women.
—Darla Wilson

I do think that when you become a public defender, you adopt a line, and you live with it. And that's why you'll find a lot of women who are strong feminists who really are not bothered by representing men charged with rape. And I think the only way that they can deal with that is they bought in so deeply.
—Emily Locatelli

I know a lot of people think I'm naive, but I do think that we can have an impact on our clients. We can make a difference, even if it just means them feeling like somebody else cares. And it goes beyond that. I think that we have an impact on the judges that we deal with. I think that we especially have an impact on witnesses, victims, and jurors. I just think that there are so many different ways that we can have a positive impact beyond just getting the guy off, and those things all keep me going.
—Fran Jones

3

Identity Formation: Early-Career Women Defenders

I was a victim of a rape when I was a teenager. And I thought about that when I first got into this line of work because a lot of these capital cases [that I was working on] involved sex crimes, and I went over that in my mind whether or not I was going to be able to deal with it, and it seems it's a totally separate event from what I do for a living.
—Annette Petroff

THE courtroom is a battlefield for wars over ideas that society holds near and dear—ideas of justice, fairness, and right and wrong. As a formal institution, the justice system decides who may or may not ultimately be a full member of society and reap the benefits of that membership. The presence of competing ideologies, values, and morals can hardly be matched in other settings— nor can the emotional conflict that extends beyond the courtroom walls into the everyday lives of the participants.

That Becky McBride and Darla Wilson are youthful and energetic is indisputable. So is the fact that their profession takes emotional and physical tolls on them. Both of these women work in the same large urban public defender's office, and they self-identify as "Betties." Becky explained that there are two distinct generations of women attorneys in their office. Darla and Becky were born around the time that the older generation of women—the "Abogadas"—were coming of age, in the 1960s. The terms that these women defenders use to describe themselves symbolize perceived contrasts. "Abogada"—the feminine form of the Spanish word for advocate or attorney—sounds serious and represents a generation deeply influenced by the civil rights movement. By contrast, "Betty" sounds trivial, conjuring up an image of women dedicated to youth, beauty, and Neiman Marcus credit cards.

However, these terms also symbolize a shared identity with other women who began work in their particular public defender's office around the same time. The name Abogada came about during a vacation. The women who now call themselves Abogadas were on their yearly trip with their families—this time to Mexico—and were referred to as "las Abogadas" by Spanish speakers on the plane. The Betties received their name by way of Darla's girlfriend, who called masculine women "Big old Betties." With time, members of the younger cohort began using Betty as a term of endearment for one another, associating it not with sexual orientation but with strength. The names, then, reflect the different identities of two distinct cohorts of women defenders that describe well two of the three distinct generations of women defenders that emerged in my study.

BECKY McBRIDE

Becky McBride is younger and less experienced than the Abogadas in her office. She is white, thirty-three years old, has been a deputy public defender for six years, and has tried ten felony cases. Of those felony cases, seven were violent, and four were cases where the violence was directed at women. Becky is very expressive, and we got along immediately. I loved the way she leaned over and lowered her voice to tell me things that began to feel like secrets—that she was embarrassed to be called a "Betty" because the name sounds so "silly" considering the work she does, or, with sadness in her voice, that she never tried to get out of a case assigned to her. There is no official policy in Becky's office that says she can't pass off a case to another attorney if the emotional effect is too great for her. As a matter of law, if a case is too repugnant for an attorney, taking it on is a conflict of interest. Like all but one of the public defenders I spent time with, though, Becky accepts whatever case is assigned to her as part of the job. She told me about the physical costs that accompany the stress of a particularly emotional trial:

> BM: I have a hard time sleeping a lot of times. I experience diarrhea. I can't eat very well. I eat hardly anything, and I get thin. I get headaches. I obsess. I think about it all the time: I wake up thinking about it; I dream sometimes about it. These things definitely

happen to me. It's gotten better over time. But it still happens. And the ways that I deal with it . . . I definitely try to exercise: that helps to clear my mind a little and get rid of those icky feelings. Actually, working helps; digging in and doing as much as I can do definitely lowers my stress level. . . . It used to be that when I'd feel that way, I'd try and push it away and sweep it under the carpet and try to distract myself by thinking about other things. And so there would just be this gnawing icky feeling. And over time I've realized that working gets you away from the gnawing icky feeling. Then you just feel like a release.

Becky's emotion work, in the most fundamental sense of the term, is evident in two places: avoiding identification with the victim, and remaining distant from her client. Her stories, which are themselves very important management tools for Becky, emphasize her abilities and attempts to vilify, dehumanize, and distinguish herself from the victim; they also speak of the power she feels over both victim and defendant.

Becky "divorces" herself from victims who are girls or women by treating the complainant's testimony as a story. She says it is not all that difficult because there is so little contact with the victim.

BM: It's more like a story that's being told when the victim's on the stand for me than it is a real-life scenario. I just got out of a trial a week ago where this woman—worst nightmare in the world—at three o'clock in the afternoon a man bursts into this woman's house. She tries to run upstairs; he grabs her by the hair, tries to rape her in the bedroom, chokes her with a telephone cord till she almost passes out. I mean, horrible. Any woman's worst nightmare. During the trial she sobbed and sobbed and sobbed. And during the preliminary hearing too.[1] I mean, she's completely traumatized. She's like twenty years old. She is so freaked out. She has been sort of suicidal. Really bad. And I had no feeling for her. I mean I really don't think I could go there.

From the sequencing of Becky's last two sentences, and the way she drops her voice, I suspect that it is not true that she has "no feeling" for the victim. Perhaps it is simply that opening up to feeling would be too dangerous and painful. It would make her vulnerable to identification with the victim. And it would force Becky to question the defense she has con-structed: "She better be sure she can identify him" is her challenge. When I ask her to explore this more with me, Becky tells me she willfully will not allow herself to feel for the victim. There is a conflict. Though she does not allow herself "to go there," Becky says it still bothers her.

> BM: It was an identification case, and the one feeling I did have that I'm sure I subconsciously nurtured was that she had no problem fingering my client when she really wasn't sure. And my client could really go away to prison for a long time. And she doesn't care. She just wants to get someone. So sometimes it's disturbing for me how little I feel for the victim.

Becky does not embrace a work ideology to keep her going, though at times she might say, "Everyone deserves a defense." Instead she embraces a feeling that will vilify the victim.

> BM: There were reasons to think she wasn't sure it was my client. And she became more sure over time. You can look at that two ways. You can say, "That's a natural human response to want to feel like the person is off the street," and all of that. And I actually said that to the jury. But I didn't feel that way. The feeling that I had was, "This is bullshit. Don't be saying you're sure about someone if you're not sure. Don't forget about this guy's life." I think any emotional outlet goes absolutely to the favor of my client.

In these remarks, Becky not only presents two ways of looking at a vic-tim's uncertain identification, she also gives a glimpse into external and internal accounts. Without reviling the victim, which she does internally, Becky might resort to the everyone-deserves-a-defense line. This is a reified cultural maxim as well as a legal ideology. Culturally it is in the same com-monsense vein as it is "a natural human response to want to feel like the person is off the street." The external account proffered to the jury is her presentation of self;[2] the internal account of nurturing negative feelings toward the victim is her emotion work. Both are strategic.

The external account attended to Becky's need to be deferential to the victim so that the jury would tolerate her cross-examination. She knew "the tack of 'this poor woman' would come off well." Becky said she did not feel "this poor woman." She would not allow that feeling in. And it takes work to suppress that feeling. Her own words, that this woman had already been subjected to "any woman's worst nightmare," suggest her fears. By not believing or overly identifying with the victim, Becky did not feel, "What happened to her could've happened to me." Instead she actively compartmentalized her gender to "distinguish" herself from the victim and was successful in feeling only disdain for the victim. The fact that it disturbed her was Becky's emotional cost. The internal account suggested a personal loss that worked to the benefit of her client through an emotional transfer of energy. Becky recognized this was not a conscious strategy, rather, "It's something that kind of happens to me."

> BM: I think that there's a part of me that I haven't gotten rid of from when I first started—that true believer. It pushes me forward and is an energy that I operate off of. And because of that, I think that my mind works out the rest subconsciously. So, for instance, going back to this woman who said my client did it. What my mind goes into and where I get my energy in all of that is, "You can't be pointing him out when you're not sure." Something I can grab onto and really believe in.

Becky uses her power to further separate herself from the victim. Consciously, Becky will not allow the victim to become fully human by disallowing the victim's history.

> BM: I separate myself from the woman, and sometimes I actually get really angry with the woman. Like this three-strikes case that I recently had was a domestic-violence case. And this man had terrorized this woman back in 1993, had done some really awful things to her, and he went to prison for eight years. Twenty days after his release there's another domestic violence incident with her. She married him while he was in prison. And so, again, what the energy goes toward is a "who is this? why is this?" angry feeling at the woman—thinking that she put herself in this position and getting angry that she allows herself to be so powerless in society and feeling like she reflects poorly on women in society. Like, "It's people like you that give women this image of being victims. Stop being such a victim. . . ." That's what I criticize DAs for doing.

Which is saying, "She has her whole history, too." Right? But that total unsympathetic feeling for her comes up for me. . . . Logically and consciously I realize that's really unfair. Because she hasn't grown up the way I have, and I recognize that unemotionally. But emotionally I can't ever imagine myself in that position, and so I don't feel a bond or a sisterhood with her, and I feel that she's just making the rest of us look bad.

Again, Becky will not allow herself to identify with the victim. How can she feel a bond with her? Becky is strong; the victim is weak and only makes women look bad. Becky may be trying to avoid seeing herself in the victim's position, but her statement that "she's just making the rest of us look bad" belies her attempt. Consciously Becky knows this woman has a history that could explain how she got to the witness stand not just once, but twice. Normally she criticizes district attorneys for divorcing people from their histories. Earlier she told me, "I don't see people as being born and then self-created. I see them as coming from a real history. . . . I mean, there's so much that makes a person who they are throughout their lives."

According to Becky, her approach is ungenerous and not her usual way of being. It takes emotion work to act against both her nature and her belief that, because of their history, some people may not have "full choice and responsibility." Becky says that most of the victims she comes across in the public defender's office, like the woman who married her terrorizer while he was in prison, did not grow up in an upper-middle-class home of a judge, as she did. Again, there is a transfer of emotional energy. In this instance, Becky gathers her strength from feeling angry at the woman's weakness.

Becky does not fear for her own safety in her personal life because of the kinds of cases she takes on, unlike some of the other women defenders. And she says that she feels more powerful than her clients, so they rarely make her feel vulnerable.

BM: Even if they think of me as some broad, it doesn't threaten me, because I never take it on. I mean, here's this person who's in custody, scared to death, maybe been a fuck-up their whole life. And if the person's kind of seeing me as just a broad, I know that has nothing to do with who I am. I feel very confident vis-à-vis my clients.

Becky says that she maintains her power over defendants by not sharing very much emotionally and keeping them at arm's length. As a result, she rarely feels emotionally fragile and is indifferent to their perception of her. Just as her class background helped her distance herself from the victim, it may have also bolstered her in relation to the defendant.

Becky told me a long story about the time she shared her emotions with a client and why it was a bad thing. She had a particular client for almost a year. He was paranoid schizophrenic and had been institutionalized most of his life: "He's a total pain. The jail hates this guy because he's a pain." She said he called her all the time. He had homicidal and suicidal thoughts. "He's really a messed up person. And I just like him." Becky said she could see all the different parts to him, and some were "really endearing." She saw him as just wanting to know that someone cared for him. And she said she genuinely did care, though she did not know why.

They were in trial and he started breaking out in a sweat and was "losing it." He wanted to attack the district attorney. Court had to recess because it got so bad, and they went back into the holding cell.

> BM: It was a cold case that shouldn't be tried; he was going to get more time. So I talked to him for a long time. I brought over his psychologist from the main jail to talk to him. And he decided to plead [guilty] in the middle [of the trial].

About three weeks later, Becky's client started to think that, because she arranged the plea bargain, she was against him. They were sitting alone in a holding cell, a soundproof, private room with a window that guards look through only sporadically. Because he was always getting into fights, this defendant was not in the customary orange jail garb, but in double red, indicating that he was a threat. It took three custody officers (COs) to move him from cell to cell. He was shackled everywhere, in leg irons, waist chains, and even bolted down to the floor; he had only a limited range of movement on his person.

> BM: He starts out by telling me how he's been beaten up, yet again by the COs which I really believe. The reason is that he's really annoying. He's pulling up his shirt to show me things, and starting to pull down his pants, and I'm feeling a little like you don't have to show me all of your private parts to tell me. You can just tell

me the story. And the COs outside are kind of looking in, wondering. So that kind of makes the atmosphere weird. And he starts telling me how he feels like I just sold him out. And I'm feeling like this guy doesn't feel like there's anyone who cares that much about him. And I really want him to know that I do. And it's important for me for him to know that. But I don't usually get there with my clients. I don't usually tell them, "look, I really care about you," because I like to keep in my lawyer role.

Because of her client's history, all that he had been through, and her "genuine feeling" for him, Becky decided to take a risk.

BM: I had already had a really emotional day to start with. I was telling him, "I did what I genuinely thought was best for you. I wasn't selling you down the river. I do care. I care a lot."

As she was saying this, Becky began to cry.

BM: And he said, "I wish I could hold you." I don't want him to tell me he wishes he could hold me. I don't want him to feel like he needs to take care of me in any way. I shouldn't be getting teared up and telling him that I care about him. That's me. I wouldn't blame somebody else for doing that. But I don't feel like that's a good realm to go into, because you're the lawyer. You're not their mother, or their sister, or their wife. You're their lawyer. Shortly after that he said, "I want you to know this is nothing against you. I like women. It's not that I don't like women." And then he said he likes to suck and eat pussy [she whispers this]. So I just felt like it was one of those rare occasions that the whole thing got completely out of control and bizarre and was not a good thing. So that's a long, long story about how I almost never get into those kinds of situations and when I do, it feels really inappropriate to me.

Her comments suggest that the emotional "places" Becky will not "let herself go" are demarcated by gender. She is protected as the lawyer, someone in charge, not affected by the emotions of a mother, sister, or wife. However, her lawyer role clearly doesn't protect her from the verbal sexual harassment of the defendant she obviously cared about, any more than the glass between her and the COs kept them from noticing the visual harassment. On the contrary, the client was powerful enough to sexualize the encounter because of her gender and her display of gendered caring.[3] Remaining distant took work for Becky, especially in the only place she could be with her client that might be considered a "backstage" region,[4] where she would be closer to, as she put it, her "normal nature."

According to Becky, the flooding of spontaneous emotions happened more frequently when she began working in criminal defense. Like many public defenders, and women public defenders in particular, she began with a juvenile calendar and cases that "depressed the hell out of [her]." Becky said that, with time, she began to feel she could occasionally make a difference in her clients' lives. However, back in the juvenile court days she was "way too sensitive. I didn't feel like we were doing the kids any good, and I felt they didn't have a chance. To see someone so young and see what looked like their future laid out before you, if it was an ugly one, it was awful. I hated it."

Becky said she cried most often at work in her early days. When she started work as a public defender she believed everything her clients told her. In her own words, "I was definitely a bleeding heart. I thought of my clients as pretty much pure victims of society and the system." She mockingly describes her own attitude of "my poor victim client" in those early days. "You come in sort of naive, you pour your heart in, and you think that these guys are absolutely telling you the truth. Then you realize that you're being manipulated and lied to, and even abused. You get tougher." Now, she says, she tries to be more objective.

That a defense attorney needs to be objective could easily rest solely on constitutional principles. That is, everyone is entitled to a defense and to be considered innocent until proven guilty. For Becky, this is part of the solution, but according to her, "It's more real than that"; the Constitution is "just a fuzzy document that's lived out on a case-by-case basis." She has learned more about the importance of objectivity through those times "when I, their lawyer, thought someone was totally guilty and found out that I was wrong." And with respect to being able to do her job and remaining unemotionally involved, Becky "tries":

> BM: I try to get out of the framework of trying to decide whether I
>   think my client is guilty or innocent and try and be a lot more
>   objective. I have an inclination to try and go there, and try and

think what I think, and try and figure it out. But I find that's not really productive, that really what you need to be looking at is, try and separate yourself out first of all from all that you know because a lot of times you obviously know a lot more than the jury. And really kind of think what the evidence is.

That Becky tries to be objective and tries to separate herself out from all she knows suggests strong emotion work. And increasingly she is successful. For her it has been a matter of toughening up over the last six years. In an office that assigns cases based on what the supervising attorney "thinks you can handle," the fact that Becky is headed for the homicide team is an indicator of her successful emotion management. Still, sometimes, Becky told me, her "nature" takes her close to those emotional places she attempts to avoid. She said the last instance was just a month before I interviewed her, when she "related" strongly to the unfairness of her client's fate. This was the same client who had terrorized a woman repeatedly. It was the first time she had a "guy go down on a 'three-strikes' case."[5]

Sentencing can be a very emotional time for a defense attorney and her client. Becky repeatedly suggested that she transfers her emotional energy to the benefit of her client through work. Clearly this is less possible when a trial is over:

> BM: I cried in court when I was a younger attorney. When I was still in my naive state, I guess. But in this three-strikes case that I just had last month, I got teary. I was able to control it, but I got teary. I was sitting there in court, and everyone was acting like it was business as usual, chatting it up about silly, inconsequential things, not disturbed at all by what was happening. And it really bothered me. It really made me feel like I couldn't relate to any of these people, and this was something really serious and tragic that was happening and nobody cared. I totally cried later.

Becky's emotion management has changed over the years. She consciously avoids emotions that are difficult to counter. Her words suggest that emotions are much like a landscape that can be traveled through, a terrain where emotional distance from her client or a victim helps to keep her in her lawyer role. Becky also fantasizes about escaping from this place. We chatted for quite a while after the interview. Becky wanted to know more of what I was finding. She appreciated the time we spent talking and said that few people understand the emotional stress of her work. She told me about a fantasy that she tells only her woman colleagues because no one else would understand. She gets in a car wreck on her way to court when she has a particularly nasty case to try. She wants to be in a wreck that will totally get her out of the trial; she'll be in the hospital for maybe a month. I told Becky about midcareer defender Jesse Madrigal's fantasy about being punched out in court by her client. Becky comments, "Yeah, but that will only get you out of that particular case. It won't get you out of all of your cases. You need an injury that's significant enough to land you in the hospital."

DARLA WILSON

Like Becky, Darla Wilson is also young, white, and less experienced than the Abogadas in their office. As I walked into Darla Wilson's office, I was struck by the fact that she was visibly pregnant. I have two children, so we immediately hit it off by talking about what it is like to be pregnant and to work, what childbirth is like, and about being a new mother. She was beaming. A huge prenatal calendar covered the wall behind her desk, a calendar made by one of her colleagues when he heard that Darla and her girlfriend were becoming parents. Large red Xs marked out the first six months, the stages of her gestation. The legal files on her desk represented anything but the celebration of life. Inside were stories of lives, and even loves, in a state of disarray—the victims usually women or children. Darla has been a public defender for seven years. By the very nature of her current calendar assignment she fit the profile of the woman defense attorney I had been hoping to interview, and this came out when I asked, "Have you ever struggled defending a particular client because you are a woman?"

> DW: Well, twice I've been on domestic violence calendars, both in municipal court and now in superior court . . . I'm on an early resolution assignment where I do sexual-assault cases, domestic-violence cases, and then, like, failure-to-pay-child-support cases. And sometimes I feel like it's difficult dealing with the guys who continually beat up on their wives, but I really can't—I mean for me to do my job—I really can't get too lost in that, so I go back to the "well they're entitled to representation too, there's another

side to this story, they need to have their bit told, they grew up in an abusive household, or whatever." But occasionally that gets to me, yeah.

Not only does she recognize the gender conflict, Darla Wilson is one of the few attorneys I interviewed who acknowledges the conflict between her role as a public defender and her beliefs as a feminist. She told me that the major concern of feminists is equality for women.

> DW: Not special rights, just equality. And I think that public defenders are primarily concerned that their client gets the best representation possible, and those two conflict. For example, on domestic-violence cases, the concern as a public defender is not, how are women being treated? Are they being treated equally? They're certainly not in those situations. And in that case, I have to wear the public defender hat and not the feminist hat. I really have to kind of consciously not be concerned with the victims in the case. It's not my job. In fact, I think it inhibits my good representation of a client there.

Darla's stance is unusual for most women in her line of work, who see feminism as a call for equality for all. Seeing this conflict does not mean Darla cannot do her job. But it makes it more difficult for her. She must actively compartmentalize her personal political beliefs and her public role. In fact, Darla said public defenders joke about "prostituting" themselves.

> DW: I mean, you have to get along with the judges and the district attorneys whether you like their political beliefs or not. It's required for the representation of your clients, I think. And so you definitely have to compartmentalize.
>
> CS: Is there any way you can expand on that more, actually how you do it, the process you go through?
>
> DW: Here's a specific example. We spend a lot of time in chambers with the judge, the district attorney, and maybe a probation officer. And there's a lot of shooting the shit, sort of schmoozing stuff that goes on. There are a lot of old white golfing men on the superior court bench in [this county]. I mean a lot of them. And it was time for their judicial Christmas party, and one of

them said, "My wife's sick." And the other one said, "You know, I think my wife's sick too." And they said, "Ha, ha, we'll have to dance with each other." Funny guys saying something that was homophobic and insensitive . . . I think that in different circumstances I might have jumped right in and said, "You know, that's just totally offensive." And I didn't say anything right then. In fact I didn't say anything at all, at any point. I was in the middle of discussing a case, and I really didn't want to make a stink when I was talking about my client. And I don't feel particularly great about that. I think that in the best of all possible worlds I would speak up immediately if I was offended by something. And there have been other times when I have said things. It's not like I have a gag in my mouth at all times, no matter what. But that's a situation where I think I needed to compartmentalize my feelings about people being homophobic and my client.

As early as her second year of law school Darla knew she wanted to become a public defender. Her coursework included a criminal law clinic where she did defense work in a metropolitan setting. As a result, Darla came into this line of work knowing she would be dealing with hard cases; she even welcomed them. Like most criminal defense attorneys, Darla believes that you "naturally fall" into one class or the other—either the prosecution or the defense. But regardless of which side you end up on, you are faced with conflict. Often a potential prosecutor is asked at her hiring interview: "Could you prosecute a death-penalty case to your fullest ability?" The comparable question for a future deputy public defender is: "Are there any crimes you could not defend?" When I asked Darla if she remembered being asked this question, she did not even hesitate to respond, "I said that I thought I'd rather have the crimes that other people don't want to defend people against. It seems to me those people, they are the whole reason we have this system, so people don't get lynched and have eggs thrown at their houses."

On the face of it, Darla's response seems to be the well-thought-out answer of a young aspiring defense attorney. But none of the other attorneys I spoke with "wanted" to take on these cases. I wondered how Darla could want them. She told me they were difficult, hard to hear about, and made her feel vulnerable in her own life. Darla told me what it is like for her to imagine being raped by a stranger.

DW: The worst possible thing is having somebody come into your house at night when you're most vulnerable and feel your safest. So I think those cases of rape by a stranger are a lot harder for us to defend against. They're awful. They're offensive.

Being male wouldn't spare an attorney from such imaginings. Darla gave an example from a man in her office.

DW: There's a male attorney in my office who represented a serial rapist. And [the rapist] always wore a mask, the case was really [horrible], and he talked to me about it. The jury was out for a long time and the ID [identification] evidence was not great, but the MO [modus operandi] was kind of the same, and one woman was able to ID him, and so they were piecing it together. And he was worried that they weren't going to convict him. And at the same time he's a fantastic lawyer, and he did a great job for the guy. I think it was a conflict for him because he has a wife and three kids, and he knew the guy did it.

A male defense attorney might express vulnerability through his protector identity in the family when contemplating defending a rapist and quite possibly take on a patriarchal attitude toward the victim that would work against his client.

When a woman defender feels vulnerable, she risks sympathizing with the victim. Darla admits this sort of sympathy is not beneficial to her client, and it interferes with her feeling of safety every day.

DW: I close all my windows at night. . . . I've read too many police reports where somebody's come into the house in the middle of the night and doing sexual violence against women, or cases where women are going out to their cars at night and they're dragged across a parking lot and sexually assaulted. My awareness is really heightened based on doing this job, and that affects my personal life because I think I'm certainly not as happy-go-lucky a person as I used to be. I used to work at a restaurant [in my undergraduate days], and I would go in at 5:30 in the morning and leave the door open, and I'd be alone until 7:00, probably cooking. And I can't imagine doing that now. I mean, never, I just wouldn't. I would lock the door, and I would be concerned going from my car, and so I think I'm a different person.

Because of her gender Darla is a member of a potentially susceptible category. She is not a generic person who routinely deals with cases of sexual assault. Darla imagines being raped in her home by a stranger. Given the content of her caseload, it is not surprising that she is in the process of installing a security system in her new home.

Darla resolves the conflict of being a potential victim and her work through a strong faith in the system. She says the system provides safeguards and a forum for justice. Without this system, we run the risk of turning into a "lawless society where people don't have counsel, and people are lynched, and there's a vigilante system, and it's not very civilized . . ." The system also provides her with a rationalization. Darla is able to put her duty as a defense attorney before her feelings as a woman, knowing that there is a "well-machined system" protecting women like her as private citizens. Again, there is a contradiction: the system is the same "huge well-financed machine that's grinding down her clients." It is a combination of all the elements of the criminal justice system protecting her—police, judges, DAs, probation—that she is helping her clients fight.

And there are costs. Darla admits she is no longer the "happy-go-lucky person" she was. Such a statement implies her inability to present a certain self to others, but it goes deeper than that:

> DW: In my mind it's a higher duty for me because of what my job is, and I accept that and really am okay with it. It doesn't mean that I condone violence against women or that I feel okay about it. I don't. And I think that the system has in place certain ways of guarding against the recurrence of violence against women. . . . People get violated[6] and get sent to prison the second time they do it. And it's a larger societal concern that we bring our children up differently so that they don't hit each other, and men especially. But for me, the way that I rationalize putting my duty as a public defender on top of my feelings as a woman is that there are other things taking care of those concerns, and that's my job.

That Darla's job is a "higher duty" implies ideological work, as does her belief that parents in our society need to raise nonviolent children. Considering my experience of motherhood while working in a public defender atmosphere, I was not surprised to hear what may have been an ideological shift on her part toward larger societal issues.

Darla, like other Betties, is very reflective. The Abogadas, women whose careers span twenty years, are often annoyed by my questions. Sometimes I feel they are telling me, "I already dealt with all that years ago. Let those feelings remain undisturbed." By contrast, their younger counterparts are right in the middle of whatever conflicts they may be feeling, and they want to talk about them. Many women defenders, at all stages of their careers, use the ideological defense of the system taking care of the public to justify their role in that same system. It is their faith in the system, of which they are a part, that becomes stronger with years of practice. Darla tells me she did not give much thought to this before she entered law school. And even during school it was only theoretical. Now the theory is effective when she describes her role to others who question her work at social encounters.

According to Darla her role is clear and simple: "To explain the legal process to my client, advise my client based on what I think the facts of the case are, and then do the best I can with the decision my client makes on how he or she wants to proceed." It was the same when she defended misdemeanor clients on traffic infractions as it is today when she represents a rapist. In the early days it meant taking a misdemeanor case to jury trial where a young African American man was pulled over by police officers who were notorious for hassling and illegally detaining people. The young man was offered an infraction with no fine: "They offered to make it go away for a slight mea culpa on his part, and he wouldn't do it." So the case went to trial and she won. Darla was very happy to have caught the officers in their contradictions.

Whether her role is the same or not, the cases Darla works on today are uglier, and she is aware of her emotional conflict. It comes out most strongly when she is working on a case that turns her stomach, for example, the case with a burned baby where the mom was accused of having burned the child. Darla thinks her supervisor assigned her this case because he felt she would be sympathetic when presenting the woman's case to a jury.

Darla told me the client she objected to most had molested his step-children. They were eight and nine when his molestation began, and it went on for a one-year period. The crime certainly bothered her, as did her client's verbal abuse and his disregard for her attempt to minimize his potential sentence. Still, she was doing her job, assessing the facts and advising the client on how he should proceed. When a woman tells me the story of a particularly hard case, only her words can get the emotion across:

DW: He was looking at an exposure[7] of something in the range of sixty to eighty years to life. He confessed on tape, and both of the girls gave taped statements which were entirely consistent with his confession in terms of the number of times that the sexual acts had occurred, the way that they had occurred, and the types of sexual acts. So the case was pretty cold against him. But the victims were sideways. They were telling a different story at the preliminary hearing, and I got him a fifteen-to-life offer, which he should have taken. And I went to see him probably three times in three weeks and kind of talk it out with him and explain to him what the evidence against him was, and he got really personally verbally abusive with me. His case was really offensive—but a lot of my cases are really offensive. It wasn't so much that. But he really attacked me, and then his parents got involved, and I sort of swore at him and the parents came in and had a meeting with my boss about how I was using unladylike language, that kind of thing. It was really ridiculous. So I explained that I chose that particular language for a reason: to make a point to explain the severity of the situation to him, and that was fine. My boss is great. But anyway, the case ended up going to trial, and he was convicted on everything. It was difficult because I felt really attacked, and he had a terrible case. It was hard on the jury, it was hard on the girls, it was hard on my client, and it was hard on me, and it seemed sort of unnecessary. That's one of the only times I've really felt kind of like I would prefer not to be doing this. This is really not good.

CS: You say it was hard on you. In what way was it hard?

DW: I knew he was going to get convicted, and I really felt like I went to a lot of trouble to get him that offer [of a plea bargain]. It would have made him eligible for parole soon. And it was frustrating to know that he could have minimized his damage and chose not to. And so in that way it was difficult.

CS: So it was nothing about the case?

DW: Oh, the case was hard too. I mean, the girls were [damaged]. . . . The mom was saying that there's no way this could have happened. So I interviewed the girls, and they clearly were very screwed up from the experience. My investigator interviewed one of them, and she ripped up my investigator's card in a hundred pieces, it was all over the floor, and it was emotionally taxing. The molest was really extreme, and he not only had intercourse with this ten-year-old, eleven-year-old, and twelve-year-old, but he hit them all the time too. So it was kind of hard to hear about, and I could see from talking to the [oldest, who was by then a thirteen-year-old] that her life was ruined. I mean, she's already sexually acting out with older guys, and she sees herself as a sexual object, and it was painful to see it.

At the end of trial Darla still believed that the lighter sentence was more appropriate than sixty to eighty years to life, and that it was her job to get that for the perpetrator, despite her insights into the effects of childhood sexual abuse on the older girl. Darla's repeated emphasis on the duties of her job shows in her words, as does the gender double bind she found herself in for using "unladylike" language. What came across to me when I heard these words was her frustration. Darla was frustrated because she knew she had to work doubly hard for this man, not because his case was compelling, just the opposite. She had to prove to herself that he had received the best possible defense, even though she objected to both the crime and the person.

Darla's strategy of proving to herself that she could give the best possible representation is a precursor to the types of cases that are transformative for midcareer women, as we will see in the next chapter. However, Darla still feels residual emotional damage after handling a case like this. The leftover problem for Darla is: "I try harder when I'm repulsed by the case. So I fight myself about it." As we saw in Becky's stories, "trying" suggests emotion work. That Darla still fights herself about repulsive cases suggests that the emotion work is not fully effective in resolving her conflict.

As we were walking out of her office, Darla asked me what I was learning about women defenders: "How are other women dealing with this emotional stuff?" At that point, I had talked with only a handful of attorneys and told her that I couldn't generalize. But what I had begun to hear was a repeated emphasis on the professional ethic and ideology of criminal defense work over emotion. I said, "Many of the women say that it's really not all that emotional, they just focus on their duty." Even though Darla also used the "higher duty" justification during the interview, her response to me was, "That's bullshit. They do something with it. If nothing else, they are just stuffing it somewhere." Something about Darla seemed very different to me in comparison to the more established women defenders I had interviewed. Her emotions were rawer, and her repeated use of lynching examples indicates an ever present awareness of the potential for violence against minorities in American society.

Yet Darla's profile was similar to those of many of the women I interviewed. She grew up in a lower-middle-class liberal household in one of the more politically progressive towns of California. She is easily offended when people are discriminated against on the basis of economic status—and even more so when race and sexual orientation are concerned. Like many of those I interviewed, at least one of Darla's parents is in a "good works" occupation: her mother works as a church secretary. In contrast, her father held a working-class job at a department store until he was fired for his alcoholism; he then became a corrections officer. That Darla was about to become a mother wasn't all that different, either. Most of the attorneys I had interviewed up to that point were mothers. Nor was the fact that her life partner worked in the criminal justice system (as a police officer). That she is lesbian choosing motherhood puts her in the growing ranks of same-sex couples becoming parents.

What set Darla apart from the other women I had interviewed was her relative youth (she is thirty-four years old), fewer years of trial experience, and far fewer years in practice (seven). Of her eleven felony trials, half involved acts of violence, and almost all of those violent crimes were perpetrated against women. Darla does not know what she does with her feelings in these cases other than that "they do get kind of pushed off to the side." She is clear they do not go away. To be effective in trial, though, Darla must believe in the case she has constructed. "Even in the case with the 'molest.' You have to . . . start believing your own argument, or you can't argue it effectively." What makes Darla different is that when she talks about the cases, she gets back in touch with the emotions she has "stuffed." It appears that the combination of her gender and sexual orientation adds to her emotional conflict and the recognition that people are "lynched" on the basis of their identity—if only metaphorically.

By the time I interviewed several women in the early stages of their careers, I found that their age, fewer years of trial experience and practice, and the fact that they might be called Betties were not all that set them apart. Their emotions made them different. Like Becky, Darla gets back in touch with her emotions. I was left asking myself if this is the result of their willingness to return to raw emotional conflict. Another question is whether this is the result of a less sophisticated ability to manage emotions. Apparently Becky and Darla rely very little on professional ideologies to narrow the gap between their emotional responses and the work required of them.

EMILY LOCATELLI

Only one of the attorneys that I interviewed was ultimately unable to narrow that gap. I introduce Emily Locatelli in this section not because she is in the early years of her legal career. Chronologically, she would be an Abogada if she worked at Becky and Darla's office. However, after eight years in a metropolitan public defender's office, Emily decided to become a law school professor. She is the only woman I interviewed who dramatically reoriented her criminal law practice because of the content of the work. Others reoriented because of changing life circumstances (e.g., motherhood), but not because of types of crimes their clients might have committed.

Emily went to law school at a prestigious university on the east coast. She says she entered law school with a desire to represent poor people in criminal cases—a desire born in the leftist politics of the '60s and '70s. For Emily, law school was an "uphill battle." It wasn't because she was a woman or that she was a person of color—Emily, too, is white. It was difficult to convince people that her goal of being a public defender was worthwhile.

> EL: I mean, [they asked], "How could you defend those people?" when they were studying so that they could go to Wall Street. I don't understand why they thought what I was doing wasn't morally a good thing. Corporations are worse than public defender clients by all means.

Emily remembers being asked if she could represent someone charged with rape when she was interviewed for a job at the public defender's office. She said she thought the question was "peculiar and annoying," and asked, "How do you feel about representing someone charged with beating up his mother? . . . or other horrible things that public defenders are charged with defending?" In retrospect, she says, she did not understand the question.

EL: When I got into doing rape cases, I did take issue with it, but not because I thought rape was worse than taking a child and putting their feet on the rungs of an oven rack, because I don't.

Emily's reflections show that for her, the difference was her perceived participation in the revictimization of the victim and allowing of possible future victims. Nothing in her reflections suggests that her job made her feel more vulnerable in her personal life or more powerful than her clients or victims. However, Emily's words suggest an inability to distance herself from the victim.

Emily began practicing law in the days when rape cases required corroborating evidence to prove that the assault had occurred beyond a doubt. Unlike other kinds of cases, a victim's testimony was not enough to convict the defendant. During the time Emily was a public defender, the law changed in the eastern state in which she practiced as well as in most states. But according to Emily, regardless of the change in law, disbelief in a rape victim's story is "still the reality in the courtroom. And I had a very hard time being a part of that. It really troubled me."

Most of the women in this study said that in sex-crime trials, women defenders are "good for the victim" because they cross-examine in a gentle way. Emily takes issue with this "line." She said, maybe a woman defense attorney is more effective approaching the victim in a sensitive manner; however, the ultimate goal is to discredit her, especially in cases where the defense is consent. In Emily's words, "The bottom line is to convince the jury that she's lying and she made the thing up, and . . . there's no way you can do that without demeaning her." Emily told me that the assertion about cross-examining in a kinder, gentler fashion is a justification that makes women in criminal defense feel better about the work they do.

Emily shares Darla's opinion about the conflict between feminism and public defense work. Emily believes that when you become a public defender, you adopt a perspective that is inconsistent with feminism. In fact, it was my interview with Emily that led me to ask the rest of the attorneys I interviewed, "When you become a defense attorney, do you adopt a view that is inconsistent with being a feminist?" In her words:

EL: You adopt a line, and you'll live with it. And that's why you'll find a lot of women who are strong feminists who really are not bothered by representing men charged with rape. And I think the only way that they can deal with that is they bought in so deeply to that line. . . . Maybe I'm being unfair to them.

In Emily's case, she felt the contradiction in rape cases when a victim is demeaned.

> EL: I didn't want to be any part of that. I didn't want to take all of these horrible stereotypes about women and . . . use them in defense of my client. I felt like a scumbag. I'd see these women up there on the stand testifying about these horrible things that had happened to them, and I could win my case by trashing her more and challenging who she is . . . "Didn't you ask for it?" and "What were you wearing?" and "You know the guy." And I could use all these horrible things to win the case. And I wanted no part of that. I felt horrible.

Like Darla, Emily acknowledged that her feelings may get in the way of the best possible representation for her client. There was one particular instance where she objected to defending a client on personal grounds.

> EL: I represented one man who was charged with statutory rape, repeated incidences of statutory rape, against his daughter. And to this day I worry that I didn't represent him, really give him zealous representation because I had such a bad stomach about the case. And I should have withdrawn, but I didn't. We ended up pleading the case and I still to this day wonder whether or not somebody who didn't have such a stomach may have pushed for a trial. Because it's possible she could have been discredited, although you know that every trial is a crap shoot. And I didn't make him plead guilty, but he did. But that case, I really had trouble with it.

I suggest here that Emily's implicit identification with the victim resulted in her inability to push for a trial where she might have had to discredit the girl. She recognizes contradictions, and often her own rationalizations, although she did not point out that she was rationalizing when she said that she "didn't make him plead guilty, but he did."

Emily revealed nothing that suggests she would have more difficulty than other women in defending men accused of sex crimes against women.

She did, however, reveal an ideology that might minimize the conflict she experienced in these cases. It is an ideology she entered practice with and one that she still teaches students in criminal defense clinics:

> EL: I believe absolutely, firmly, that everybody deserves a defense. And if they insist that they didn't do it, no matter what the evidence is, and no matter how convinced the lawyer is they did it, that it's the lawyer's job to go in there and present that defense. If the client doesn't want to plead guilty and wants a trial, you're entitled to a trial, and a jury is the institution that decides the case and not the lawyer. And so, I believe that.

Despite the fact that Emily "believes that," I noted that she did not speak in the first person. It appears that her belief is not enough to counter the troubling aspects of some of her own cases. When I asked her which cases she found most difficult, she described the aftereffects of two.

The first was a rape trial that resulted in an acquittal. One of the jurors told Emily that she believed the defendant was innocent because Emily was able to stand up on his behalf. A year or two later the defendant was arrested on multiple counts of rape. (The only time Emily ever declined an appointment was when she was assigned to represent this defendant on the new charges. She said she was excused because he threatened her.)

The second case was a young woman who was charged with child abuse. Emily told me that initially the woman's baby was taken away. At some point during the trial, she was given her baby back.

> EL: We went back to a hearing, and I found out that she hit the child again, and the child had another injury. And I was still preparing to defend this woman at her trial on the first injury. And then she got pregnant. And I felt such a . . . it was very, very hard for me. It was very troubling for me. This was towards the end of my career as a public defender.

Emily was haunted by these outcomes. In her words, "These things began to build."

When I asked Emily about the atmosphere of her office, she said there was a lot of camaraderie, but also a "macho attitude." The environment, she said, was not receptive to hearing about the problems she was having.

Her colleagues would come back from court with "war stories," and Emily said she was "right up there with the rest of them, smoking and joking."

> EL: But really, when it comes down to it, like a sensitive thing like where a person's really torn up about a client. It's not the kind of thing you [can] readily go back and say, "I'm really troubled about representing this person." And there were some really bad cases. Shaking baby cases. Really horrible cases. But I know I personally struggled with some of them. And the rape cases . . .
>
> You do it because you have a passion for the work, and you care about the clients, and you understand that the system needs you, or they need you. So there's a certain sort of wearing the white hat, if you will. And in these cases I didn't feel that way.

Emily said she recognized that to discuss her negative feelings would be to stigmatize herself.

> EL: I was a little afraid to do it because it was like coming out publicly, taking an unpopular position among people who I respected and who respected me as a public defender. I mean, there was something about sticking my neck out to say, "Well, I'm a public defender who doesn't like . . . who sees these rape cases as different."

Emily's words are a very interesting example of accountability to sex category (i.e., doing gender). I suggest that she was "coming out" as a woman, and it is "women's nature" to identify with the victims of such crimes.[8]

If we are concerned with the social processes that keep a woman in this line of work, what about those that may lead her to pursue other specialties? And at what career stage may this occur?

Darla and Emily share the opinion that there is a conflict between feminism and public defense work. Both acknowledged their feelings may get in the way of a "zealous defense." They share other commonalties. Both are lesbians in long-term domestic partnerships where they are raising children. Both also are partnered with women who work in the criminal justice system. Darla's partner is a police officer, Emily's a criminal defense attorney. However, their work environments are very different. Darla has an informal support structure as part of her everyday work life. She told me that if she gets back from court at 5:30 P.M. and "You're, like, aaack! You want to scream," there are people around for "you." If her three close friends, all women, are not around, she has several men friends who will talk with her. Based on her description and on my own experience in the public defender's office, I suggest that these are the times that criminal defense ideology is fortified, when people begin to adjust their beliefs to bring them in line with their desired feelings.

Emily's stories suggest that to be a full member of the public defender culture, one must adopt the "line," to use her word. I suggest that Emily's inability to believe that line was limited by the culture of her workplace and her identities as a feminist and a lesbian. This combination curbed her ability to do the emotion work required for her job and ultimately led to her seeking out a new field. But limiting Emily's reflections to emotion would mean neglecting the stress she described. Stress is a big part of the job (as Darla's "aaack" suggests).

Emily was gracious enough to invite me to her home for the interview. When I asked her what sort of stress working at the public defender's office added to her life, particularly those difficult cases, she responded, "I'm going to have a cigarette for this question. Should we sit on the side or out in the back?" We went outside, and she started:

> EL: Stress, stress, stress, stress. Well, being a public defender is extremely stressful. I can tell you that because somebody's life is in your hands, and the stakes are really high, and everything that you do . . . you're constantly on. So not only are the stakes high, not only is it important, but every minute of every day that you're in a courtroom, you're on. The jury's looking at you, the judge wants to know what you think, you need to know the law. It's very stressful. It's very stressful to be a good trial lawyer, a trial lawyer that cares about what she's doing. That's very stressful.

Emily has not been in public defense for some time. The description she gives of the stress she encountered in the job is the larger picture of defense work, stresses that have become magnified for those women who remain in the field with the changes in law during the last ten years or so, including California's mandatory sentencing and three-strikes law.

FRAN JONES

Fran Jones told me what a day in the life of a public defender has become since mandatory sentencing and three-strikes laws have taken effect. She said these political changes in the law and their repercussions have changed her attitude toward her work.

> FJ: I think we have much more of an obligation to make sure that the clients understand the consequences of going to trial and losing. Whereas before the consequences were, if you shoot somebody, and you go to trial, and you lose, you're going to get four years. Now, you have a gun in your possession, it adds ten years; if you shoot the gun and you miss, it adds twenty years; if you shoot the gun, and you hit, say you wing somebody in the finger, it's twenty-five to life on top of whatever. So the sentences in this game are so much higher now, that I think that it is so much more important for us to spend time with our clients getting to understand the importance of it.

Fran told me delivering the news of probable sentences is extremely taxing. She comes out of the jail sometimes and wonders why she is so tired; after all, she has been sleeping and eating. "You don't realize the emotional energy that you put into work, because it's just what we do. And then Thursday night you're so exhausted you fall asleep at eight o'clock." After she described a really stressful day, it is understandable that she would head for bed so early in the evening.

> FJ: I remember going to court one morning, telling a client basically the best I could get for him was life, and then I had to go talk to another client, tell him he was going to lose his motion, here's what the deal is, and then I had to go to the jail and tell another client how the best I could do for him—and this was a great deal—was twenty years, it used to be seventeen. And he was very suicidal, and we started talking about it. This is a client who I had inherited from somebody else. He had stabbed his common-law wife seventeen times, and by the grace of God she didn't die. Thank God, because otherwise he was a three-striker, and I had done everything I could to get them to strike a third. [A conviction on a third strike would

mean he was facing a possible life sentence.] So I had to convince him that that was the right thing to do. And I got done, and it was 3:30 in the afternoon, and there was a new animal shelter right next to the county jail, and I hadn't had any lunch, and I'm starving, and I head on in there, and I end up with some kittens out of it. And then I thought, I can never go back to the animal shelter. Yeah, with all those animals, I'll be one of those cat ladies. It's like that is a very typical day for me, and the kind of cases I'm dealing with.

Fran told me her goal in criminal defense was to get "what is fair and just and right." She reiterates some version of this phrase seven times in the course of our conversation. Given that she believes her goal is to get what is fair and just for her clients, it is not surprising that the three times she remembers crying in court all involved perceived unfairness. One time was her first murder case. She told me she was asking for involuntary manslaughter, which she got.

FJ: The courtroom was packed—every lawyer in the courthouse is there—and so I get this verdict, and I'm very happy by that. And then the judge remands my client into custody. Why am I sad? I've just won? And he's getting remanded into custody, and I'm crying over that. And people were like, why are you upset over that? And I'm like, that's not the problem. I cried because it was unfair that he put my guy in custody because he could get probation, and he had already had the equivalent of two years [time served while in the local jail waiting for trial].

The second time, she had a client for two and a half years. Again it was a murder case. At the first trial for this offense, the jury could not decide between voluntary manslaughter and second-degree murder. The result was a hung jury. The second trial ended after seven days of jury deliberation.

FJ: The jury convicted him of second-degree murder. And we both cried. It was a really hard case. It was long, and it was hard. And I had done such . . . I had worked so hard, and I felt like I had done a very good job. And so then for the jury to come back with a result that I thought should come back manslaughter, it was really difficult. And knowing what that meant to the client, sixteen years to life.

Her third time, Fran cried during what she described as an awful case. She said her client was wonderful, but "basically he had done horrible things to his girlfriend." Domestic violence was a burning issue of the day—with the O. J. Simpson trial. In this case, Fran said she tried to get her client "to do what was right" through a plea bargain, and he wouldn't.

FJ: And so I put together this big package on why they should reconsider and give this guy a better deal. And two weeks ahead of time I gave it to everybody—the judge, the DA, everybody to read. And the DA didn't even have the file with her when she came to court, and the judge hadn't even read it. And I was so frustrated by it. And I was back in chambers, and I was like, well, "Why didn't you guys look at this? That's why I gave it to you." So the DA came up to me and said, "[Fran], you seem to be a little upset, what's wrong?" And I got tears in my eyes. And the judge came out, and I had tears in my eyes. So I bolted in the back where [the] client was kept in custody, and the marshals are trying to drag him out. But the judge felt really bad after that. And he felt bad that he hadn't read things. I would have been mortified years ago having cried, but then it was, screw that. I was upset by it. He needed to know I was upset by it. He likes me. If I was upset enough to cry, which I don't usually do, then it has an impact, and hopefully I got something way better for the client. Since I don't do it often, I think it has an impact.

Rather than seeing her heightened emotional state in court as a weakness, Fran learned that women defenders' public display of emotions in court can be a powerful strategy in "the game." Fran portrayed her performances in courtroom competitions as extensions of her athleticism. She told me she began playing basketball in the Olympic development leagues in southern California. She went on to play college ball at a top school, where women's basketball is prestigious. In both instances, especially in the development leagues, the women playing were primarily Black or minorities. Fran was not. She could not figure out why these women who were respected on court were treated differently off court. Fran translates her desire to work against that fundamental unfairness to the game she plays in court.

Fran wants to be the one who can perform in court in such a way that she can get comparable sentencing outcomes for the "cute, nice client" and one she described as a "scummy old Black guy." Superficially, Fran's comments about the clients may suggest a lack of consciousness of any kind. I suggest, however, that her apparent lack of consciousness is a representation of the criminal justice system's ideal of blindness to difference. In other words, the apparent unconsciousness is quite the reverse.

FJ: For me, I want to be on the line once I put the ball in my hand. I want to be the one representing that guy. I want to be the one that can introduce him to the jury and save this man's life. Because I think I can do it better than 99 percent of the people out there.

If Fran needs to use her emotions as a strategy in the game to get "what is fair and just and right," she will. As a woman defense attorney who understands performance, strategy, and playing a game, she feels she has the advantage in court. Fran gave an example of how the woman defender "does gender":

FJ: I think part of lawyering is about communication and learning how to communicate with people. And I think so many of us go in with the idea that you've got to be a tough broad, you can't let anyone see you flinch at all. And I think so much more of it's about remember who you're talking to and how you can interact with them in a way that they are going to like you or want to talk with you. There's this one judge who's been around forever, and he adores his wife. The big thing he does every year is take her on a shopping spree, and the other thing he does is cruises. Well, you know, it took about five minutes to figure this out about him, but men never take the time to do that. I ask myself, "If he's just another person on the street, how would I communicate with him?" If you can figure out what makes a guy tick and be able to communicate with him on that sort of level, then when it comes time to start talking about your case you're going to be at the same level, you're not going to have all this tension.

I can go into a judge's chambers, or I can go in front of a jury, and I can make arguments that are based on passion, and compassion, and win those, but a man could never do it. And I feel sorry for them. I think it's a gift that we have, but I think that we [women] have to use it. I don't know, I just think that we have to have control over when you put it out there. I can go in and walk the walk and talk the talk because I did play sports. And it's all a game with the added benefit that it's not hard on your knees.

It is obvious that Fran, more than any of the other women to this point, developed the use of her gender in the courtroom game. Fran learned quickly the rationalization that what she does in court is to "perform" whatever the client says happened. Her toughening over time includes a willingness to let her gender-displayed emotions work to the advantage of her clients.

When Fran had been in the office for only about six months, she got a case handed to her for trial with notes in it that read: "Don't get close enough to this client for him to hit you because he will." Reluctantly she went to the jail to meet her new client.

FJ: There was this big, ugly, mean, Black man. He was accused of stealing stuff from Grand Auto, and he had a whole bunch of different counts. It was on video tape. And so I went and met the man and he just growled. But in the day or so that I had to prepare the case I found that if I talked to him and tried, I could get his viewpoint of what happened. The first question I put out to the jury was, "Could you understand being in a situation where you were charged with a crime and felt that you were wrongfully accused? Can you understand that if my client feels that way, that he may not act very happy in this courtroom, and he may come across as being very upset? Are you going to hold that against him?" As soon as I put that out there he was like a cat eating out of my hand.

Fran told me that of her sixty felony trials, probably ten included violence perpetrated by men against women. In her first rape case, the man was facing three separate charges with three separate women on three different occasions, and, as Fran put it, "Everything stacked up against him." Ultimately she argued convincingly that the man was not properly charged, and she got an acquittal. What helped her get through this case was seeing how much damage could be done to someone's life when the person is innocent—and in this case she believed he was. At the same time, she has represented people that did commit rapes. In those cases she rationalizes her participation in the case by saying that she has "ended up sending people to prison [through plea bargains] for more years than a lot of DAs do, but again it's trying to get something that's fair and right."

Before I even had a chance to ask her how she felt about her gender as a conscious strategy in crimes involving violence against women, Fran says that she "likes it the other way around. I like to represent women who have been accused of killing men they've been involved with—battered women."

> FJ: I think there are so many women out there who are abused. I'm trying to get what's fair and just and right for my client. And I feel like the system treats women different than men. Sometimes you just don't send a woman to prison if she's got to support her babies. But when it comes to women perpetrating violence on men, it's the opposite. They are much more severe on women that attack their partners. I don't think it's fair. I don't think it's right. It's kind of nice sometimes when women stand up and defend themselves against these guys that have abused them for years and years.

Fran makes it clear that she does not necessarily like it that women kill. "I'm a feminist, and I don't like crimes against women, but I don't like crimes against anybody." But if she had to choose between defending a man who beats and kills his wife and a woman who has been beaten for years and then responds, she would choose the latter. According to her, this is a place where she can have a positive social impact.

Fran is a classic example of the woman defender as a tempered radical, someone who may bring about change in the criminal justice system just by being who she is—her gender challenges the status quo. In representing women who kill their abusers, she can bring about fairness and use her identity to help her own. (This is a precursor to the type of identity display performed by men of color prosecutors in the appendix.) Fran is also about to undergo a career transition. With ten years of practice behind her, she has just been promoted to one of the senior positions in her office. She is now in the position to supervise a death-penalty case and perhaps even a branch office of public defenders in her large county.

FJ: Our current boss, I think, has been very good in trying to promote people other than white males that are qualified to do the work, and so that has a big impact on things. I think that a lot of these old boys don't do things as well as women. I don't mean to be anti-men, but we are [not only] kick-ass trial attorneys, but we're also perceptive about what makes a good work environment for people and how to support your people. A lot of the guys that have been around forever, they're just like, "Well, you've got it tough, too bad." So that's something that's been difficult, but we're seeing some of that change now.

When I asked Fran what her most emotional case was, she replied, "The most recent. It's an ongoing thing . . ."

ANNETTE PETROFF

One of the women I interviewed, Annette Petroff, began her legal career as the second chair on death-penalty cases, meaning she was not responsible for the handling of a case, as Fran will be, but contributed by writing legal briefs, doing investigation, trial work, and working with the victim. Annette worked on about eleven of these cases, the majority dealing with female victims.

AP: One case involved a large number of victims, many of whom were female sexual-assault victims. The others, one case involved two male sexual-assault victims. And then I would say maybe two others involved female sexual-assault victims.

The only case Annette says she was hesitant to work on was the one involving the multiple murders and sexual assaults. But she follows by saying, "I mean, I never felt that this crime is too horrendous; I can't be involved in it. As a matter of fact, I think the more horrendous the more they needed representation." Later she adds the rationalization, "It didn't somehow bother me the number of victims, etc. It just was a larger scale of single killing." Annette, however, did not rationalize away the sexual assaults, or that the case was huge and the client difficult.

In the course of our conversation, Annette suggested that she experiences minimal conflict in her work. She herself was the victim of a rape as a teenager and wondered whether she would be able to work on capital cases because so many involve sex crimes. But she sees that trauma as "a totally separate event from what I do for a living and [one that] doesn't interfere. . . . It really hasn't been a source of trouble for me." What Annette's comment shows is an excellent ability to "compartmentalize."

> AP: I think that some emotional involvement probably helps put together a compelling case. But in terms of not letting your personal feelings, or emotional self, or your background interfere with erecting all the roadblocks you need to erect to defend a person . . . I don't know, somehow it hasn't been that difficult for me.

Annette's effectiveness in separating her personal, maybe emotional, reaction to a crime in order to be able to focus on her job reveals a sophisticated ability to use beliefs in combating a potential emotional dilemma. This is especially true for someone with her personal history and limited experience practicing criminal law.

One element she was not able to compartmentalize was her gender. Annette is very attractive by American standards of beauty in the early 2000s. She is young (thirty-seven years old), white, athletic—a marathon runner—taller than average, and thin. Annette realizes that on certain cases she was chosen to sit at the defense table next to the male defendant as a strategy but says that she did not feel "used," because it was something she would have done if she had been in charge of the case. At the same time she realizes that it is a "man's world" in criminal defense work.

> AP: And so you're conscious of it, of your femaleness in that setting. Whereas, for instance here [on this park bench], I am not aware of gender. My gender doesn't enter into my thinking here. Or I'm not aware of it, I guess. It's not a conscious part of my doing what I'm doing here. It was, there.
>
> CS: When did you realize that?
>
> AP: On day one.

I shared with Annette that I was consulting at that time on a rape case and that the first day we went to court the attorney called me to the defense table and had me sit next to the defendant.

CS: It was such a strange feeling because it is what I'm studying. I know it's a strategy. I know what's being done, and all of a sudden I am that person. You're not really being used, and you don't object to it. But you realize there's a certain utility involved.

AP: And it works. I had interviewed jurors after this one lengthy trial who were very aware of the strategy.

CS: What kinds of things did they say?

AP: I remember one juror outright saying, "We know exactly why you were sitting there next to him the whole time and looking like you're really friendly with him." Which I was—it wasn't an act. I had known the defendant for a long time and was close to him. It wasn't an act, but they perceived it as that. The strategy did not go unnoticed.

CS: But they didn't say something like, "We knew he wasn't guilty because otherwise how could you be sitting there?"

AP: Oh no. In that case guilt was not an issue. It was clear that he was guilty. The issue was life or death.

Sitting next to a client in the courtroom with a bailiff nearby offers an amount of protection not guaranteed in locked interview rooms, another place Annette is keenly aware of gender and resulting tensions, especially with men who have spent so much of their lives in prison and have had so little contact with women. Not unlike the sexualized encounter Becky found herself in, Annette experiences the double bind of gender in these settings even though she concentrates on setting up emotional and physical boundaries with her clients.

AP: I remember being in a locked holding cell on numerous occasions with this one client who was very aggressive. Not in a hostile or threatening way, but in a very friendly, very juvenile, trying-to-touch way. I was so concerned that the bailiff would look in while he was reaching over or something. And I was almost feeling myself like I was in collusion with him some way. Because at the same time I was trying to keep him under control. I couldn't, I wouldn't have called the bailiffs for help or reported that he was misbehaving or something.

Her response was to say, "You do that again, and I'm just going to get up and leave." Annette chalks this up to dealing with "pretty limited and damaged" people and moves us in the direction of an emotion work technique that includes turning the defendant into society's victim.

Annette has practiced law only seven years, but her reflections are similar to those of Sally Tan, who has been in practice twenty-two years and who is court-appointed only on homicide cases. One could argue that Annette has not been the first chair (i.e., responsible attorney) on difficult cases, so she has yet to experience the conflicts of other women defenders at this stage. Another factor is that she works in a small, liberal county, where death-penalty cases rarely make it to trial. She tells me, "We just don't get death verdicts, and none of our clients have ever been executed." The goal of her team was to try to settle a case for a sentence of life without parole, or less, before the trial so that the client did not risk getting the death penalty.

There is also the important fact that Annette was a contract worker who had the "luxury" of not having to take on any of the cases she worked on, and that these were high-profile cases where the county and state put a great deal of money into the defense. As Annette put it, "There was enough money to do the right investigation and do everything that should be done. In other words, it really comes down to money. Whereas a lot of counties are restricted financially from putting on much of a defense." Add to that the notoriety of the defendants and cases she was working on—one an infamous serial killer, another involving two children who killed their parents. The celebrity and publicity brought excitement and travel to her day-to-day work that can hardly be compared to the average day Fran described.

Still, I think the better explanation is that she was immediately thrown into a death-penalty work environment. My own observations suggest that people who do this kind of work are adamantly opposed to the death penalty, and that opposition, more than any other ideology, drives their work. As Annette explains her work to others:

> AP: A lot of people, if you point out how many people have been innocently accused, will understand a little bit better why it's so important that we don't judge people instantaneously, like we did 500 years ago, and [we don't do] summary executions. Because a lot of innocent people get caught in that net.

Such a strong explanation requires less internal work than needed in cases where the stakes are not as high. Especially in death-penalty cases, she says, "People are entitled to someone speaking on their behalf. . . . I just do it." That is her ideological work. Annette's emotion work is "not getting too emotionally wrapped up by the particulars—just trying to focus on the bigger picture of what you're trying to do."

Annette has just been hired to the dependency unit of her county's juvenile court office, where she will no longer have the luxury of turning down cases. Becky's account of the toll juvenile defense work takes on the public defender was telling. Her assignment was less emotionally taxing than the one Annette is about to take on. Annette will represent parents in cases that involve Child Protective Services, parents whose children are removed from the home due to allegations of abuse and neglect. Some of her new clients have sexually violated their small children. "It will be tough," she said, "but I just believe so strongly . . ." I ask her if her role in this new work will be clear and simple. Annette's response is, "Defend them if possible; get an acquittal if there's any way to do it."

> AP: It's not your role to judge them. You're this person's advocate, and you can't judge them on any level, as a person, as what they did, as what they didn't do. . . . Once you go down that road, I think it would be very difficult to do it. So maybe that's my rationalization. I am not the judge. That's not my role. I think that people who say I couldn't defend someone who did X or Y, in essence, are making a judgment about the person. So I guess that's my process—not to judge the client. Otherwise you can't do it even when it's completely clear that they did what is said to have been done.

There will be nothing glamorous about her new job—or her new office. Despite the fact that she works in an affluent county, her new office is dark and shabby and must be shared with one, if not two, other deputy public defenders. Old tattered furniture in olives and oranges rests on a floor with too many years of polish, and cheap paintings in the same colors line the walls. But Annette is now in charge of her own caseload—no more second chair. Time will tell whether Annette will maintain her ideological adamancy. As it stands, even though she is still in the early stages of her career, Annette's explanation of her work and her staunch ideological position is more closely associated with the "seasoned woman defender" (chapter five) than it is with the Betties—or even with women who are in their midcareer, whom I consider next.

You have a duty to be a zealous advocate, and you're the only one who knows in your heart if you can do that. And if you get to the point where you feel like you can't do a good job for someone because of your personal feelings, it's up to you to stand up and say, "I can't do this." And they should honor that.
—Meg Lowe

I'm contemptuous of the law. . . . My attitude about that is that it's just a hurdle to get over. . . . And I'm pure emotion. I don't get comfort from some sort of intellectual syllogisms. Emotional lawyers suffer from much more burnout because they're constantly being slapped down and hurt. . . . It's my Achilles' heel and my strength, and that's just the way it is.
—Kay Owens

No one really understands the nature of the work we do. We're the few people who can joke about child molestors and some really ugly things because part of it is just to release tension. I've never experienced such beautiful camaraderie. You know that your audience really can empathize with you. So we have therapy sessions here, actually, or at the corner bar.
—Gina Rossi

4

Identity Transformation: Midcareer Women Defenders

What makes me really mad are the self-righteous contradictions—to see a district attorney very intense about something one day and then the very next day turn that whole principle on its head. . . . That part makes me very offended. And that probably sustains me, too. I realize that if you don't have someone who's willing to go to bat for you, and to kind of push and push, if you just go along with the program, everything stays well hidden. But it's not until you rub a couple of stones together do you see a spark.
—Holly Porter

As I proceeded with the interviews, I found distinctive patterns of connections between emotions and ideals that occur at different times and stages in women defenders' careers. The patterns imply a longitudinal trajectory. However, the trajectory of fixed stages in a "moral career"[1] becomes complicated in the lives of women defenders, especially those who have been practicing criminal defense law for eleven to fifteen years. They are the older "sisters" of the Betties and the younger sisters of the Abogadas—the "Abogaditas," if you will. They attended law school in the early '80s, and their reasons for entering the profession vary.

I argue that midcareer is a period of transformation. I find the woman defender reaches "a new plateau when [she] learns that she can survive" her career.[2] Most of the women who have just learned this lesson are in their early to mid-forties.

MEG LOWE

Search-and-seizure issues brought Meg Lowe into criminal defense work. She is forty-two years old, has been a public defender for fifteen years, and has taken twenty-five felony cases to trial. Given her years of experience, she should have had more trials in that period of time, but Meg told me that she has spent most of her career on research for pretrial motions to suppress and dismiss evidence. Considering her legal interests, Meg's office is well located, directly behind the law library in one of California's largest public defenders office. On "research row" she is surrounded by silence; the attorneys nearby tend to be newcomers and stay in their offices writing most of the day. She says, "I started out as the lowest kid, and now I'm the mom on the hallway." Meg has an obvious maternal relationship to the newer research lawyers. She knows to have a box of chocolates and Kleenex on her desk at all times. If a lawyer comes to her upset, Meg will close her office door to give him or her a place to vent.

> ML: Obviously, it's women that tend to cry more, but people can come in yelling. A guy that has left the office would stomp in using the worst language you ever heard. He would come in and just scream and rant and rave, and sometimes he'd throw stuff. I'd just go along with the program until he was done agreeing that what happened to him was fucked. When I first started in this office, you needed to hide to cry. I was told by other people that if [the administration] saw you crying, you'd be held back because it's wimpy. People have recognized that it's okay. Still, you don't want to be crying in the lobby or in court, but nobody thinks less of any women who express their emotions back at the office.

Meg grew up in the Central Valley of California, in a middle-class neighborhood and a conservative, Republican home. Before an internship at the state public defender's office, following her first year of law school, Meg thought she would become a prosecutor. That route made sense for someone who volunteered as a sexual-assault investigator in a district attorney's office while earning her undergraduate degree in criminology. Her college friends went on to become police or probation officers or prosecutors. Meg told me that the prosecution direction would have pleased her family, who saw her intrigue with defense work around illegal searches a phase Meg would outgrow. "I was flabbergasted," she said, "when I finally got out of my neighborhood to find out that not everybody was treated like I'm treated." It upset her to find that the police did not talk to Black men the way they spoke to her and that a friend from El Salvador had a gun pulled on her during a routine traffic stop when she reached over for her purse.

ML: I grew up believing that the police were the good guys, and most of them are, but a lot of them lie, and they lie primarily about poor people, and poor people tend to be more minorities than white poor people, and it just really offended me. . . . I was kind of embarrassed that I had lived this life where I never knew anything. So what interested me and got me involved was illegal search and seizures and the lying cops. The thing that makes me happiest in the world is to get to take on a lying cop, especially if I've got some evidence—if I've got the pictures of the intersection that show that he's lying, or I've got the dispatch tape that he doesn't know I have so that I can prove to the judge that he's lying. I mean, there's just nothing that makes me happier than that.

I could see Meg was thrilled by the way she rubbed her hands together as she said, "It's like, 'Give me a lying cop, a new lying cop, a nice young one.' That's what I like the best."

As a "motions person," Meg rarely ends up taking cases to trial. She tells me she tends toward "paper cases" (i.e., arguing cases through legal briefs or motions), with good outcomes. The only cases she took to trial had problems that could not be addressed solely through legal motions, such as unreasonable district attorneys or clients unwilling to accept prison terms that came with plea bargains. "Very rarely did I try cases where I had someone who I thought was truly innocent, or where I had a great defense." Good defenses that arise with compelling legal issues can be argued on paper.

Meg recalled that the most emotionally stressful case she ever had was a sex case—actually the only sex case she has tried. This was also the only case that Meg ever requested be assigned to another attorney. The administration knows not to assign her familial molestations if the defendant is an older man and the victim is a little girl. Meg told me that an elderly relative molested her as a child. That one "type of defendant," in Meg's words, "just gives me the heebie-geebies. And that is my issue." Other kinds of sexual assaults, whether rapes or stranger molestations, she can handle, but Meg told me this particular case was different. I asked how she got past her objection. "They told me to. I didn't want the case. I didn't think it was my turn. And they said, 'Oh no, you're taking this one.' And so I did." The facts of this case are best told in Meg's words:

ML: It was three counts of rape and two forcible oral copulations. He followed a fifteen-year-old girl at night, strangled her, dragged her into an orchard and told her he was going to kill her when he was done. And he didn't finish. The police arrived and he didn't stop. They had to pull him off of this kid. . . . You can tell from the facts there wasn't any sort of a defense. You've got a bus driver who sees him following her, you've got her testimony, you've got all these police who arrive, you've got these horrible statements that he makes. The only thing they didn't have was a video tape. And I think we tried the case for his pleasure. So it was really just a miserable experience.

CS: He asked for a trial, so you took it to trial. You had no choice.

ML: No, you don't. And I think the only reason we went to trial was because he wanted to watch her squirm, he wanted to watch me squirm; he wanted to watch the female prosecutor. I think he just was really a sick human being.

It's horrible for anybody to watch the victim of a crime have to talk about it because it just is a very painful thing. It's painful for them and for everybody else. And the district attorney wanted to make sure that the jury got the full impact. And so she pushed this girl using icky words—pushed her, pushed her, pushed her, until she broke down. It was really not necessary . . . I mean, it was an overkill on the part of the DA . . . but she wanted the girl to break down in front of the jury, and so she made it happen. I did not do it. I was very gentle with her. There was no reason to be confrontational, and strategically I didn't think it was a good plan. But when the girl broke down, she started to go, her chin starts to quiver, you can see that she's barely maintaining, and then she lost it, and then she kind of put her hands over her face and then folded up and went into a fetal position off of the chair, actually went down to the ground in a fetal position. Which was just the impact the DA was hoping for, but it was like a horrible thing to do to this kid, I thought. So I asked for a recess, just because I wanted everybody to get out of there . . . I went out into the hallway . . . it was just awful to watch. . . . And I had to leave the felony team with an ulcer after that, which I always kind of thought was his ulcer.

It is hard to imagine an attorney that would not find this case difficult. Not only was the crime truly horrendous, but the defendant behaved abominably toward Meg. She said his attitude was horrible, and he said awful racist things to her or whispered sexual things and made noises.

> ML: He kept sending me on wild goose chases—maybe he took medications from his mother and took them that night so he wasn't culpable for what he did. So then I'd have to track down his mother to find out what kind of medications she had. Then I'd have to get his blood analyzed to see if any of those medications were there. Or he'd say, "Well, maybe she was a teen prostitute, and maybe I had some coke and maybe she wanted it." [I replied,] "Well you know what, they analyzed her blood and your blood, and neither one of you had any drugs in your system."
>
> As a lawyer I wanted a defense. I wanted something I could talk about. I spent all of this time combing through [the file] trying to find something to hang my hat on. And he kept coming up with all of these different reasons why he had not victimized her. He knew she was giving it away elsewhere. Why shouldn't he take what's being given away for free? And we're talking about a fifteen-year-old girl. . . . There was no question that this girl was not a prostitute, or anything. . . . There was a big racial element to what he was doing and why hurting white women was a way of getting back at white men.

With her history, there was no way for Meg to lessen the social distance between herself and the defendant. For her, there was no way to get beyond the feeling that her client "was just a bad person." Meg told me, "I couldn't do this if I couldn't see the good in people. And he was really something." And the client was not about to let her get close to him. "He was never going to like me," Meg said, "because I was always going to be white and a woman, which are the two things he hates most in the world. But he and I had a working relationship."

The only time in her career that Meg said she nearly broke down in court was in this case. By her own description of the courtroom drama, the person she wanted to help was the victim. In this instance, Meg was empathizing with the victim and no strategy of emotion work was completely successful in avoiding this. Just being gentle in the cross-examination of the victim was not enough to overcome the negative feelings she had for her client, or the emotional and physical stress she was enduring. According to Meg, the girl would not even take a Kleenex from her when the courtroom was cleared. It had to be passed by the district attorney who subjected the girl to unnecessary pain. The only way Meg could get through the ordeal was to persevere.

Still Meg reflects back on this case with pride.

> ML: I felt afterwards like, if I can do that, I can do anything. And I did everything I could for that guy, and he couldn't have had a better attorney. I wanted so bad to make sure I was not being unfair to this guy. . . . I really did feel like I have withstood the test of fire. I can do anything. And nobody could have been a more difficult client for me, and I did it. So there was a pride at the end and in what I had done. There was pride in that but it was very unpleasant.

This case happened, in her words, "a long time ago . . . [but] it's not something I'll ever forget."

There are women defense attorneys who are in their line of work because they want to stand up for those people who don't know how to stand up for themselves. As Meg sees it, "You're helping someone other than the victim of a crime, which is also a helping job."

> ML: It's almost always someone who's been kicked around and hurt, and so many of our clients just really need a friend, someone to stand by them and say, "Look, I'll help you, I'll help you get through this." Many people who commit crimes have done something bad, but they are not themselves bad. They're people who need help who don't know how to get help, who may want help.

She says that just maybe she can turn someone's life around. Meg sees herself as the victim who survived to go on to do better things, and she believes her clients can too. This is most evident in her determination on search-and-seizure cases where there's a question of a "lying cop." One could argue that Meg sees herself as the victim, questioning the legitimate authority who is abusing his power—not unlike her position as the victim of molestation by an elderly relative.

Like Becky, Meg's emotion work is evident in her attempt to avoid identifying with the victim, which may in her case take extra work, considering her childhood trauma. Unlike Becky, in order to do her job Meg usually identifies with the defendant and sees him as the victim, even in domestic violence or date-rape cases:

> ML: I have a hard time believing that domestic violence is entirely one-sided. And that's where you do get into demeaning or challenging the credibility [of the victim] or pointing out other instances where this person has made false reports or has instigated problems or whatever . . . and you do it in those cases. And my experience has always been that I believe in what I'm doing. It's not like, "I think I'm going to make fun of her today." You don't do that. But you start gathering evidence, and you start feeling like, wait a minute, my client is the one who's been victimized here. . . .
>
> You see [date rapes] over and over again, where you've got people going out on a date and then a few days later he hasn't called her. She calls the police: she was raped. And then you think, wait a minute, what's going on here. Is this a woman who's embarrassed that she had sex on a first date when she shouldn't have, or is this someone who was really raped? And you don't know. And it is very difficult. But for the most part when my clients get arrested and put in jail on a rape charge, it destroys their lives, it destroys their homes. . . .

The beliefs that brought Meg into this line of work, "grew stronger over time." And her desire to help has been transformed into part of a professional ideology. As a young lawyer, she realized that there are people who do not have the advantages that her white skin and middle-class standing offer.

> ML: They can't defend themselves, and somebody needs to stand up next to them and say, "I'm willing to stand up next to this person. I will be their champion. I'll help them." I mean, everybody needs that. And I don't care what they did, everybody needs that.

Ideologically, Meg asserted,

ML: To be a good public defender . . . you have to be able to handle things that are unpleasant to you. And you have to do that whether it's murder, or whatever it is. . . . It's like, the First Amendment: I may not like what you have to say, but I'll defend to the death your right to say it.

Ultimately, Meg adds that being a public defender has colored her political views more than the other way around: "I'm not a member of Mothers Against Drunk Driving. I don't like those organizations, and I don't like them because I'm a public defender."

GINA ROSSI

Gina Rossi's sophisticated appearance belies the class background she described for me. I had been waiting for Gina for some time in the lobby of her office. The time gave me a chance to dry out from the rain that hit just as I left my car in a dash for the huge, bleak box of a building that houses her metropolitan public defender's office. As in most of these sorts of buildings, a guide is necessary to make it through the maze of offices. As I waited for my escort, the public defender clients tried to figure out what I was doing there. I don't look like the "typical" public defender client; maybe I'm an attorney. Some asked my legal advice only to find (to their disappointment) that I was a sociologist. A new receptionist took over the front desk while I was waiting. She didn't know who I was either—perhaps a new attorney or an intern waiting to be processed. I let her know I was waiting for Ms. Rossi, who burst into the office just about that same time in her well-planned rain gear. Here was a woman who knows her city and its weather, unlike me (suddenly feeling like a drowned rat). At a glance, I could only be taken for an attorney by the down-on-their-luck folks lining the lobby. Realizing that Gina and I were the only whites in the reception area, including the secretarial staff, I experienced one of those moments of strangeness when the race reality of the criminal justice system revealed itself once again.

At thirty-eight years of age, Gina is the youngest of the women defenders in my midcareer category. She has practiced law for twelve years—ten of them as a public defender. After two years of working for an insurance defense firm, she applied to a large public defender's office solely for the trial experience it would provide. She told me there was no political motivation behind her career move.

> GR: It ended up being a true miracle that this was exactly what was waiting for me, because I love the job, and I can't think of anything else I'd rather do. . . . I didn't come here for ideological purposes. Maybe that's why I ended up loving it so much—because it evolved into something else for me.

During Gina's time as a public defender, she has taken approximately fifty cases to trial. For the past three years, she has been a member of a complex litigation unit. Rather than having the run-of-the-mill felony burglaries and robberies and a full case load, she is assigned to five serious cases at one time.

As in all of my interviews, I asked Gina if there were any events in her life that would make certain types of cases difficult, if not impossible, to take. The following story is the first thing that came to Gina's mind when asked. In the process of responding to me, she painted a picture of her early years and family life.

When she was seventeen years old, Gina was living in her hometown in the Central Valley of California. Her grandmother used to live on "First Street," the main street of this farm town. After she became widowed, the grandmother moved from the farm to a little Italian neighborhood. Like many ethnic neighborhoods, First Street eventually deteriorated. Living next door to Gina's grandmother was another elderly Italian woman, "Nana."

> GR: She was the sweetest. She was like my grandmother. When I'd go see my grandmother, I'd go see Nana. And every day they'd be out on the porch talking. It was just wonderful, like one of those beautiful childhood memories.

These two little old ladies were the only two Italians that survived and kept living in the neighborhood over the years. Eventually Gina's grandmother died. For the next few years Nana still lived in the same little house next door. When Nana was about ninety years old, a man broke into Nana's house, stole her social security check, and brutally raped and murdered her. She told me she has not thought about this in a long time, although it feels like it just happened yesterday: "Obviously I have very strong emotional feelings as they relate to Nana."

At the time, Gina decided that she would become a police officer. She fantasized about apprehending the suspect, who was never caught. On a human level, she said, she wanted to kill that person; instead, she imagined apprehending him. For Gina, becoming a police officer would have channeled her desire for revenge. She never joined the police force, but these events led to her interest in the criminal justice system. The way she redirected her urge to kill Nana's murderer through her dream of enforcing the law is similar to the way she approaches her role as an advocate. It appears Gina easily counters intense emotions by taking practical steps:

> GR: I have always thought I've been pretty good about separating what I do from what I believe. If it's the job, if you can't take the heat, get out of the kitchen. And if you can't do it, you shouldn't be doing it. And I just guess those are strong values, working-class values. I don't know what they are; those are just really strong beliefs that I've always had. It may be how I was raised. You've got to have discipline. If you've got a job, you've got to do it.

Gina reveals two things through this story. First, she counters her strong emotions of revenge with a rational fantasy—police work. Second, Gina gives a window into her childhood memories of small-town Italian working-class culture—the work ethic and the values of her community of origin. She ended by saying, "All the other kinds of things naturally follow." In other words, the strong work ethic rationalizes away the emotional content. The ethic is not limited to a certain career; it is her cultural discipline for work. While this particular ethic is not coated in higher ideals, its ideology emerges in another one of Gina's stories.

When I asked about her definitions of fair and unfair, Gina related a long story about a public defender Christmas party. She said she was leaving at one or two o'clock in the morning. There were a couple of cops outside the monstrous downtown public building. A friend and colleague said to her, "You know, I'm so glad I'm a white woman." Gina was quick to defend her friend's comment to me and adds that it is okay for public defenders to say something that might sound racist

GR: . . . because we don't say them with evil motives, because it's the truth. You know what? No one's going to mess with you. You know what? You are in a protected class basically. You're a Black guy leaving a party, a young Black kid, you know what? Chances are, if it's between me and him, the cop's going to stop him to see if he's intoxicated or if he's got drugs on him. And you talk of it because that's the truth. You're white, you're in a protected class, you're like a Black kid in the projects, and you look suspect, you're going to get stopped. That's just how it is. People are still harassed. It's race and economics, then it's where you live. That's unfairness to me.

Gina described an issue of equality that "started with childhood and my basic belief of where I came from. It was just a natural progression to take it to my profession. That fundamental concept formed itself in a bigger thing in the Constitution and the right to representation." Because of her working-class experience, she truly believes that people should be equal regardless of their socioeconomic status. Growing up, it always angered her that somebody from one social group was more privileged than a person from a lower "class." Now, she told me, it should make her mad but, "it probably doesn't, because I assume that's a given. I assume the client is getting screwed. That's why they've got me. I just consider it part of life, and part of why I'm there to do the job." In essence, Gina uses equality as the rationale for why she is needed and anger as an emotional fuel. Her response is similar to Meg's with regard to her Salvadoran friend's treatment by the police. The difference is that Gina finds the need for equality rooted in her working-class background, whereas Meg's comes through recognition of her white middle-class privilege. For each, an early recollection of socio-economic disparities in how people are treated provides the energy for her work. Ultimately, those recollections help combat internal conflict.

GR: I'm very proud to say in front of a jury, "I am a deputy public defender." You know what a good feeling it is afterwards when they say, "I thought you were a private lawyer," because it goes back to the equality issue. It makes me feel good to think that this schmuck over here who has no money, no one who cares about him, no resources, that you're the only one in this world who's

going to care about him. And you know what? You're just as good
as all the money can buy.

Other aspects of Gina's background underlie her attitudes toward defense work. After growing up in a Republican household, Gina feels she
understands the mentality of conservatives. Her father is a retired farmer
from California's San Joaquin Valley. Both of her brothers also became
farmers after brief attempts at college. Gina was the first person in her
family to graduate from college—and to adjust her political views. While
her family has been supportive of her career, she says that she would kick
any of them off a jury for their beliefs. Gina was the first professional, the
youngest, and a woman. She said, "That was actually a kind of big deal in
my family because I would imagine from childhood it was just assumed
that I would grow up, get married to a farmer, and live in the Central
Valley." Instead, her parents divorced and, as the youngest child, Gina grew
up in a "less traditional kind of lifestyle" than her brothers did. She did not
marry a farmer, like her mother and grandmother before her. When it was
just the two of them, Gina's mother showed her that she could live life as
a woman on her own. From her description of growing up in a household
supported by a mother who worked first in a cannery and then as a retail
clerk, life was not easy. As Gina put it, "It allowed me to be kind of different, to have an alternative kind of life." Still she's never lost the working-
class notion of work as productivity. Coming from a farming family, Gina
believes work should produce a tangible object.

One case in particular, Gina said, gave her pause about the conflict
between her understanding of "work" and what she does as a criminal defense lawyer. She was representing, in her words, "a gentleman" on an un-
solved rape case. The man was from Louisiana and had a long history of
rapes, "lots of priors." The Department of Justice matched one of his fingerprints to the crime scene and extradited him back to California.

GR: Basically, they thought he was a serial rapist. This was a case with
a woman who lived on [California] Street. Regular neighborhood.
She could have been your friend, my friend. Just a nice woman,
working, just a nice woman. Obviously it wasn't a case about fabri-
cation, or it wasn't rape: she obviously was raped. The defense was
obviously "misidentification"—they only had a fingerprint. Interestingly enough, I fought really, really hard on that case. And the

jury, some of whom I talked with afterwards, said they were amazed at how hard I was fighting because "how could you fight so hard for this client?"

Gina told me she actually wondered the same during the trial. It wasn't so much that she could fight for this man. She was fighting for him, and she thought she was winning. The question she had was, "What do I produce as a criminal defense lawyer? Isn't it a strange job I do?"

GR: In my case, to be effective, to be productive, means that I theoretically could get this man off who's done this terrible thing. And like somebody who's on a production line, or an assembly line who's making widgets, or who's a computer technician, or a physician, or who's doing things that really benefit society, what am I doing, really?

That was a moment, and I remember discussing that with one of my colleagues, saying, "You can't think about what you do too much, what it is you produce. Why do we have so many of us, and isn't it really a sad commentary on our society that they need us, when maybe we could be using our talents elsewhere, to produce things, to make people's lives easier and better? Why is this my role to get this guy off?" And he got convicted. And I was surprised. Well maybe, I guess not. But in any event he got convicted and he got thirty-eight years. And he took it. It was no big deal for him. It was the only life he knew, except when he was out committing rapes.

That was the only time in my life when I just kind of thought about the whole thing. About what we do, about what our goal is. . . . It wasn't to the extent that I couldn't do the case. Because I think the guy got some pretty good representation. I mean, I really fought hard and did my best. But I guess I thought about that after having the case and knowing that I was working so hard and that I could potentially walk him. I mean, it didn't happen, so I didn't have to worry about it.

Gina is the only attorney I interviewed who questions her work in terms of what she produces. When she used the word "widgets" I thought of undergraduate lectures in classical social theory on Marx. Professors love to use "widget" examples when teaching Karl Marx's early essay, "Estranged Labor."[3] From a Marxian perspective, fundamentally what it means to be a human being is to work, produce, and create, and to do it all with fore-thought. Labor, or one's life energy, is objectified in the process of producing a material object. According to Marx, this is all fine as long as the worker controls the object she has created. However, in capitalism the worker is haunted by the fact that the object that she has consciously created—that which embodies her sense of being—belongs to another. In Gina's case, she recognizes a fundamental disjuncture in her own labor process: she produces no tangible objects as a farmer or cannery worker would. However, she is not completely separated from her production either; her participation leads to a sentencing outcome. The outcome for the rapist will not come back to haunt her, though she suggests that possible alienation from her hard work had the client gone free.

Professor Hochschild's insight into the connection between "the commercialization of human feeling" and becoming an "instrument of labor," is present in Gina's reflections.[4] But I wonder more about her rationalization of the work process, work ethic, and job duty in order to counter the deepest human feelings. It is her sense of work that spares her the emotional turmoil.

Gina told me that the reason she was late for our meeting has the potential of troubling her for quite some time. Rather than fearing a client might get off (as in the case of the "gentleman" rapist), now she represents her clients while confronting what she sees as unfair sentences based on California's three-strikes law.

The day before we met was an unusually difficult day for her—the first time she had a client sentenced to life in prison. She told me twice, "It was life *with* possibility of parole," as if to lessen the severity of the sentence—and it does. Gina is assigned to the complex litigation unit of her office. Her clients with their multiple felony charges are exactly those one would expect to have sentences enhanced under the three-strikes law. As pointed out in earlier chapters, the sentences that result from this law are twenty-five years to life. The fact that Gina has lost only one client to the three-strikes law speaks to her effectiveness as a criminal defense attorney. It also speaks to what a loss this trial was for her.

Gina told me that this case preoccupied her for the last three years. The facts are, in her words, "really bizarre." The defendant and the victim were romantically involved but in the process of splitting up. The victim, a young woman, was beginning to see someone else. According to Gina, both the victim and the defendant "were kids that were into all that kind of mystical vampire stuff." The night of the crime, they had gone to see the movie *Interview with a Vampire*. After the movie, the defendant told the victim, "You have to die tonight." The young woman was stabbed thirteen times; she almost died and was in the hospital two weeks. According to Gina,

GR: The issue was, did he really intend to kill her? Or was he psychotic and thus guilty of something lesser than the most serious of serious? I've never had a case that was so replete with evidence of psychosis. But the problem was that the prosecutor politicized it: it was domestic violence, domestic violence, domestic violence. Domestic violence is bad; I mean, I'm a feminist. You'd want to kick me off a jury in a domestic violence case. But the thing is you shouldn't have these knee-jerk reactions to labels. That the victim was trying to see someone else was not the impetus for what occurred. What happened was a psychotic break. And that's what bothered me about the case. There was this tunnel vision. Let's call it domestic violence versus penetrating the veneer and seeing what the case is really about.

During some of the testimony there was a suggestion by me that something else was going on. Maybe not S&M, but basically the conversation when he was stabbing her was more like, "You have to die." It wasn't like, boom, boom, boom [gestures heavy strike]. He was crazy. There were all these puncture wounds, and she was qualifying [her protests about the pain] like, "[Joe] this hurts too much. Take the knife out now." Instead of saying, "Get off of me! What are you doing!" She was really calm, so I was suggesting there was something more to it. They were young kids who were into alternative kind of things. I wasn't saying she was deserving it, but I was [asking] in some ways, "Why would she qualify it so much?" I mean the focus of the case was clearly that had he wanted to kill her [he could have]. None of the injuries penetrated more than two centimeters. The woman was very small. She was like 105 pounds, 5'3". Tiny, petite woman. Now, you've got a six-inch blade, and if you want, it wouldn't take much to kill the woman.

And then he calls 911. The testimony came in that he told her to tell the [dispatcher] that a Black man did it, and when the police officers responded [the defendant] was there. He cleared the way for everybody to come in, and he told the police officers that a Black intruder had done it. And that was a big problem in the case. Now this is interesting, and this didn't come in as evidence, and I'm thinking maybe I should have done it. Do you remember that woman several years ago who drove her children into the lake?

CS: Susan Smith. She blamed it on a Black man.

GR: Well that happened right before this happened. It shows he was suggestible and that was part of his mental illness. The movie, he was suggested. It sounds ludicrous, but people suffering from bipolar disorder are highly suggestible. People think of mental health defenses as excuses. And that was certainly a theme that was addressed throughout the trial [by the prosecution] during jury selection. I mean, the Theodore Kaczynski "Unabomber" case was going on. And O. J. ruined it for everyone, right? I mean, we're not going to let another person get off on domestic violence. There was a numbness out there that unfortunately this client became a scapegoat on. I underestimated how powerful this whole thing about domestic violence is.

CS: What was the jury like?

GR: I obviously did not pick a jury that I thought I had chosen. I left on people that I thought were smart. One woman was a nurse, and I typically kick off nurses, just because they tend to be conservative. This is a woman who seemed to be liberal, and so I thought maybe she would be sympathetic to this, and I thought because she was smart she would be a stronghold. And there was another guy there, and he happened to be gay, and I generally kick off white gays because they tend to be conservative. And I thought he was smart and he would be a stronghold. And I had a Japanese woman, older Japanese woman, married, family. Couldn't kick her off because I ran out of challenges. And I thought, well, she'll just go with the flow. And then I had a couple of Filipino women who I thought, you've got to keep the ones who you think are not going to be strongholds. And unfortunately, the person who turned out to be the floor person is somebody I should have kicked off. It was a young woman—intelligent—and she seemed from her appearance to be kind of liberal. So I thought she'd be sympathetic. But what I didn't realize was she by nature would sympathize with the victim in the case.[5] Being liberal, it works both ways, right? Domestic violence is a liberal issue, and she's the one who became most vocal. I thought the guy was totally on my side. Everyday he would smile, and I thought, "Oh, he's in my camp." All I need is one. He totally, like, screwed us. The jury was out only four hours, which from my perspective wasn't much at all given the fact that there was a lot of technical evidence in the case.

So that was the case and I think that the times are changing. I hadn't tried a case for two years, and I did think, "I can win." I thought the jury would just basically believe what I could sell them. And that they were going to believe me, and that I could not lose it. And I was . . . I was not shocked by the verdict, given the fact I knew I had lost them. Because at that point I realized something really bad had happened. But, I mean, going into it, I felt I kind of got caught in the headlights. So that was what I'd consider a really great loss.

Gina told me the stress she experienced during the trial energized her. The stress she experienced the day after the interview "is a different kind." It's not the kind that fuels her. Rather it is the kind that comes with a big loss, an example of what really hurts in her job. Gina's attempt to distance herself from responsibility emerges through her use of the passive voice (e.g., "During some of the testimony there was a suggestion by me"). She further explains away the pain by blaming the loss on the juror who "screwed" her, on the prosecutor who "politicized" the case, and on the ripple effect from the O. J. Simpson and Theodore Kaczynski cases. It is painful for her to think that she chose the wrong strategy. Gina asked for my opinion on whether she should have brought in the Susan Smith case to show just how suggestible her client was.

GR: Do you think that would have helped if you were on the jury and heard, "Hey, he got the idea from somebody else?" Would that have shown more lucidity?

CS: Well, I have a tendency to think situationally and that things hap-

pen because of the times they happen in. So, yeah, it would have
helped me.

GR: Because you're a sociologist. Okay, so you'd probably get kicked
off by the prosecution, right?

CS: It wouldn't take long.

Gina was honest about what she was thinking and about how badly she had
misjudged the situation. Losing a case where the jury deliberates only four
hours can be humiliating.

Erving Goffman writes that social life is organized around ritual.[6] In
certain situations, when a person breaks the rules of her group, she must
perform "remedial work," such as apologizing or offering explanation to
remain a member of the group. This is especially so when a person's deepest
fears of incompetence are revealed. Gina's account of this case sounds
much like the remedial work Goffman describes. She did not see the verdict
coming; she was the proverbial "deer caught in the headlights." From Goffman's perspective, Gina is willing to "perform [her] own castigation."[7]
While her story of the case is not a formal apology, it shows aspects of one
when she repeatedly says she should have done things differently. Gina's
ability to understand why other public defenders might criticize her legal
tactics and accept blame implies that she is a rightful member of the club
of defense attorneys. I am uncertain whether a man in Gina's position
would have been as self-degrading as she was. However, she countered that
self-degradation when she told me that part of the job description is to be
strong.

GR: When I dealt with this client being sentenced to life, I felt as
though I had done something wrong, especially after the verdict. I
took the long route back to the office, because you can never show
emotion. You're not supposed to. You can never shed a tear, never.
You just sit there, you take the verdict. I couldn't stay with the
client because I felt as though I was going to break down and cry.
And then I got back to the office, and you say, "Live to fight another day."

For many of the women I've spoken with and observed, perceived unfair
sentences and the increase in sentence exposures faced by clients since
the three-strikes laws have made the emotional content of their work more

difficult to manage. I compare Gina to Jesse Madrigal, whom I have interviewed several times. Each time we meet, she tells me how much she wants
to get out of criminal defense work. The laws have, in her words, "become
way too draconian," and she doesn't want to be a part of the system any
longer. Jesse says she did excellent work on tort law in school and she now
second-guesses her choice to go into criminal defense. Even immigration
law in California sounds better to her these days.

By contrast, while Gina may second-guess the strategy she used on a
particular case, she never questions her chosen profession. For her, the need
to beat the odds against harsh sentences only adds to the need for tough-
ness in this line of work. The point, she told me repeatedly, is that there is
a "natural progression" to the woman defender's feelings about her job.

> GR: It's where you get experience, and you're more comfortable with
> the kinds of cases you're handling. And once you get to that point,
> and you're handling more serious cases, it just naturally falls into
> place that you're going to be able to rise to that occasion.

My interviews with other women defense attorneys do not support
Gina's assertion that the orientation of the woman defender "just naturally
falls into place." Emotion and ideological work help make it fall into place.
Indeed, Gina herself is engaged in ideological work when she tells me about
the "natural progression" she experienced. If ideology is represented in the
cultural maxims instilled in childhood,[8] we can imagine that the saying,
"When the going gets tough, the tough get going," would be present in
Gina's social history. Put another way, Gina explains her attitudes and behavior as "only natural" for someone like her.[9]

An individual deals with the beliefs she brings into a situation in relation to the practical pressures of that situation. If her beliefs are based on
dispositions shaped by childhood[10] that are compatible with the requirements of the situation, the potential for ideological or emotional contradictions is minimized. Ideological work takes place when individuals try to
cope with opposing ideas. Gina's reflections on her work minimize the contradictions she faces by the value she places on work and her working-class
acceptance of the job. She told me, "It's the job. . . . If you can't do it, you
shouldn't be doing it." I asked Gina, like the others, when she had this
realization. Luck would have it I interviewed her the day after the vampire
case.

GR: I had a lot of cases before, but [this case], because of the complexity of the issues, because of the political issues involved, and the hurdles I really did have to jump over [including] a court compelled psychiatric examination, which we took on appeal. Everything came into this trial. His character was totally assassinated from the get go. Yes, this was the case which I think covered almost every potential issue I've ever had to deal with, including losing somebody for a very long period of time.

When it comes to, "How can you do this?" Isn't it fundamental to the foundation of our whole democracy? Obviously I don't think domestic violence is a good thing. But my role as an advocate, why can't I do the job just as well as a male can? Why can't I separate my feelings, my ideas from what I do? And why can't we all rise to the occasion to know that everybody has a job to do, and you respect it. It doesn't mean that I don't think that ultimately people shouldn't be punished. I just think there are some things that are so fundamental that they're basic. And I think that's an intellectual stance.

KAY OWENS

Kay Owens said she is ready to quit. She wanted to get "away from the office," so we met at a delicatessen where we ended up spending the entire afternoon. Kay told me the job is emotionally painful for her. She sees more and more mentally ill clients in a system that offers them incarceration rather than the institutional care they need. Kay said she was "feeling more tragedy" about how her clients are handled these days. She is forty-five years old, has been practicing criminal law for fifteen years, and has probably taken that many felony cases to trial. Almost all of those cases included acts of violence, but Kay cannot remember trying any sexual-assault cases. According to her, the public defender's administrators may have been protecting her from such cases.

From Kay's childhood history, a sociologist might predict that she would move into a care-giving occupation. She is the eldest of five children. Her father was a lawyer who absented himself from the family; her mother was a "bon vivant," an "adventurer," and an alcoholic. Kay picked up her parents' slack and took care of her four siblings. She told me that caregiving work is what she knows how to do, and she has always done it to her own detriment. Growing up, she was a parent to her siblings, and now she is a parent to her clients.

> KO: I have a very much maternal approach to the job, and I'm just a hands-on, take charge, I'll-solve-this-problem type, even when they're not really solvable. But I think that's probably how kids look at things. I've got to solve the problem. And that's translated into my adult life.

Kay told me she identifies as a social worker as much as or even more than as a lawyer. She sees almost all of her work this way because in California there are fewer social services all of the time. Her approach is to use the law as the means to address social problems.

> KO: Some kid, she's up in juvenile hall, she's drinking a lot, she's already had a kid, she's running away, she's acting out, and I ask my colleague, "What's going on?" He says, "It's alcoholism." I say, "No, no, no. What's going on with her? She was raped." There's always something. A kid is not just an alcoholic. There's something else that happened to them. In my opinion, when somebody crashes like the girls do at juvenile hall, or the women downtown, it's because they've been so violated for a variety of reasons, whatever they may be. Rape, incest, ongoing sexual abuse, prostitution . . . And we send them to a drug program, an alcohol program. The drinking is a symptom of what's really percolating underneath. And if there were services for the girls when they fall . . .

The contrast between her view of the law and that of the typical seasoned woman defender is extreme. Kay recognizes that some people love and believe in the law, but she does not. In fact she distances herself from other participants in the criminal justice system by saying, "I am not one of those. I'm contemptuous of the law. I don't believe in [it]. I don't believe in the system. My attitude about that is that it's just a hurdle to get over. It is not something that really protects us." Part of Kay's attitude comes from the political component of the criminal justice system. She told me that she tends to dislike judges because they "buy into" the law.

KO: They use the law in what I think is a fairly unconscionable way . . .
they just sit there and administer justice when the people that are
brought to them aren't the people that ought to be prosecuted.
The people that are brought to them are the hapless, helpless,
poor, sick, wounded, [and] uneducated, who can't make it. The
law is just trying to get them out of the way so they don't wreck
things for the rest of us. And I despise that.

As we talked, it became apparent that some of Kay's views result from how
she views the different players in the system, such as district attorneys,
using the law as means to "unjust" ends.

Kay kept returning to the mentally ill. She told me the story of a client
she saw the day before:

KO: He's borderline personality. And he's very bright. He's committed
a whole lot of crimes. He's been institutionalized basically his
whole life. [When] he's out, he's very, very depressed. He can't
cope out. He wants in. So he makes himself a little bomb and he
calls suicide hotline, and he talks to them for an hour . . . and they
get permission from him to call the police. He gives it because he
wants in. And he gets arrested. And he's now facing twenty-five to
life.

The reason that this client is facing a twenty-five-years-to-life prison sentence is the three-strikes law. It is clear that Kay's frustration with the new
law is compounded by what she sees as the breakdown of the mental health
system in California.

KO: And so here I am, the district attorney says to me, "It's twenty-
five years, that's what the offer is. . . ." And I looked at him, and I
just started screaming at him. He said, "That's the law, gee, what
am I supposed to do about it?" And I'm like, "That's the law. I
think that's what the Nazis said too. All those people that stood
by and let all these people get destroyed. That was the law, too,
and that's what they hid behind. This is not right. This guy was
trying to commit suicide, and you know it." And I'm really, I'm,
like, yelling at him.

Kay spoke passionately about this case, describing an incident where she was driven by moral outrage, not legal ideals. The district attorney becomes a moral adversary—a "Nazi."

We were eating lunch at the delicatessen, and I could easily imagine the scene she described. Kay is a tiny white woman, perhaps 4'9" tall and perhaps 100 pounds. The woman who suggested I speak with her described her as "feisty"—a term Kay herself used. Despite her passion, she kept talking about giving up. She told me how nerve wracking dealing with her mentally ill client was the day before, watching him "smacking his head, ramming his head against the wall. It's like, 'Aye! Aye! Aye!'—I'm having hot flashes here. Oh my God. He brought on hot flashes."

Kay is working in a system where she says she "can't do a damn thing." This is a woman who says she chose to become a public defender because she wanted to be able to do something "in the system to help these people." Now she's disillusioned.

> KO: Why do I have to put up with this shit? Our jobs have gotten more and more complicated because of [the mentally ill]. We can't relate to the client. Here I am trying to do the best I can for this guy, having a hissy fit with the DA, talking about how he's a Nazi and all that, you know just really totally extreme behavior on my part. Trying to defend this guy, and I can't communicate to him because he's so ill.

Kay is very aware of her extreme behavior. She paints a picture of an adult woman throwing a tantrum in court. Ultimately she is not even effective in making her client feel better.

If a case does make it to trial, Kay said she must then deal with "the politics of the jury."[11] After her part in a trial is over, after she has done everything she can, Kay "relinquishes all control over to a jury of idiots, most of the time." Kay said she does not usually feel "contempt or disdain" for the client sitting next to her, nor does she feel political conflict about what she does. Any social distancing on her part comes from her dislike of other actors in the system: judges, who "defend their lifestyles at some level"; district attorneys, who unreflectively follow the law; and jurors, who do not care what might be wrong with the defendant, "they just don't want [him] out on the streets where they might walk into [him]." Thus, Kay distances herself from those who sit in judgment—the judge, the district attorney (who may offer a plea bargain), and the jury. She does not distance herself from the victim or feel threatened by her clients.

> KO: I'm not judgmental about why they did it. I'm not the victim. And I tend not to see the blood and the gore. I don't see them in a rage. I'm not frightened by them because they need me, so they don't usually make me fearful of them. But I just care. I just feel pain. I've never hated a client. And I've only just rarely disliked clients.
>
> The clients that you tend to dislike the most are the little nitwit white people who think that they're special in the system. And they whine and they cajole, and they have no concept of taking responsibility for what they did. Whereas most of our clients who have been in and out of the system, they know exactly what's going on. They're not whining about it. They just take it. This is their life.
>
> Some of the most egregious criminals make the best clients. The worst contract killers—they're professionals, they know you're the lawyer, they know what your limitations are, they let you do your job, they don't whine about it, they're appreciative for what you've done, and they accept what happens to them.

On the whole, Kay sees the law as disposing of society's unwanted: "Because they can't make it on our terms, we put them away on our terms."

I asked her if she ever had a case that was pivotal, a case that made her believe that, if she could do that, she could do anything. She responded, "No." Kay said she has had the kind of cases that were either going to "break your back" or "destroy you." For example:

> KO: [There] was a guy who committed five burglaries, and during the first of the five, he shot the victim in the leg. Very unusual circumstances though, because he was really trying to get away from [the victim], and he tried to leave the house, and she caught him in the house. He immediately fled, and she fled. She got in her car and was sort of trying to regroup when she saw him walking down the street as if nothing had happened. And she became so enraged that she followed him. He finally got in the car because he couldn't outrun her and ended up shooting her in the leg. And then he

committed four other burglaries [and] was caught. There wasn't one shred of room to defend him. There were fingerprints in every house. There was property from every house in his storage unit, with his name on it, he kept notes of what he'd done, so there were notes indicating what places had been easy to break into. He left his backpack in the woman's house he burgled, with his fingerprints on it. And when he was arrested, her husband's pen was in his pocket. This guy was so completely dead in the water. But he insisted on having a trial because he had no prior record. He was in his thirties and was a complete virgin in the system. He was not going to take the offer of seventeen years that first time out and so he went to trial. And I had to figure out how to stand there and defend this guy where there wasn't a single thing to say that was going to help.

Kay described another instance of a woman defender contemplating how she could possibly go to court without a credible defense. Once again, her client was mentally ill and she described his history—one that has all the makings of a serious motion picture:

KO: He was eight years old when he discovered his mother, who had asphyxiated herself in the garage, and he found the body. So at eight he already was exhibiting symptoms of mental illness himself. Apparently he had a gender disorder, so he wanted to dress in girls' clothes. His father was a military guy, very unemotional, kind of hard fellow. And here he's got this gender-disoriented eight-year-old who's just discovered his mother dead in the car. It went from bad to worse. My experts believe that the discovery of his mother created a post-traumatic stress disorder in the kid that had the result of totally fragmenting all of his personality. So he has every possible character disorder that you can imagine. He's obsessive-compulsive, he's got some anti-social traits, he's got severe depression, he also has a seizure disorder, so he's got some organic brain damage besides, and he's going to go to prison for a long time. So it's one of these situations where this is not an animal, but what has happened in his life has so completely twisted his ability to survive. I mean he's a sick guy; it's just been hideous, and I'm not going to be able to do much for him. In fact I had a sleepless night last night worrying about it . . .

The effect of such a case on Kay is not transformative in the "test of fire" sense Meg described; it is emancipatory.

> KO: My feeling about this trial was that this was one of these impossible situations that I survived. I mean, I'm still here. And so there was a liberation in some sense. You think, "I just can't possibly cope with this. The consequences are catastrophic." But pushing through it gives you a sort of sense that time marches on. So I guess it wasn't a sense of power so much as the inevitability that time will keep going, and I'll keep going.

She told me that, over time, "You desensitize yourself." After a while, she said, you reach a point where you do not feel the same kind of pain about outcomes, and then "you're able to cope better." But at the same time that she learns to cope better, Kay said, she loses some passion for her work "because the easier it is for you to cope, the harder it is to motivate yourself to do what it takes to make a miracle happen, if that's possible. So there's a trade off. It's sometimes better not to cope well, as long as you can get up and keep going the next day. We have a phrase, 'We live to fight again. We live to fight another day.'" Kay has worked in the same office as Gina. Not surprisingly, they both fall back on the same saying.

In the hours Kay and I spent together, she never spoke about a client as if she or he was a criminal. For each one (just like the storage unit burglar), there was an explanation for why they got to where they were:

> KO: Nobody does things without a reason. It may not be a socially acceptable reason, it may not be a rational reason, and it may not even be a good reason. But they had a reason for why they did what they did. My relationship to them is in understanding why they did what they did.

Kay never described crimes as being so horrific that she could not defend the person who committed them. Rather, she speaks with empathy, if not over-identification, with her client's pain.

I asked Kay to describe a case that was particularly painful for her.

KO: I had a case that the woman was mentally ill, and she ended up going to prison for seven years, and she never comprehended what she had done wrong and why she was going to prison. There was enough ambiguity in the facts of the case, when you factored in her mental illness, that she didn't have the intent to commit the crime. It was just awful.

CS: What was the crime?

KO: She had bipolar disorder, and she was starting to go into a mania phase. And she got kicked out of a shelter, and she felt she had been wrongly kicked out. She wanted the police to intervene to help her. So she left the place in a huff, but she was moving into this really mania phase when she called 911. And was just rambling about how unfair it was, and she wanted the police to come immediately. She saw the police a block away, and she assumed, of course, that since she had called they were coming for her. But they weren't coming towards her. So she ran down the street, and as she ran, there were these tourists, she grabbed the woman's purse but didn't take it and then kept running in the direction of the police. She was a huge woman and the woman that was victimized was elderly. So had my client wanted the purse, she could have clearly gotten it. And the husband intervened and tried to grab her, and she kicked him. And meanwhile she was sort of chanting about how she had been kicked out of the center. "I need the police" sort of thing.

So my theory of the case was that these people didn't even factor in. She was unaware; they were in the way of her getting to the police. When the police actually arrested her, she was still talking about the incident in the shelter as opposed to anything happening on the street. And so it was clear to me that she wasn't intending to take this lady's purse but that she was trying to get attention so that the police would come and take care of her problem. And she was ill. The jury didn't see it that way. They convicted her of an attempted robbery. She had a prior serious felony, so she had to be sentenced to no less than seven years.

CS: What did you do with your emotions during that period of time, do you remember at all?

KO: Oh yes. I wept. At the time she was convicted, I wept. I walked out into the hall, and I was crying in front of the jury, which I've never done before. And one of the jurors was trying to be kind to me and said, "It's all right." And I said, "No, it isn't all right. This wasn't all right. This woman is going to prison, and she doesn't belong in prison." I was beside myself. And then I got depressed. And then I stayed depressed for probably a couple of months. It affected my ability to get back on course and keep going, but I did.

Kay said she may feel like she has reached her limit after something terrible like this, but when she walks into an interview room where someone else needs her, "You all of a sudden feel, 'Okay, let's get to work. I get it. I want to help you. I see that you need me. All right, I'm ready to go.'" Kay's "battery" is recharged, "but it's not as strong."

Considering Kay's disdain for the law and scorn for the system—and arguably her role in it—I asked her what her motivation was. Apart from the belief that her work is that of the "ultimate Christian," she answered this question with the closest approximation to an ideological maxim I heard from her—a saying that she learned from her father, the lawyer: "I don't take on the system, I just represent one person in the system." Kay told me that she remembers a discussion she had with her father when she was in high school. She said she believed him then, and she believes him now. He told her, "You don't ever want to practice law from a political point of view. You represent one person. And your job is to defend one person at a time, not to fend against a systematic abuse, because that doesn't help your client."

Kay said she is constantly wondering how the people around her cope, whether they are in trial or are going through an average day. I asked her to describe both, beginning with a trial. She started by telling me that everybody has diarrhea when they are in trial, whether they admit it or not.

KO: People are sick. It's lonely. It's stressful. And you feel it physically. And you hide it because it's very important how you go in. You're an actor. You own the world, you're in charge, and if you go into a courtroom setting and you're not in charge, then you're not going to win. Everybody has to look at you and be riveted on you. And you're the one, you've got the answer here, you can lead them through the maze of conflicting information and tell them the truth. So, you have to put that on.

CS: Where do you take it off? For example, the way you described crying in the hallway. When you start feeling like that, where do you go?

KO: To the bathroom, to the stall.

CS: How about going back to the office?

KO: No [sad inflection in voice]. I don't want to cry in front of my colleagues either.

CS: Do any of them cry in front of you?

KO: No. No, I haven't seen that. You might go to your car and just take a ride. It's like a wounded dog. You can't share that with people. That's a hiding time.

I then asked her to describe her typical day, which, she said usually begins with a fight with one of her kids about homework or some sort of chaos about them being late for school, which makes her late for court:

KO: So I rush to court, and I sit there because everyone's queued up; I'm the last in line, but I have four departments to go to. Start there. Then wait. When you finish there you go to the next one, they yell at you, "Why weren't you here?" "Well, I couldn't be two places at once." Wait there. By the end of the morning, one of the five or six cases you've had you've got rid of. Four of them just sort of went off into nowhere. And you still have to deal with them. Go back to the office, have lunch. And you have forty messages on your machine, so I'll either answer the phone, or I'll go interview a client or two. You can't get into the jail because all the interview rooms are full. So now you can't interview the clients because you were stuck in court all morning, and you shouldn't have had lunch. I say to myself, "I should have been more organized. Why did I have lunch? I should have just gone then. I didn't want to go then. I was too tired. I was frustrated. I was angry." So then at four o'clock, you rally. You've done your phone. You've done a little bit of paper work. And you go back to jail to start interviewing your clients. And you could be interviewing clients till seven, eight o'clock at night. And then you go home. The next morning starts again. But you haven't accomplished anything. You haven't prepared for trial. You haven't gotten investigation done. You're just barely sustaining. In the meanwhile, more cases keep coming in, and it has reached a point of [becoming] absolutely intolerable. And it works if you can finesse it so that nobody gets hurt. But with the law the way it is, you can't finesse it. They're going to get hurt. You never have a sense of confidence. You haven't done anything. You've just stood there and let it happen. You haven't had enough time to try a case and win it and just have somebody walk out the door. Or really done something creative where you've saved somebody from what would appear to be inevitable. And when your life is every day just getting by and never having gotten a professional sense of accomplishment of really doing a great job, really studying a case, really preparing and winning . . . I got to the point in my office where I just felt I was worthless as a lawyer. I wasn't alone in that extreme frustration. Four lawyers quit last month, so I'm definitely not alone.

I asked Kay again how she copes with the stress, frustrations, and emotions of her job. She told me there are times she does it well, and there are those times she does it poorly. Kay told me she was feeling the latter on that day.

KO: I'm not as confident as I was. I'm not as naive as I was. I'm not as protective as I was. And I'm actually more realistic, and I'm thinking maybe I should get out. I've done it. I'm spent. That's how I'm feeling. And maybe this will result in an epiphany where I push through and stay forever, or maybe it'll result in my leaving.

Kay sees a reverse evolution in her work ethic. Early on, her attitude was, "I can, and I will. I will do everything humanly possible to save them." Her job now is "very small. My job is to treat my clients with dignity. That's about the best I can do." Lily Tate, another midcareer woman, has a similar outlook. Lily began her career believing that everyone deserves a dedicated counsel because of the Constitution but said with time her work began to take on a religious expression. Although she is not devout in a conventional religion, she said she was raised "to give back." While she recognizes that her perception of "simply being the person who's there for someone" may sound grandiose, she said she truly believes her work is "not unlike Mother Theresa's . . . that simply to be with the poorest of the poor is simply a virtue in and of itself."

In our conversation Kay said nothing to indicate that she relies on an ideology to help bolster her confidence or to rationalize her role. Where most of the women who are in this line of work for as long as Kay explain their dedication through a strong belief in the Constitution, she, like Lily, relies on a spiritual sense of authority:

> KO: There's a spiritual paradigm to it. It is the spirituality of a Christian thing, or a human populist thing of just stopping to give a pat on the back, or to say one more thing. To slow the process down long enough to say, "good luck," and look at somebody, or to hold their hand, or to sit and talk with them. I do think I'm doing God's work. And I do believe that. I do believe that I am the ultimate Christian. . . . I think I've always had that. It didn't develop, it's always been there. It's very little, but it's enough to be kind.

Ultimately she rationalizes to herself that if she cannot save her clients, she can at least be kind to them in a system that she says "has gotten crueler and crueler and crueler." Unfortunately, Kay sees herself playing a role in legitimizing the system. "And you've got to walk home at the end of the day and say, 'What's the point? What are we doing here?'"

Kay and I continued talking long after the interview. She told me about her kids, the children's theater company she has founded, her husband, who used to be an "arch conservative" prosecutor, and her fears. Her work has invaded her personal life to the point that she looks for signs of schizophrenia in her children, "I actually worry about this. As a parent it's the most heartbreaking thing in the world. They're really ill. There's no stopping it. You've got a bright articulate track star, and all of a sudden they start hearing voices, they drop out of school, they can't cope." As her husband became more liberal, Kay's home environment became more supportive. She no longer must relieve tension by playing fullback in an adult soccer league as she did in her early years of criminal defense work. She also told me that the interview was therapeutic for her; it was a relief to talk about these things.

I left wondering how long she would last in this line of work. By her own admission she is "the emotional type of public defender," who is more prone to burn out. I felt the same about Jesse Madrigal, who finds her work so depressing since the harsher sentencing laws came into being. I was in touch with both of these women two years after the interviews. Each was still practicing in the same office where I found them so many months before.

HOLLY PORTER

I never wondered how long Holly Porter would last doing criminal defense work. However, when I tried to make one last contact with all the women in my study she was the only one I was not able to reach. She is an extraordinarily busy woman. At the time I interviewed her, Holly was in trial on a double homicide. While a serious trial like this is all-consuming for most attorneys, Holly carved out an hour to meet with me during a lunch break.

When I walked into her office, I let the receptionist know I was there to see Ms. Porter. She told me that she was Holly and that she needed to finish up one last thing on the computer for court that afternoon. The phone rang, Holly answered it, and I overheard her end of the conversation: "Micah, this ain't going to do you good. You're all hyped up. . . ."

Holly attended a first-tier law school in California and has been practicing law for twelve years. She is only thirty-seven years old and has taken about fifty felony cases to trial. She began her legal career as a public defender but after five years went into a solo private practice. While other attorneys have gone into private work—including two midcareer women, Jesse Madrigal and Iris Egan, and three seasoned women defenders, Nina Kanter, Sally Tan, and Vivian Samuels—Holly is the only woman to enter into practice for herself.

The story of her landing in a successful solo practice hinges on two unsettling trends she saw in the public defender's office where she first began. Holly is an African American who works near the community where she grew up. Her philosophy for the type of law she practices can be traced to the oral tradition of her family and community. Holly described times that her extended family would come together to hear "story after story" of social injustice.

> HP: And then you heard of all the community heroes who took a stance and made sure that things changed or something happened. And I think just being exposed to all of that constantly, [going into public defense] was just a given. It wasn't even something I second-guessed. I just thought law was the one vehicle where you had

a say. Where you did have some control, you did have some power to make a difference.

The stories Holly heard from her extended family included the limitations that were imposed on previous generations of African Americans. Her grandfather was never allowed to read, and her grandmother took care of households when her own was suffering. Her mother lived a better life as a homemaker and a home care worker for the elderly, and the stepfather who raised her worked in the shipyards. Holly felt that "they made it so I could do what I want to do, and I owe that. My success isn't limited to me, and I owe something back."

As Holly talks, a different ideology emerges, one that combines civil rights and community. It goes beyond Lily Tate's and Kay Owens's religious expressions of wanting to work with the "poorest of the poor" and treating one individual at a time with dignity. Holly says her role is to play a part in a person's life that will have an impact on the community.

> HP: I want to know this person was treated like a human being when they went through the process, and they feel better about themselves now. Maybe they won't be a different person, but their kids are going to be different as a result of it. So that's just kind of self-sustaining.

Entering criminal defense work with the philosophy that she had been given the opportunity to make a difference and that she owed the community eventually led to Holly's dissatisfaction with the structural constraints of the public defender's office. Holly saw that "the seven-year track" to partnership practiced in private law offices was replicated in the public defender setting. She told me that, out of the 140 attorneys in her public defender's office, there were only five women of color. And although close to 50 percent of the attorneys in the office were women, the white men were moving up in the hierarchy quicker and were getting the better assignments.

> HP: I saw that there were no women and no people of color who were administrators. And I was kind of surprised to see that here was a group of people who thrive on representing [the] downtrodden,

representing the inequities . . . yet [they] perpetuated some of that same structural feeling within their own environment.

More important, Holly says that she had social commitments to her community that were not compatible with bureaucratic rules.

> HP: I started getting feedback from supervisors saying, "You can't go to that neighborhood because our insurance may not cover you." Well, this is the neighborhood I grew up in. I'm not concerned about walking through the projects, or if there were things I thought my clients needed by way of assistance and I was willing to do the extra time to go out and find what community resources were available for them, I didn't like feeling restricted in that regard, knowing that someone was going to start watching my work more closely just hoping to see that, you know, "she's neglected this over here because she's become this glorified social worker."

Considering the emphasis Holly places on the social significance of her job, I asked whether the limitation on her community involvement was the reason she ultimately left the public defender's office. She says yes and that if anything, she felt her background as a Black woman who grew up in the projects gave her a better understanding of her clients and their cases: "I mean, having seen poverty up close and personal, having seen dysfunction, I think I have a better understanding than the investigators that might be allowed to go into my neighborhood. I just feel more 'bilingual' from a social aspect because of experiences."

Holly told me she had taken the first real vacation of her life. While in the tropics she prepared for a big hearing on a homicide case. When she got back from vacation, her first appearance was on this case. She heard from the judge that her office had "conflicted out" of the case, and the defendant had been appointed a new attorney. Public defender offices conflict out of cases when they have opposing interests. For example, the office might already be representing a codefendant or a witness. Holly told me that this conflict of interest was unusual. Rarely does an office conflict out of a major case that is already being worked on. It appeared to her that the reason was economic. The office probably saw a conflict because of a subsequent case and backed out of the first case because it might require a great deal of resources.

Given that Holly had developed good rapport with her client and had the case prepared, she felt the change in attorneys was not in the best interest of the defendant and that the effect on him had not been considered. She described him as devastated because of the trust he had put in her.

> HP: For him, facing a life sentence on a case, he at least deserved to have known there was going to be this change, this transition. I don't think that people who practice in that arena for a great deal of time remember that maybe it's not new for you, but it's new for this person that you are representing. And the amount of trauma and stress that you may put that person through, there's something inhumane about that. And that was just something that finally got to me, where I just said, "I don't want to practice law like this. I don't want to think of people as mere numbers, and files, and just parts of the machinery."

An attorney in the courtroom saw what had happened with her client, and he approached Holly. She said he told her that she had enough experience to handle the case on her own. And though she was not confident she had the background to start a business on her own—"nobody in my family's ever even gone to school let alone tried to run a business"—the defendant's family hired Holly as a private attorney. That was the beginning of her solo practice.

An attorney in private practice is in a much better position to avoid cases that generate emotional conflict. While at the public defender's office, Holly remembers several cases that were highly emotional for her. The first case was difficult because she is African American; it was a cross-burning case. When the case was assigned to her, she tried to get out of it. Holly said she met with "a lot of heat" from the administration because she said she just wanted out. Fortunately, "The client took care of that for me. He came to court and just basically told the judge I'm not going to be represented by this person."

The second case involved a serial rapist. According to Holly, the unnerving part was not so much the crimes. Rather, Holly was uneasy working with such a "sophisticated client."

> HP: In reading the case file, some of the things that the women had experienced were a little unnerving. It was definitely one in which, you know, it was kind of like that Ted Bundy thing, where the person that they were describing was somebody who was like your next door neighbor. It wasn't the scary jumping-out-of-the-recesses-of-the-stairwell kind of thing. But someone who these women had either gotten to know, or knew of, trusted, or just wouldn't have expected anything from. And that was troubling because that all of a sudden started to creep into your own environment a little bit. You're saying, "Gosh, I can't be as detached here because I could see that this could be a problem. This could be a real problem." So I felt on edge. That was probably about the only time where I think I had some really strong reactions.

In both examples Holly could not separate the crime from the person, especially in the cross-burning case; she told me she could not be detached from it "at any level." Neither of these cases was as emotional as a domestic violence case.

> HP: It was the first case in which I represented a woman who was being abused by another woman, a domestic partner as opposed to a husband or a boyfriend. And trying to convince the court that this was a true domestic situation . . . She had actually fought back her partner and it resulted in the other woman becoming paralyzed and losing sight in one eye. And my client had a horrendous history of mental illness. During one part of the trial she actually withdrew, and we watched that unfold. Seeing her on the witness stand and all of a sudden becoming totally removed from the whole process was pretty frightening because I had just never seen someone actually go through that. So that was probably one of the most disturbing experiences I've had. It was an attempted murder charge, and I think she fell on an assault with a deadly weapon. I've actually seen her since she did her time. The exposure she had was significantly reduced. She still has grave mental health problems that have gone untreated that all stem from something

that happened very early in her own childhood that was very trau-
matizing that never got disclosed until she became an adult. She
didn't have the support of her family when she did disclose some
of the abuse she had experienced. So, that one was pretty troubling.

In private practice Holly does not take cases that require the type of
emotion work she described in separating herself from the crime as she
needed to with the cross burning and serial rape. She told me she would
either price the case high, knowing that the defendant couldn't afford to
hire her, or let the client know she had a conflict in her schedule: "I'll pick
up on something that I know will make it unattractive to them to hire me
as their counsel as a kind of mechanism of amicably parting ways. That way
the person doesn't walk out feeling that they have a scarlet letter on their
chest, and that I've made some kind of judgment call of their case." Iris
Egan, another former public defender now in private practice also quotes
high prices when she has "particularly repugnant crimes that I don't want
to invest the emotions. I know if the price was lower I'd be defending him."

By pricing cases, both Holly and Iris get the word out on the street that
there are kinds of cases they will not take. Iris is limiting the number of
rape defendants she will represent, not because she will not defend the
crime—even though she was a near rape victim. Rather, she does not like
the reputation she is getting in her small county of being "the lady rape
lawyer." Holly will not defend drug dealers:

HP: I don't represent drug dealers in transactional stuff. Now, if there's
some whodunit shooting, they know I'm probably inclined to take
that kind of case. But if it's a transaction thing, they know not to
even bother.

Holly practices criminal law because she believes she can help make a difference in the lives of people in her community. Unlike Kay Owens, she believes she is still an effective force in her work. One of the reasons may be
her ability to choose cases. Consider her reason for not defending drug
dealers:

HP: People who are drawn to selling drugs tend to do it because it's an
economic thing . . . it's a way to get them out of some very dismal
circumstances. I find it frustrating because I can't offer anything

that's going to be more attractive right now than this immediate gratification that they've chosen, especially when I know that education isn't an option, jobs may not be an option because by now they may have a series of felonies, or just because they don't have transportation. I mean there are just all these other social infirmities that I can't find a solution for. So maybe that's just a part of the practice that I just find too troubling. And I decided that as a private practitioner I want to feel good at the end and know that I've either changed somebody's life in some kind of small way or at least made the system honest. That area just seems like it's too complicated in terms of having feelings about the people involved. So that's just an area I stay away from.

Holly does not see herself as a feminist, from the standpoint of being fueled by a political agenda, "so much as across the board I just think there are inequities, and if I can see an area where I can alleviate that, that's where I want to put my energy." Being, as she calls herself, "a feminist by default," Holly does not see defending men who have committed violent acts against women as problematic.

HP: I think that as a woman representing men who are charged with that kind of crime, I can tell them very straightforward, "This treatment is not going to go over, and you need some help, and these are some things that you need to correct in your behavior." And since they've come to me for representation, I know that they're going to honor my opinion. So I think it's a good thing I'm there because I can see where there are problems. I can see where they didn't get along with their mother, where they had coping issues, where they had control issues, and be able to say very candidly to them, "This is where the problem is. And aside from tactically what you might want to do in this legal arena, if you want to sustain a constructive life, you're going to have to make some changes here. Or you're going to encounter these problems again and again and again." So from that regard I think that I'm remaining consistent with the feminist theme. I'm letting the world know it's ugly, and I think it's ugly. "So what are you going to do about it now?" So that's how I look at it.

Despite the fact that Holly is in a position to be selective about the cases that she takes, she is still working in a highly emotional field. She told me that in some ways private practice can be even more draining, because clients open up to her more completely. Holly said she knows so much more of what their futures may hold. As a public defender she was not able to avoid drug cases. In fact she describes her early days when she was in a group of "baby public defenders" being pitted against "baby police officers" on the drug task force. But in public defense work, she said, clients in drug cases participate in a "code of silence": they "just tell you enough to represent them." She finds private clients to be much more candid.

There are several possibilities why Holly's private clients open up to her more. First, she is a respected member of her community—no longer the "baby" public defender, but someone who gives trusted advice. Second, paying clients may feel a greater right to professional consultation than indigent defendants. Either way, Holly said that she does not want to hear about it, suggesting the vulnerability she feels in relationship to certain aspects of her community, especially with her growing family. She told me she tries to remain anchored in her family—she has two small children— and her community. The walls of her office are lined with plaques of appreciation from youth clubs, athletic leagues, and service organizations that promote women and women of color, testifying to her connection to the community. Without an outside focus, she finds her work gets "very, very emotional." She said that if a person gets too caught up in criminal defense work, she tends not to realize that it is a part of a bigger picture. Having it become the whole picture can be overwhelming. In keeping with the oral tradition of her family and community, Holly left me with a metaphor:

> HP: You have to understand that this is just a paragraph in just a long, long story. And you've got a lot more paragraphs to go, and a lot more stories to hear, and a lot more stories to tell.

The real feeling, like everyone's entitled to a defense, comes out of my political background. A certain thing as to what happened in college and the political events of the time, and a feeling that the police were overbearing and were arresting people for political beliefs, and the poverty and racism, and all the rest of the evils of our society were impacting people very negatively.
—Rose Carr

Politically, I sort of grew up with an eye of skepticism towards what I was being told, and that's why I think that now when I read a police report, I don't necessarily believe what's in there. I'm somewhat skeptical about what somebody writes down as necessarily being true. Politically, I've always been for the underdog and have always been aware of the people that are oppressed.
—Olivia George

The criminal defense attorney is the watchdog of our society and of our judicial system. And I really do believe that. I still believe that, twenty-two years later. And I think that it will hold to be true that this will be the last bastion of the group trying to protect individual rights.
—Sally Tan

Part of proving yourself, for a lot of women, is how they handle sex cases. There are those who argue that it changes the gender of some women. "Is it really a woman?"
—Trudy Kaufman

5

Identity Reinforcement: Seasoned Women Defenders

You fail in your representation of a client unless you convince everyone within your way that your client and what happens to him or her matters to you more than anything else.
—Vivian Gold

SEASONED women defenders share strong convictions of social justice, awareness of the history of racial inequality, the political climate of their college years, age, and years in practice. These women came into criminal defense work keenly aware of the constitutional ideal of equality and the everyday reality of social inequality of the criminal justice system. They are idealists in the original meaning of the word: these women see social change occurring at the level of ideas. They also recognize their public roles as key to the protection of individual rights. Driven by many of the same ideals they entered legal practice with, their ideals have grown stronger over time. This has reinforced their identities as women defense attorneys and their rigid adherence in the dominant ideology of their profession.

Rose Carr and Olivia George are seasoned women defenders—Abogadas, by actual group membership. They work in the same office as Becky McBride and Darla Wilson (from chapter three) and were on that vacation to Mexico when given the Spanish name for "the women advocates."

ROSE CARR

Rose Carr is the best legal mind in the office. So I am told by two deputy public defenders that work with her. She certainly speaks fast and eloquently. I can barely keep up with my note taking and am grateful for my tape recorder as she fires off answers to my questions.

Rose tells me she is a product of the political climate of the '60s. She graduated from UC Berkeley in 1971 and experienced the politics of the day—the Huey Newton trial, the Black Panther Party. Rose saw the potential for a police state, that people were oppressed, and she wanted to help.

> RC: You wanted to serve the greater good, do something that could make a contribution in this world. And being a lawyer, and then fighting for people, which is what it felt like we were doing. All my friends were of the same philosophy, so it was something that was thought of as a very good thing.

She made the decision to become a public defender in her last year of college. Rose comes from a conservative family. "My family is military," she told me, "career military." The family was happy that she was going to be a lawyer; a paternal uncle had been a superior court judge, so being a lawyer was a respectable thing to do. Her conservative father was perhaps even happier that she would move away from Berkeley for law school and leave behind its leftist politics. Rose landed at one of the better law schools on the east coast. To her father's dismay, she returned to an even better San Francisco Bay Area school a year later.

That was almost thirty years ago. When I interviewed Rose she was still a public defender in the same office she began in twenty-two years before. During this time she has probably taken forty felony cases to trial. She has never felt that she was excluded or discriminated against or thought less of because she was a woman. Several other women were hired at the same time she was. Rose was assigned to a misdemeanor calendar for her first eleven months at the office and has been dealing exclusively with felonies ever since. Today she is the head of the office's homicide team of eight lawyers.

Politics still motivate Rose, although she tells me she is no longer the naive, "bright-eyed, big-eyes, wide-eyed" young woman who entered public defense work to "help defend the poor and downtrodden."

> RC: Not everybody is poor; not everybody is downtrodden. Even if you are, that doesn't mean you get to hit somebody over the head and take their bicycle. There are other motivating things, like feeling

this person might be a bad person, but twenty-five years for that's too much, it's wrong.

As we spoke, the politics of fair sentencing was the issue Rose returned to repeatedly. While some attorneys, like Kay Owens and Jesse Madrigal, find their work almost too depressing for them to go on since California's 1994 sentencing enhancements, Rose told me the new "horrific penalties" motivate her: "It gets much easier to represent people." This is not to say she does not find the work difficult. In fact, she says, the job gets harder, "because it's painful to watch your clients go to prison for twenty-five to life when you know that's just the wrong thing to have happen."

For Rose, stressful cases are any of those "that are triable, that you believe the outcome should be a certain way"—and for which your belief is at odds with sentencing laws. For example, a person is "looking at 200 years. . . . Based on a lot of things, maybe what you really believe is they ought to do a prison term of six years. Some of those are sex cases. I've tried several rape cases that I believed the defendant should be acquitted."

Not unlike Holly Porter, Rose says that she transforms the stress around big sentencing exposures into a concentration on the larger picture that makes her job all the more important. The more Rose is needed to right a societal wrong, the easier it is for her to represent "unpleasant" people. She says, "The longer the penalties, the more part you can play to be able to assist in fixing this."

As Rose spoke it became apparent that she uses her beliefs or ideals on fairness in outcomes to mitigate emotional stress. Her work is far from pleasant. "I represent people that kill people," a group arguably worse than sexual assailants she says to those who question her ability to defend rapists. Almost all of her murder cases have been women victims. She's handled "all varieties": A rape/murder case, a man who killed a woman he was dating, a man who killed a woman in a robbery, a woman who killed her mother.

Rose said that in her office everybody needs to take her share of difficult cases. In her office, a public defender is allowed only infrequent objections: "If you exercise it too often, you should expect someone in the administration to sit you down and find out whether this is the right line of work for you." Nonetheless, life circumstances may lead lawyers to ask for the option not to take certain types. For example, one attorney's wife was raped, and he does not take rape cases. Another lawyer's father was killed by a drunk driver, and she does not take felony drunk drivers. And Rose will not take forcible child assaults, and this has only been in the last two years since her daughter was sexually assaulted. With time, she can imagine taking a sexual-assault case with a child victim, but not until she is able to talk about sex cases again in front of her husband and daughter.

> RC: Right now, in terms of my feelings of what happened to my daughter and my husband and me, and everything else, those would be hard cases for me to take home. Because they would be hard to talk about at home. And I talk about my work with my family. So that would be hard for me to get to be able to do that.

As a public defender, Rose is unique in that she "takes her work home"; by talking with her entire family she helps work through work emotions. Some women defenders will talk with their husbands, especially if they work in the criminal justice system. But none of the other women told me that they regularly spoke about their work with their families. Rose also seems to have more control over the cases she takes. The office had no objections when she asked that another lawyer be assigned to a particular client after he struck her. Rose actually experiences a scenario similar to Jesse Madrigal's fantasy of being punched out by a difficult client to get her off the case. But more important, Rose is able to maneuver assignments. Arguably her ability is based on her seniority, position as head of the homicide team, and status as the "best legal mind in the office." Rose has said, "I just don't want this [assignment], give me something else." But her request was not based on the severity of the type of crime; it was based on her life circumstances and the fact she has been assigned so many difficult cases over the years.

> RC: One was a serial rape case a number of years ago. It was a very difficult, complicated, and high-publicity case. I mean, I've handled lots of rape cases. It's not that there was anything special about it other than it was a whole bunch of rapes. It was a very difficult client, and I just didn't feel like I needed that right then in my life. I mean, I handle my share of big, serious, hard, high-publicity cases, and I said, "I just don't want this one."

Rose is also in the position to help relieve other women in the office of assignments they feel they cannot handle. She told me about a woman colleague who came to her at the start of a rape trial. The colleague was having personal difficulties and said, "I don't think I can do this." Rose told her, "Then you shouldn't." They walked down to the administrator who assigns cases and Rose "got her out of the case," saying, "I'll handle it if necessary, but she needs to not do this."

But, given the nature of public defense work, there are times an attorney must take a case that she does not believe she can handle. Rose faced one of these cases many years ago, when she returned to work after a six-month maternity leave.

> RC: Right after I came back from having my daughter they gave me a really bad child-abuse case. A mother who just terribly abused her brand new baby. And I gave that back to them and said, "Give this to someone else, you've got the wrong lawyer for this." I had trouble reading [the file]. The woman who was assigning cases at that point said, "I really need you to do it." And I did, and I felt very sympathetic to this young woman who was going through postpartum depression. I convinced a close friend of mine who also had a young child that she needed to take this case to superior court and handle it, and she did. I mean sometimes the first thing is, "I can't do this." And then you take a step past that and realize, "Yes I can, there's lots of ways I can, and reasons why I should."

Rose first needed to use her situation to sympathize with the defendant—the new mother was in a postpartum depression. The "reasons why she should" defend this woman stem from a professional ethic that suggests a public defender should be able to defend any client and any crime. The reason that she could find a way to help was her self-identification with the mother.

In this instance, Rose related a joint effort with a colleague to take on a case that was problematic for them both as mothers.[1] Rose did not directly represent the new mother, but she illustrates what is for many a pivotal moment in their careers: the attorney says, "I can't do this," only to find that she can. Whether as a new mother able to represent a woman accused of child abuse during a postpartum depression or an African American assigned to a cross-burning case, she is able to handle a difficult case that pits her duty as a lawyer against a competing identity.

RC: If I'm sitting next to this guy who's charged with doing this horrible thing, patting him on the back, talking to him, and not seem-
ing afraid of him, and feeling like he's a positive, nice person, then
that communicates something to the jury. I can essentially get
evidence into the courtroom that's almost like character evidence
by who I am and how I respond to my client.

In fact, I observed Rose giving "indirect character evidence" in a preliminary hearing on a death penalty case.[2] There were four codefendants, each
in a unique sitting arrangement in relationship to their attorney. Two sat
next to their attorneys at the defense table in traditional fashion; the other
two sat in the jury box with their attorneys. (Interestingly, both attorneys
in the jury box were women; at the table were men.) The other woman
defense attorney, Sally Tan, who appears later in this chapter, sat with a
space between her and her female client. Rose sat right next to her male
client, slouched in his direction.

Another case Rose found in her assignment box when she first returned
from maternity leave was the case of a man charged with the kidnap and
sexual assault of a young girl. As it happened, he was also charged with the
same crime in a neighboring county. In that county, the victim was the
daughter of family friends, someone she had known for years. Rose said
she looked at the case and said, "I can't do it. Give it to somebody else."
The administration gave it back to her and said, "Please do it. All you need
to do is the preliminary hearing." Rose said, "And I did. And then somebody else got the case after that. And I was able to do it." How could Rose
possibly maintain her friendship with the family whose daughter was also
victimized by this man, especially when the account of her assault was horrendous? The world of public defenders is small. The father of the victim
in this case was a public defender in that neighboring county. While he
curtailed his own work for several months to help his daughter and family
heal, the family understood Rose's job duty.

The type of case a lawyer believes that she cannot handle indicates
situations in which—at least going into the case—her usual emotional or
ideological strategies are insufficient to allow her to cope. Whether the case
relates to her life history or current circumstances, such a case holds the
key to the development of her moral career. When the attorney realizes
that she can handle the "impossible" case, her professional ideals and her
ability to manage emotions through them are fortified.

RC: I would say the two high-point cases of my career were a rape case that I litigated on a speedy trial issue all the way to the California Supreme Court—and won it. It's a published opinion that's a very good defense opinion. I'm very proud of myself for that. It was a case that basically I got from the beginning, and I did all the work on it all the way up. And this case is cited in speedy trial law all the time, and I'm very proud of it. Yeah, and [then] there was the nurse who killed her mother.

Rose volunteered to represent this woman who, as she described it, drove for over three hours and then waited outside her mother's home until her mother opened the door so she could strangle her to death.

RC: She then confessed to the police that it was premeditated. "You better believe it. I killed her because she was a monster." And she was convicted of voluntary manslaughter and served a year and a half in prison, and she was looking at first-degree murder with special circumstances, and with lots of work, the right result. Well, I'm not sure it was the right result. I thought she shouldn't go to prison at all. But she got the mitigated least amount of term in prison and was convicted of the least things she could have been convicted of. I was very proud of those cases.

Rose's particular view of justice and her role are strengthened through victories. She said her job is not about trying to get the guilty free as much as it is about getting a fair outcome. As we talked, Rose said little about feeling vulnerable as a woman. She said there are those clients who have made her feel uncomfortable, but that makes sense to her, considering the business she is in. She told me she once had a client who was charged with rape who asked her if she felt she could represent him because of what he had done to a woman. After talking with him a long time Rose answered, "Yeah, it's not a problem. My concern for you is that you did this. I know that, they can prove that. But I'm not sure you should go to prison for the maximum. I think you should go for [another length of time] and I can do that." As Rose put it:

RC: Quite frankly, charges of sexual assault carry such incredibly significant penalties and arguably more than crimes that are of a more serious nature in terms of long-lasting things. I think you stand up in a courtroom and are at a disadvantage representing anybody charged with a sex crime.

I asked Rose if she finds her view of this case to be consistent with the goals of feminism.

RC: Part of being a feminist is caring about people and wanting the right thing to happen and to be able to help those that are in trouble. Just because somebody does something bad to a woman doesn't mean assisting them in helping making sure that their constitutional rights are protected, and that they're treated fairly in the system, doesn't make me not a feminist.

And I represented people on some really ugly, ugly cases. The stranger rape cases, those are the scariest, where you go into the market at six o'clock at night to get some butter for your family, and you're abducted and raped repeatedly and strangled and left for dead. And that was a case I represented somebody on.

This was the first time in our conversation that I recognized unsuccessful emotional distancing or even vulnerability on Rose's part. She suggests that stranger rape cases are the worst to imagine, and then attempts to distance herself from the victim by shifting the pronoun. The problem is that Rose's use of "you" specifies an indefinite person that might include herself.

Despite her emphasis on fair outcomes, Rose does not go into all cases feeling strongly about the right outcome. She told me, though, that she does a good job convincing herself.

RC: Different cases you believe in at different points. It's those that you read from the initial interview that you say, "This case is going to go to trial, this is a good case, this is right, and this should happen."

She told me those cases make it easier for people to see "you're not trying to get the guilty free as much as you're trying to have a fair outcome."

RC: There are others that take longer to get to that point. But by the time you're in trial in every case, you believe in it, and certainly by closing argument; because if you don't have belief by then, you're in real trouble. Then you sit down, and you've even believed all of this. And your friends say, "You believe that. Bullshit. I can't believe it."

OLIVIA GEORGE

Rose's success has earned her the respect of other Abogadas. When Olivia George, an attorney in the same office as Rose, questions her own performance on a case, she told me she thinks, "What if Rose would have handled that? I bet she would have known what to do. I bet she could have figured out something." As Olivia was comparing herself to Rose, I was struck by the contrasts in these two women. Rose presents herself with confidence both verbally and physically. She spoke so rapidly I could barely keep up with her. Olivia is soft-spoken, and it is hard to imagine that she could ever intimidate anyone in the courtroom.

Olivia may verbalize doubts in her ability, but she never expressed uncertainty to me about her reasons for doing public defense work. Like Rose, the issue that motivates Olivia is politics. Olivia's politics and sense of justice grew from her family experience.

Olivia's father was Native American. Although she was not raised on the reservation, like her father and grandmother before her, Olivia grew up with a skeptical eye for certain aspects of American culture. When she was a child, her father would tell her why in their house Columbus Day was not a day of celebration. When she was taught the story of Father Junípero Serra and the California missions—the standard curriculum for every fourth grader in California—her father gave her another version that included the near genocide of California's Native Americans. Olivia told me that thirty-five years ago she learned to disregard what she was being taught in school and to tell her teachers her father's interpretation of history. The response she got was, "Your dad's nothing but a drinking Indian."

By the time the American Indian movement became a political force around 1969, Olivia was sending off money for their efforts. She believed "in all those causes, like the Indians should be on Alcatraz, and they took our land away and tried to cover it up." That is why "I think that when I read a police report, I don't necessarily believe what's in there. I'm somewhat skeptical about what somebody writes down as necessarily being true."

Olivia told me she felt the need to be a fighter for the underdog early on and recognized that people in authority will at times cover up the truth to protect their own way of life. She equates her teachers' use of racist slander against her father to invalidate the version of history he presented her with the comments of those who now say to her, "Ninety-nine percent of your clients are guilty, so why do you even listen to them?" Olivia said every person has a story to be told. The lessons of her childhood carried over into her early adulthood and her work as a public defender.

While in law school, Olivia interned at a public defender's office. She told me she knew she wanted to be a public defender a couple of weeks into her internship. Her job was to conduct the initial interview of clients referred to their office by the court.

> OG: It still sticks in my mind that there was this man that was about eighty years old who came in and he was charged with petty theft. He had taken some batteries or something, and he was almost blind. I remember just thinking that this is just really terrible that this eighty-year-old half-blind man is being charged with this petty theft for a $1.69 pack of batteries, which he said he forgot he put in his pocket. I originally thought that I could [be either a public defender or a district attorney], and it was real quick into my interviewing that I decided. How could I work on the other side?

No one in Olivia's family objected to her choice. Her husband was also a public defender and, "my mom was always a public defender at heart." Looking back on her life, Olivia said it surprises her how much her mother's way of interacting with others influenced her. Throughout most of the interview she identified with her deceased father instead. She related a recent episode of her mother's and asked me to keep in mind that her mother was widowed (alone) and not young. The story seemed to amuse Olivia as well as cause her concern.

> OG: [My mother] got up one morning, she went out in her garage, which is detached [from the house] and there was a man sleeping in her car. Well my mom just starts yelling at him and tells him to get out of her car. So he gets out of her car and runs away. Then she noticed that his baseball cap was left in the car, so she puts it out on the mailbox so that in case he's walking by later he's going to get it. I mean, she didn't call the police. She just told him to get out of there. She was mad that he was there, and

then she puts his hat on the mailbox. So it's like she had a homeless person living in her backyard for a while. Now that I'm older I see her influences [on me]. I think my mom would have been the last person to talk me out of [becoming a public defender].

Olivia works in the same public defender's office she began in sixteen years ago. She is forty-four years old and has taken somewhere between thirty-five and forty felony cases to trial. She told me that her gentle demeanor often determines the type of cases she is assigned. The mental health calendar has turned into her specialty: "Anytime they ask me what calendar do I want now, I say mental health." Many public defenders offices have someone assigned to represent mentally ill clients who are conserved by the state (or sometimes by relatives) because they are not able to care for themselves. My experience is that rarely does a public defender seek this assignment. Considering that the mental health calendar in Olivia's office is broadly defined to include mentally disordered sex offenders (MDSOs), her willingness is even more surprising. Olivia told me that part of the reason she chooses this calendar is that the clients are so compelling. And even when she is on a felony rotation, about 30 percent of her clients are mentally ill.

OG: My heart goes out to them, and they do things for me that other clients wouldn't do. They paint pictures for me at [the] state hospital, and they make me craft items and send them to me. I really get to know them pretty well. . . . Since they are in the mental health system, whether they're insane or not, and since they usually don't get better, I keep them for many years, so I follow them.

My name is out there. So if there's somebody who is mentally ill that needs a public defender, a lot of times I get the call first. Then I do the intitial interview. If I really want the case, I keep it.

Sometimes these clients do get better, and Olivia feels a real sense of accomplishment. She told me that not long ago she was in the checkout line at a store. The cashier was a man she had represented at a restoration of sanity trial. "He recognized me right away. I thought, 'He's got a job, he's out of the hospital.' It just felt good."

Olivia told me that two of her greatest victories came from cases that were assigned to her because she was a women and on account of her personality. For both trials she had clients who needed extra handholding—the kind of treatment they would not have received from a male attorney. Just recently she tried a child-molestation case. According to Olivia, "Child molesters are usually the most pathetic kind of clients. They'll cry and all. They've probably been molested themselves, and they're just very needy clients. The child molest case that I just did, he was clearly someone who needed a lot of attention. And he was a very easy person to work with." The case was complicated. Olivia shared what she was up against in representing this man:

OG: It was a three-strikes case, and my client's strike priors were child molests. He had this one alleged victim with two counts of child molest on her, then he had this other alleged victim who was actually his girlfriend. It was statutory rape: she was sixteen, and he was twenty-one. It was a really difficult case because I had no defense to the statutory rape. They ended up getting married in the middle of the trial. She went to jail rather than testify and all this stuff.[3] He was acquitted of the child molest, which was to me incredible because the jury knew about those two prior child molests. There was nothing I could do on the stat rape, and that was still twenty-five to life even though they ended up getting married in the middle of the trial.

Her parents had been the ones to basically blow the whistle. She was eighteen by the time the trial rolled around [they could get married without her parents' permission]. She was very estranged from her parents. Once they arrested him on the stat rape and started looking into all of his activities, that's when they arrested him with the activities with the eleven-year-old. And I really believed that he wasn't guilty of the child molest. So then I was facing twenty-five to life on a stat rape, even though they were married and she was only four years younger than him. The judge struck a strike [making a third-strike conviction impossible]. I mean, it started out 100-to-life, and he went to five. Even though five to me is outrageous for stat rape. I really thought the guy was going to go away for the rest of his life, and he was only twenty-two years old. I don't know how many stomachaches I had over that case. I was really happy with the outcome.

Olivia's comment, "I was facing twenty-five to life," gives us a sense of just how much she identified with the defendant.

The other case that Olivia described in detail involved a childlike defendant, a "slightly retarded" woman who was charged with hand-to-hand sales of methamphetamines to an undercover police officer.

> OG: She was living in a house where there were people dealing drugs, and an undercover cop came to the house several times and bought drugs. She would do things like let him in [and] show him to the back room. A couple of times she said, "That's good stuff, you'll like that." But I really believe that she didn't really have the intent to be aiding and abetting in those sales, and she was looking at a mandatory prison term with no record. She kept crying in the trial. At one point she said, "Mom, they're saying bad things about me," and she went running back to her mom in the audience. They found her not guilty, and when the judge was looking at the verdict form before it was read, he gave me a big thumbs-up. It was just like justice, okay! It was hard, though, [taking on] an undercover cop.

In both of these cases, Olivia described good rapport with her clients. She told me that when she represents someone, what matters is not the accusations, but how easy it is to get along with the defendant. "It's how they relate to me and treat me as a person. Completely." Olivia said she has felt fine sitting next to someone who has committed a horrible violent crime and uncomfortable sitting next to someone who has committed a burglary. In fact, Olivia's most difficult client, just six months into her career, was someone charged with a misdemeanor for drunk driving. The client repeatedly demonstrated his hatred and lack of respect for women. This was the only time Olivia had a case transferred to somebody else: "It was just in the best interest of the client." Clearly this statement could be read as her rationalizing away conflict, and it would be an example of ideological work to combat emotional conflict if Olivia regularly rid herself of obnoxious clients.

Normally Olivia's first step in representing a client is to give him or her extra attention in order to get them to cooperate and trust her. But there will always be those clients that do not want a woman defender. In her last "felony tour" Olivia was assigned to represent a man charged with serial rape. Like Holly Porter's cross-burning client, who refused to be represented by an African American, this man spared Olivia the disagreeable task of representing him. Instead, he hired a private attorney. Olivia said the client has since fired the private attorney and is back at the public defender's office—this time represented by a man.

It has been fifteen and a half years since Olivia asked that the woman-hating client be assigned to a man. In those years she has moved through several "tours of duty," an apt descriptor for the warlike nature of the job. In her office, each tour means a year's assignment to a particular calendar. Olivia has moved through many rotations—from juvenile, to misdemeanors, to drugs, to mental health, to felonies. While she gladly volunteers for the mental health calendar, only once does she remember asking to skip her turn on felonies: "I was just personally having a lot of problems right then. I had three miscarriages in a year. And I just asked not to go back to the felonies right then. I didn't think I could handle it." In the interview, she did not attribute the miscarriages to the stress of her work.

When Olivia finds herself in the difficult position of working with a disagreeable client, she avoids personal contact where she can and concentrates on the technicalities of the case.

> OG: I just back off and start working on the case, get the case ready, and try to look at it as though it's a paper case rather than a personal case. I enter into the legal aspect of it, and I don't do something less for him. It's hard though. I have to say, if you really like the person, there's just a natural instinct there to work harder and to pour your heart out. If you're getting up in front of a jury and you've had a person sitting next to you who swore at you the whole time, and bad mouthed you, and called you names, it's real hard to get up at closing and act like you really care. And I would say 95 to 98 percent of my clients I feel very connected with. It's just a small percent that I just cannot stand because they are so abusive to me. It has nothing to do with their crime, it just has to do with they way they treat me. It's amazing; sometimes the easiest defendants to work with committed the worst crimes.

Olivia stays connected to her clients by looking skeptically at even the most egregious charges against them. Because so many of her clients say they did not commit the crimes they are accused of, Olivia said she approaches them with the attitude that she is there to represent their version: "I don't care what it is, in fact, the more serious it is, the more worried I am about the fact that they could be wrongly convicted." She believes that the numbers of people being released from prison on exonerating DNA evidence only bolsters her approach.

Olivia acknowledged that holding onto the belief that "maybe they didn't do it" can be stressful. She described a case of spousal rape:

> OG: I had a guy last year who raped his wife and choked her out and she was unconscious and all kinds of stuff. Well, he was denying that. It's her word against his. Maybe she's lying. Maybe he's lying. I don't know. But I'm going to look at it as though he's telling the truth, and I'm going to present it the best way I can.

According to Olivia, cases are difficult for one of two reasons: either the crime is "ugly," or she is not able to develop a solid defense. Olivia said it is difficult to "sit there and have a victim that's very believable, who's very upset, who's crying, [and] who you're trying to show is lying." She feels badly for people who are upset about what has happened to them. Olivia told me it does not necessarily upset her that a man has committed a crime against a woman: "Even in burglaries people get pretty emotional when you put them on the stand." Olivia sympathizes with "people." One might suppose that Olivia's use of the generic—that is, people—indicates social distancing from women victims. But based on the time I spent with her, I would say work for Olivia requires much emotional labor in that she must distance herself from the larger category of all victims. The only mechanism Olivia described to fall back on when she over-sympathizes with the victim is to know that she will get the information from the person while treating that person humanely:

> OG: It's something that I think women are really good at, because I can cross-examine a child. I'm soft-spoken, and I'm not that threatening to them. I can get the information I need, and I think I gain from the jury because of that. I don't think beating up a victim gets you anywhere unless you have a victim, an alleged victim, who comes across as unbelievable.

Guilty verdicts are even more upsetting to Olivia than compelling victims. These are the times she relies most on her friends—the other Abogadas. She described a true sociological cohort—people united in the same struggle:

> OG: Generally there are five or six people hired around the same time. And you move through assignments with them. Our families are friends, our kids are friends; we're going on vacation together next week. I think when you start, it's so difficult, and it continues to be difficult. You develop so much camaraderie, and you rely upon those people. When you feel good, they're going out with you to celebrate. When you feel bad, they're there holding your hand, and they're talking to your jury for you.

Most attorneys will interview the jury after a trial to see what made the case go a certain way, for future reference. Olivia said she now will have another attorney find out what the jurors have to say when she receives a guilty verdict: "And I have a lot of them. I'm so mad, and I'm so upset. I don't want them to tell me, 'Well, you did a good job,' or whatever. I just don't want to talk with them." Although Olivia may be critical of her performance when she loses a case, she recognizes the odds she is up against when going to trial. As we were talking, she started laughing at herself when she told me how wrapped up she can get in the case she presents to the jury: "It bothers me sometimes that I'm so upset at the end, because I know I didn't have a prayer going into it, but by the time I get done, I think there's reasonable doubt here. Why couldn't they see that? I know there's a fingerprint, but the fingerprint expert could be wrong." To combat her unsettling feelings, Olivia first estranges herself from the jury and then laughs at how seriously she takes a loss she anticipated in the first place. Ultimately, she returns to her duty as a defense attorney, which includes defending the guilty, but not setting the guilty free. As Olivia described it, this duty determines how she approaches a case.

> OG: I don't think I ever look at getting a guilty person off; that never crosses my mind. I don't start by looking at the case and asking, "Did they do it?" I'm not going to decide did they do it, because that's not my job. I can say, "Sure, maybe they didn't do it," because maybe they didn't. You can think, well, if this is true, if it's true exactly as it reads in this police report, that's really bad, that's horrible. If he did that, it's horrible, and he should go to prison

for a long time. If they tell me they did it, then ethically I'm going to do whatever I'm responsible for doing, and I'm going to try to settle that case, and I'm going to try and get the best resolution.

I think some people think that we're trying to get these people off. To most people, somebody charged with a child molest is absolutely the scum of the earth. And it's lower than scum. The people that talk to me sometimes and ask, "How can you represent such creeps?" totally shut off the side that maybe the person didn't do it. That side is shut off, and I think that's really very narrow-minded. I have no problem with the idea that if somebody does horrible things to children, that they go away for the rest of their life. You know it may be very sad because they may have been molested. But, yeah, if this person is a sexual predator then what can we do except lock them up? You still have the side that is like the public feels: lock these criminals away and throw away the key. We all feel that way [at my public defender's office]. There's nobody there that would say, "Yippee, a serial rapist got out." But we're able to see the other side of the case.

Olivia said this part of her duty is consistent with public sentiment and, in some ways, with feminism. She considers herself a feminist but not to the same degree that other people view themselves. Olivia believes some feminists lose sight of the bigger picture of inequality. She said a good example would be the movement on University of California campuses several years ago to change the skirted symbol of a woman on restroom doors. According to Olivia, it is that sort of nearsightedness that leads the same people to ask, "How could you represent a rapist?" However, there is another part of her duty that is "on this higher plane of our Constitution, and enforcing that Constitution. We're protectors of the Constitution."

OG: I mean, we're not specifically trying to get somebody off that's committed a rape, because I personally don't want somebody that committed a rape to go free, and I think they should be punished accordingly. But if that's the way you're looking at it, then you're not seeing the broader picture, which is what I think some feminists do. You're above that, you're a defender of the Constitution. The person may not have committed that rape, number one. And how terrible to be convicted of rape when he didn't commit it.

Second, if he did commit the rape then he still has the rights that the Constitution guarantees, just like women want the guarantees the Constitution gives to them. I don't see it as being sympathetic to a rapist or somehow being disloyal to my gender, because I'm not. We talk in the office about, "Oh, I hope you don't get that guy off." And the date rape thing, I think that's probably something that feminists would have a little trouble understanding. Public defenders and myself are more skeptical about a date rape. I don't doubt that it happens. I don't doubt it should be punished. But I think it's abused too. We see the side where we get women who cry date rape, and it's not date rape—it's not a rape at all. It's just they're in trouble at home or wherever, and that's what they say happened. And so we see another side of that. I think that's something feminists might have a hard time seeing that women do say they've been raped when they haven't.

Olivia told me that she personally and politically believes that her duty includes being open to a broader view of someone's story. "Maybe they didn't do it. Maybe it didn't happen like it's written." The skepticism of written authority that Olivia learned from her father carried over and has been reinforced in her work as a public defender. The irony here is her use of the Constitution to combat the contradictions inherent in her work. Olivia's childhood experiences would lead us to expect her to be critical of the Constitution, given the history of the United States' atrocities against Native Americans. Instead, she lets us glimpse how a person works with her beliefs to make them consistent with what she is trying to feel.

We ended our conversation with my asking if law school prepared Olivia for any of this. She started to laugh—the usual response to this question. But for such a quiet woman it was a loud laugh. So I asked, "Just what did they teach you in law school?" Her response was simply, "Nothing I'm using today, that's for sure. Tah. I think I could have just skipped law school."

SALLY TAN

Given her strong convictions of social justice, awareness of racial inequality, the political climate of her college years, her age, and her years in practice, Sally Tan is the quintessential Abogada. Although she never worked in the same public defender's office as the Betties I interviewed,

Sally was a deputy public defender in various California counties for more than sixteen years. She shares biographical history with Rose Carr and Olivia George, although Sally went into private practice six years ago, after the birth of her first child at age forty-one. She told me if she were unmarried and not a mother, she would still be a public defender: "I'm certain of it."

> ST: It's like an extended family. People are very enthusiastic. They are very supportive. We're all doing the same thing. Everyone gets into everyone's trials. They'll help each other. There's a lot of camaraderie. You know, we all used to stick together because we were like the underdogs in the whole system. You really are. And so there's this nice sense of community within the public defender's office.

Sally did not leave public defense work because of its accompanying emotional stress. Rather, she needed time to raise her son. She still does work as a court-appointed attorney, handling indigent clients facing the death penalty.

Like Olivia George, Sally's sense of justice grew from her family's experience. Sally is Asian American. Her parents grew up in the '20s, '30s, and '40s.

> ST: There was a lot of prejudice against Asians in those years, especially after World War II. I think that some of my empathy for the underdog comes from my own family background and being an underdog also in that I'm Asian.

Sally tells me that, because of their experience, her parents raised her to be a real individual and "to be a person who stood up for her rights and did what she had to do." From 1966 to 1970 Sally was in college. In the values passed on by her parents, she found a receptiveness to the civil rights movement and women's liberation movement of the '60s.

Sally elaborated on the importance of feminism to her own life, telling me she has held onto her first copy of Ms. magazine, a symbol of her dedication to feminist principles and her place in the generation of young women in college at the moment the movement took off. She described her work as a continuation of the ideals of feminism she incorporated into her life during her college days:

ST: My job in the system is to make sure that the government does not get out of hand. That is, the police, the prosecutors, the courts, probation—every arm of the government better play by the rules, or they're going to have to contend with people like myself. We're here to keep the balance. That is really important. And that's important for women, too. Because women are also in the groups that have been discriminated against throughout history and will continue to be so. I think we're regressing, personally. I think that women are losing a lot of ground. And as long as you have the defense bar out there maintaining an equilibrium, then everybody has a better chance—feminists, foreigners, immigrants, the criminal defendant, people of color. I think it's extremely consistent with how I view my job. And that is to make sure the government doesn't trample on people's rights, whether it be in the private arena, the economic arena, criminal, etc.

Sally told me her strong convictions about the underdog and the Constitution are what led her into public defense work. She wanted to work with people who "really needed help, and obviously, as a public defender, you're working with indigent people." This is still her philosophy. Now she is able to compare the difference between the paying defendant and the indigent client. By and large, the court-appointed client is easier to deal with:

ST: Indigent clients, public defender clients are really the bottom of every list—economically and socially—they really need help, and they appreciate it. The private middle-class, Anglo client is a pain in the neck because they believe that they are better than everybody else in the system. And they can't quite understand why they're there. The middle-class client is a very different client. They have a superior attitude about themselves and think that only indigent people, like public defender clients, belong in the system, and they're quite indignant and righteous sometimes.

For Sally, they're a lot harder to deal with because they normally have two distasteful personality traits: they are unrealistic and are whiners:

ST: Those are the worst two combinations in a client. It's someone who, after I tell them all the evidence against them, and go through every argument as to why they don't have a triable case, or why they should take a plea agreement, they won't accept it. They whine about everything and won't face the facts.

She has a good base for comparison of clients. Like all women defenders who have worked in the field over fifteen years, Sally has handled thousands of clients. In her twenty-two years of practice, Sally has taken more than 125 felony cases to trial. This is more than double the record of any of the other seasoned women defenders. About 60 percent of those cases involved acts of violence and "maybe only 10 percent" were acts of violence against women. Unlike most other public defenders, Sally began requesting serious cases early on, which helps account for her many trials. "In the beginning I always wanted to do homicides. I've always wanted to take any case that's triable." She told me she would go after the interesting cases, and homicides are intriguing:

ST: They really are. When someone kills another person, there's a dynamic there that is so unusual that it's interesting. To take another life is a really profound act. And it's a drastic act. And it's interesting to see why people do it. So homicide cases, sure, I've always asked for them.

My knowledge of Sally as a powerfully effective trial attorney led me to this interview. I wanted to understand her relentless ability to remain professional and focused on cases with horrendous facts. And most of her trials fit into that category. The trial she was preparing for at the time of the interview was typical for Sally:

ST: My client is a husband. He stabbed his wife to death. Now I don't spend a lot of time saying, "This poor dead woman." It's not that I don't empathize. When I read the reports I think this is a tragic case. It is so tragic that it should come to this end. But I don't linger on the issue that this is a woman who's been killed by her husband. I realize that there is a case that can be made for manslaughter, and I'm looking at both sides.

This case can be distinguished from the victim–battered woman case. There are many women that are just plain victims. They've been battered all of their lives, mentally and psychologically—physically by their husbands. My client stabbed his wife to death. This particular case falls into another category that I've seen throughout my work as a public defender and a defense lawyer. There are women out there who are violent, that actually engage in violence with their husbands that precipitate the violence, that start the violence, okay? In this particular case, this is a very volatile relationship, and they were both physically violent with one another. The way I approach a case is to look at it and say, "Is there something here that I can reasonably argue to a jury that precipitated the heat of passion in this man so that he just went off?" I mean, this man did not plan to kill his wife.

They were having a barbecue. There was a big fight between his brother, her brother, and himself. After everybody left he and his wife continued to argue. Two children were in the house, a four-month-old and a two-year-old. And they continued to argue. There's a lot of history behind this, okay? But he got so angry that he stabbed her to death. When you listen to what everybody around them has to say about them, the one thing that they say about their relationship is that that's all they ever did, was argue. It was a love-hate relationship. They always went back to each other. She was physical with him. She used to slap him in front of people and scratch him. And he was physical; he used to punch her, too, but . . . they always went back together. And this time it just went too far. Which I think is common in violent relationships. But this man, in his own home, stabbed his wife to death. Now people don't do that because they just don't like their wives or they're planning to get rid of her because they are going to get a divorce. This is a heat of passion. And he has a long history.

He's been to the joint twice. He was in gangs all of his life. He started out in the Youth Authority. There's a very violent history from his own family. And her side is the same way. Her family are dope dealers and they live in that culture, in that milieu. And when you put it in the context of their lives, I think that I can get a jury at least to think about the fact that this was a heat of passion. The other thing that everyone says about this man is that he loved his wife, that they loved each other—they just quarreled like cats and dogs. They didn't know how to relate. Everyone that was interviewed said they both really loved their children. So this is a case where you have a woman who is dead, viciously stabbed. I mean, she was stabbed—clearly he lost control—he didn't just stab her once. He stabbed her twenty-nine times. He was out of control.

Very few times am I taken aback by a client because I've seen so many clients. . . . But this client I was a little wary of when I first saw him. He is literally covered with tattoos—his forehead, the sides of his head, arms. He looks really tough. And it's going to be hard to get a jury to realize that he isn't just a mean son-of-a-bitch who just decided to kill his wife. That there were some dynamics, lots and lots of dynamics going on here. He didn't intend to kill her. He lost control.

There are several rationalizations in this account that might be interpreted as emotion work. Most apparent is the way Sally distances herself from the dead wife by maligning her character and that of her family, as though it would somehow assuage the husband's guilt. First we are told how violent the deceased woman was, even in public, and that her aggressive actions precipitated her murder. Second, even though the defendant is an unsavory character, a gang-banger who has been to the joint twice, his wife came from a family of drug dealers and the same culture of crime. Sally used another form of emotion work as well by focusing on what the jury might accept as explanation.

ST: Even when I was defending child molesters, it was on the same level as everything else. Anything dealing with children, it's always more difficult to keep your emotions intact and to be professional. And you do it. It's not a pleasant task, but you do it. And you try to focus on what's good for the client.

I spend a lot of time preparing the case before it goes to trial, and I'm so immersed in the case itself that I don't consider what my personal feelings might be about aspects of the case. Because if you dwell on that, or if you let it interfere, then it just distracts you. So I try to get very focused on what my job is and how I present the case.

This is the same emotion management technique that the younger women use. But their use is not nearly as well established as Sally's. There is also an aspect of her emotion work that incorporates her professional duty. I saw this most clearly when I asked her if she felt different when she was in trial, sitting next to a man who may have raped a woman.

> ST: No, I don't allow myself to do that. There are times when I look at clients and I think, "This is despicable." I allow myself that private thought, or the ability to say it to my own partner, my husband, who has the same type of work that I do. We can say it to each other and know that we're going to go back and do a good job. My job is to make sure they get a fair shake. Period.

I recognized that these short emphatic statements in Sally's responses had also appeared in the interview with Rose Carr, especially when she spoke about representing the man who kidnapped her friend's daughter: "And I did. . . . And I was able to do it." I heard another such statement when I asked Sally if it is a conscious strategy to assign women to cases where there's been an act of violence against a woman.

> ST: I think that it's a very effective thing to do if you get the right woman with the right case. Absolutely. I think it was a matter of practicality that it evolved in public defenders offices or criminal defense lawyers' offices: if they have a group of people, they'll take a look at them. If they're thoughtful about the case, they try to evaluate the type of case and the lawyer they're giving it to, and one of the factors would be, if it's a rape case, a woman. People that do this work all the time know that it's beneficial. It just is.

What can lead a woman defense attorney who self-identifies as a feminist to say in this situation, "It just is?" The ability grows from a woman's strong ideological conviction of the value of her work. Sally's certitude is represented in her philosophizing about individual rights during her interview.

> ST: I really think that it's evident in society now that there is a tide, there is always a tide—it used to be an undercurrent, but now it's a tide—of people who want to take away individual rights. They

always start with the lowest group on the totem pole, which is criminal defendants. Historically, if you look at the law, that's the area where people try and whittle away individual rights. They justify it because these people are criminals. So I think it's really important to protect everyone's individual rights, and one of the main areas is through the criminal process. I've always felt that if you didn't have defense lawyers, our system would really be horrible. And you'd have, I hate to say, a Nazi situation—very, very dangerous.

Sally's conviction is also present in her reflections on her professional duty: "I have a strong sense of who I am and what it is I do. Regardless of what the crime is, or who the defendant is, I have a clear focus of what my job is. I think it makes it easier for me." I heard hints of emotional distancing with statements like "They always start with the lowest group on the totem pole, which is criminal defendants," or "these people are criminals." She also goes on to say that sometimes she lets emotions out by badmouthing a client, a witness, or a victim: "But in the long run it's a waste of energy and it doesn't get you where you have to go." That Sally's professional ethic "makes it easier" is an indicator of effective ideological work. Again she tries to focus, and it is an ideology that helps.

Focus is also what Sally requires of her clients. Help comes from the description of the preliminary hearing where I observed Rose Carr. Sally represented a young woman charged with a murder committed during the course of the same robbery. The nature of that charge made this a "special circumstance" case, one in which her defendant faced the death penalty if convicted.

Four defendants faced the same charge, all of them in their midtwenties, two Anglo women and two African American men. The men were allegedly the triggermen, but Sally's client was the only defendant fingered by a snitch. While in jail, Sally's client was housed with a "friend," who went to the police with statements allegedly made to her by the client, implicating the client in the robbery-conspiracy. Even though the snitch said on the stand, "You don't have friends in custody," the young defendant was visibly shaken by the betrayal of someone she believed to be her confidant. The scene was highly charged. Sally sat a seat away from her client, silently scribbling notes. The client was bending over, crying.

Sally's self demand—"I can handle it"—was evident in her presentation of self in the courtroom. Also evident is the similar demand that she places on her client. To be most effective, presentations of emotions need to be matched between client and attorney. Sally reached over and nudged her client to sit up and compose herself. The client wiped her eyes and continued to sit through many more hours of incriminating testimony by her "friend" without breaking down again. What Sally demands of herself, she demands of her clients.

Strict maintenance of a professional face is clearly a form of emotion work for Sally—especially when a woman has been subjected to male violence. She told me that she has a tendency to empathize more in these instances because "it's more pathetic and more difficult to accept." But once Sally makes it in front of a jury, she concentrates on her presentation of self: "Psychologically I have to maintain the same decorum all of the time. It is not my job to judge my clients or to feel anything for their victims."

Sally's focus on her professionalism, sense of duty, and beliefs in "higher goals" have enabled her to take an extremely high number of "difficult and challenging" cases to trial with good results. By all appearances, she doesn't seem to be losing her energy for this type of work. She recognizes that "women that are drawn to this type of work and stay with it have a similar core sense of what it is they're doing." Sally also recognizes that "sometimes you change your work when your life changes." For her this has meant a move away from child-molestation cases.

> ST: Now that I'm in private practice and have the luxury of saying no to cases, I don't choose to handle those cases. And that's become recent, in having a child . . . I just don't want to handle those types of cases. But that's the only area [I won't take].

Entering criminal defense work with strong convictions did not mean that Sally was spared emotional stress in her early years. During the interview I asked if she could recall any cases that were particularly emotional and how she handled the accompanying stress. She couldn't think of any. Eight months later Sally called to inform me of an upcoming trial. She also wanted to tell me about a case that she started thinking about after our first interview. She felt she was suppressing her memory of the case because it had been very traumatic for her at the time.

Sally had spent two years at a district attorney's office before landing a public defense job. After law school she wanted to be a public defender, but when she was not able to get a job, Sally decided to learn how the other side works. Going over to the defense was a big change. As a prosecutor Sally had more societal respect. Even a former law professor (now a federal judge) who wrote her letters of reference said at the time, "[Sally], you really should just remain a prosecutor. At the end you'll be in much better shape." But she said it was where she belonged philosophically. Work as a prosecutor gives criminal attorneys little personal contact with defendants and the ramifications of sentencing on their lives. The case she remembered was a "rude awakening, a reality check" about the kind of work she was doing. Six months into Sally's career as a defense attorney she had an eighteen- or nineteen-year-old youth as a client.

> ST: He had committed all these burglaries, and the judge sentenced him to state prison. It was traumatic. I was devastated and cried. I felt horrible that this poor kid should have gone to prison even though he had tons of residential burglaries. Because of his youthful age I thought he should have been sent to the Youth Authority, or dealt with in a different manner.

Months later she found out the young man had committed suicide in prison.

> ST: I realized this is a very serious profession because we deal with really tragic situations, and people commit suicide over them. If it happened now, I would be upset but not devastated. I could handle it better now. Back then it was traumatic.[4]

To deal with this sort of emotional stress, Sally draws on "political beliefs and ideological beliefs, because sometimes those are different." The emotional example she gave dealt with sentencing ramifications. Outcomes are more difficult for the defense attorney to manage. Clearly it is more difficult for the woman defender to transfer her emotions into a technical focus on work once the trial is over. The trauma was there twenty-two years ago and it still is, even though it may have been suppressed. It would not be as difficult for her to deal with today, Sally says. Common sense might suggest that over the years a woman toughens. But in the case of Sally and the other seasoned women defenders, strong ideologies also guide them. As

Sally puts it, "It's higher goals and how they function on a daily level with my job."

Conveying the stories of women who have been criminal defenders for so many years is difficult. Part of the problem is that as seasoned litigators they have excellent abilities to debate across all sides—even with themselves. Their emotion work is so effective that their strategies to suppress undesired feelings are much less evident than they are for women early in their careers. At the same time, the ideological-emotional relationship becomes all the more apparent. While the two women that follow do not have as much to say, what they say demonstrates the correlation.

TRUDY KAUFMAN

Trudy Kaufman looks quite professorial sitting behind her desk. Her law school office stands in stark contrast to most of the public defenders offices I have been in. It is large, well decorated, and feels like a judge's chambers. Diplomas and pictures of a girl through various stages of childhood hang on the walls.

Trudy tells me that she has a set of responses all prepared for those folks who ask about the moral dilemmas of criminal defense work. She practiced criminal defense law for over two decades and has been a professor of trial advocacy and criminal litigation for the past eleven years. As a practicing attorney Trudy was very "single-minded" and did not have much of a life outside work. She left that behind when she was forty-two years of age to have a child. "I wanted to have a life in which I didn't have to go to trial." However, she did not leave behind the questions on defending the "evil" in society. They continue in the classroom, and she is ready for them.

As Trudy sees it, moral dilemmas and the resulting emotions crop up everywhere in defense work, and they come up in context. She told me that when a lawyer takes an oath to represent someone, his or her job is to do it zealously within the bounds of the law. Trudy's logic is clear, and it repeats what many women defenders have said: "If you can't, you shouldn't do it." But she does not mean a defense attorney should not wrestle with her emotions. Quite the contrary. According to Trudy, emotional conflict is necessary for the job. Without verbalizing it, she raises the question, "What kind of person would have no emotional response to the things defense attorneys see every day?" I was reminded of Becky McBride's words—"We're looking at the underbelly of life, the most depressing part, so much ugliness, so much pain, screwed up lives, and nobody being a winner"—and the thoughts of Vivian Gold, the last woman I will discuss— "We deal every day with the very fabric of life, with sex, with greed, with fear, with weakness, with regret." Without her emotional reactions intact the defense attorney would be out of touch with the prevailing sentiments she faces in court.

> TK: You have to understand that [the way you are feeling] is the way a juror or a judge is going to react, too. You have to find a way to get to the hard truth of your client's story and tell it so that it responds to those unspoken, sometimes racist, sometimes sexist concerns.

In every difficult case that she had as a public defender, Trudy said, she sifted through her emotions looking for the truth. And she had some hideous cases—a sociopathic client, who poured boiling water on a girlfriend, another client who raped a seventy-four-year-old woman while she was kneeling and saying the Lord's Prayer, an extortionist who used sex photographs to get money out of a naive young woman, and an old man who molested two little children.

In the case involving the man charged with molesting the children, her job was to show the judge all of the circumstances that surrounded this man's contact with the children and his own situation to try prevent him from going to prison. As she saw it, "A sixty-five-year-old man with a molestation jacket would be raped and killed in prison."

> CS: Would it have been any different if he weren't sixty-five?
> TK: Everything is situational. Every case depends on its own particular set of facts. That's where I think a lot of the misconceptions about the criminal justice system arise. When we hear the term "child molester," the image that comes to our mind is not necessarily a sixty-five-year-old man who had a wife in a wheel chair, who worked as a short-order cook to support her, who lived in a hotel with a woman next door who was a Hell's Angel girlfriend who would leave her two children unattended three or four days at a time . . . the children were four and six, and she would go off with a boyfriend, and the kids would be by themselves . . . "grandpa" next door would take care of them, get them to school on time, help them with their homework, feed and clothe them, and one

night he messed with them in the bathtub. It's not simple; it's not black-and-white.

He had been clean for twenty years—no record for twenty years. But twenty years earlier he had been arrested. He was a pedophile. But he suppressed it and didn't act on it for twenty years, and then this opportunity happened. Life's not so simple. Which is not to say that he didn't inflict terrible harm on these kids, and that he should not have been punished. But what good is it going to do to send that guy to prison? [What] if I had approached his case by what he had done, saying, "Child molester, ooh, forget it, I won't work on this case"?

While Trudy is not identifying with her client to the extent some of women at the midpoint in their careers do, she does an excellent job separating him from his crime. That is, the molestation was an opportunity that happened.

In law school Trudy thought that she would never be able to represent a man charged with sexually assaulting children or women. But when she started working in a public defender's office and was assigned a client accused of putting out someone's eye, she had an epiphany.

> TK: I thought, "If I can defend this person charged with this crime, how can I not defend the man who's assaulted a woman?" I mean, on what logic am I drawing the line here? Because I'm not defending the act; I'm not saying it's good to tear someone from limb to limb, or put out their eye, or rape them. I'm defending the human being's right to a fair proceeding, a human being who's alleged to have committed the act.

She told me about sitting in a jail cell with this client, who was a "speed freak," an addict who had grown completely paranoid and insane as a result of his addiction. According to her, it was the methamphetamines that caused him to hack up his friend, who was also a junkie.[5]

> TK: You know, there is a perception in our society that criminal defense attorneys represent really evil people, and that our prisons are filled with really evil people. That is just wrong. The vast majority of clients are just poor people who do drugs or alcohol. The percentage of violent, beyond-redemption folks that I represented is some-

where around 2 or 3 percent. Another way to look at it is, that was the price I paid for the privilege of representing the rest.

Trudy acknowledged that there is a cost to being a public defense attorney. The most difficult case she ever had was the extortion case. Her client had taken photographs of a young woman that he was sexually involved with while she was performing oral sex on him. As Trudy explains, he arranged the camera—"bless his twisted heart"—so only the young woman could be identified. Then he threatened that unless she gave him money, he would send the pictures to her mother, even post them at her school. This was a young Latina with a very religious mother.

> TK: So she paid, and she paid, and she paid, and she paid. Finally she went to the police. And I had to represent this guy. I found him to be one of the most reprehensible people that I've ever met in my life.
>
> So, you know how I handled that? I acknowledged my feelings, and I talked about it with friends, about how much I loathed this guy. I maintained a very professional relationship with him. Sometimes with my clients I would be warm and friendly. But I worked very hard [instead].

Trudy told me that she knew that it would be a devastating experience for this young woman to be cross-examined, especially since she had written a diary detailing her affair with the defendant. Trudy had the diary subpoenaed and translated: "Even the translator was horrified, and she didn't translate it correctly." Before the trial Trudy proposed a deal to the DA, explaining it would be a terrible experience for this woman to be cross-examined.

> TK: For her to testify to all this stuff would be just as bad as had he gone ahead and published the photographs. And we both had an interest in avoiding that. So I worked out a deal where he pled guilty to something—I don't remember what it was—as a felony but it would be reduced to a misdemeanor on the day of his sentencing if he paid her back every penny he had taken from her. He didn't have any money, but I worked it out so he could get a loan from someone. So he paid her back, and that meant that he didn't

have a felony conviction, which was good for him, and she didn't have to go through with the trial. But I wasn't protecting her. But I think part of good negotiating is figuring out what's in the other side's interest and making the other person see that it's in their interest. And the DA wanted to protect her.

It makes sense that Trudy, who defends the person and not the crime, found her most difficult case to have, in her words, "the lowest kind of a human being" for a client.

There has long been the distinction in criminal justice studies between offender- and offense-centered sentencing. Given that so many women defenders identify with their clients, not the crime, sentencing—to judge by their stories—is the most difficult aspect of their work. I suggest their experience is easier when the crime is punished. California's TSL is a combination of both offender- and offense-centered sentencing for second strikes. A defendant's prior criminal record is considered, and the sentence is based on the most recent crime committed. However, third-strike sentencing is offender-centered: a defendant may receive a life sentence "for petty theft as well as aggravated murder."[6] Arguably this becomes more difficult for the woman defender when she identifies with her client. It is what Trudy would have been facing were she still actively practicing criminal defense law.

My final interview took place over the phone. It was combined with the woman's video-taped testament of her lifetime career as a defense attorney.

VIVIAN GOLD

Vivian Gold began law school in 1961, before the women's liberation movement, a time when women accounted for only 4 percent of practicing lawyers in the United States.[7] Women were only 3 percent of her law school class. Humor pervades this sixty-one-year-old woman's reflections on her over thirty-five years as a defense attorney, beginning with her early law school days.

> VG: In my class at Boalt Hall our equity professor informed us how he would treat women equally. So in a room of 100 students, three of which were women, he would alternate and he would call on

woman, man, woman, man. And it was incredibly demeaning, but we just sat there and accepted it. We were very blissfully ignorant.

I graduated in 1964, the year that the equal rights act passed. And the only kind of lawyer that I ever wanted to be was a criminal defense lawyer. I wanted to be a public defender.

As Vivian said, fortunately for her, no one else wanted such a job in those days. Her first boss described public defense work as "exactly like traveling down a sewer in a glass-bottom boat." She had gone from the dark ages of law school to the dark ages of public defense work. Vivian would not end up staying there for long.

Early in her career at the public defender's office Vivian was admonished by the administration for signing a declaration against the Vietnam War. With time, she felt overly constrained by the bureaucracy of her office and a boss that wanted to control her legal maneuverings in court for fear she would alienate the judges. In 1969 Vivian moved into private practice: the timing could not have been better for her career.

VG: The skirmish in People's Park in Berkeley occurred thirty days later. Army tanks were lodged in front of my office in Berkeley. Criminal defense and my practice took off. As few women as there were in law schools, there were virtually no women lawyers in the courtroom when I started. I was always the only woman. There were many egregious examples of sexism that pervaded those early years. Once, in an open municipal court trial I raised my voice to the judge, as I often do, as I was arguing. And the prosecution said, and I quote, "Don't mind her judge; she must be on the rag."

The importance of the historical moment could not have been greater. Vivian said that women's rights, civil rights, and her rights all played a part in how she practiced law—as did the rights of those living on society's margins.

VG: In 1972 I received a terrific break when, as a still-young lawyer, I was appointed by the court to represent a man described by the prosecution as Ralph Sonny Barker's chief lieutenant. Sonny was the national head of the Hell's Angels motorcycle club, and he, along with my client, was charged with murder and arson. In that case the defense team exposed to national publicity the fact that the police department had an ongoing policy of giving favors to the Angels for the turning over of weapons. It turned out to be a major national expose, helped gain an acquittal, and secured for me an ongoing relationship representing the Angels. I learned from that case that it's right to take on the establishment, to take chances when it assists a client.

Throughout my interviews, women reflected on their most difficult cases and how they dealt with them, most of them involving sexual assaults against women. Interestingly, Vivian never talked about a sex case when she spoke—for nearly an hour—about her long career. The case she described as the most difficult was not related to the nature of the crime (although it was a nasty homicide), nor the reprehensible character of her client (a wealthy developer accused of soliciting a murder); rather it was related to being a woman navigating her way through the masculine legal world.

VG: The media built the case as the crossbow murder case. The defendant was accused of hiring two former university football players to kill a former business associate. A killing which had been accomplished by the use of a crossbow. The preparation and trial in this case took over eighteen months—six months preparation alone for the cross-examination of the key witness, which examination took a month. And what had begun as a very difficult and complex trial turned into a war between the sexes.

The male prosecutor was dragging into the case every dirty trick and insinuation that might rattle [my law partner and myself] and cause us to lose this case. Every time the prosecution [could, he] tried to tell the jury in subtle and not so subtle ways that we were strange women, who wore pants to court, . . . who were too aggressive, . . . who were too tough, . . . who were too bitchy . . . that we could not possibly be real Americans.

We had done our homework on this guy. We had purposely chosen a course of aggression knowing that nothing else would work. His leaving the courtroom during our questioning to go to the bathroom across the hall; his flushing the toilet for all of us to hear, including the jury; his objecting to almost every single question we would ask—we persevered, and we won the case. We felt in some small way we had also won the battle for women, too.

From Vivian's description of the prosecutor's sexism, we might imagine this case took place in the early years of her career. However, it happened in 1991 and 1992. She had been a practicing attorney for over twenty-five years and was still enduring the gendered insults that were directed at her when she entered a nearly all-male profession in 1964. Still, she believes that women are naturals for this kind of work. The combination of being a woman and a defense attorney means always being in the minority and in the role of the opposition: "This keeps us tough."

Vivian has had her triumphs in the legal business. While Iris Egan and Rose Carr have made their ways to successfully arguing in front of the California Supreme Court, Vivian is the only one to have endured the anguish and ecstasy of arguing in front of the United States Supreme Court.

VG: It was January in 1987, and I was going to argue before the United States Supreme Court. The powers that be wanted to take whatever was left of the Fourth Amendment and apply the good faith doctrine to warrantless searches. They took our case. It was a complicated case involving a probation search that produced a large drug lab. The problem was that the defendant had never consented to being on probation.

I sat down in the United States Supreme Court and waited to argue. The court crier comes out—it's just quiet. I was dying inside. Then the court members come out. They sit. The Solicitor General gets up to begin his arguments. I am terrified. The Solicitor General barely gets his introductory sentence out when the thundering presence of The Honorable Thurgood Marshall makes itself known. And he bellows into the microphone to my opponent.

The Justice: When did the respondent first know of this probation business?
Solicitor: He was told at the door.
The Justice: That don't give you any problem do it?
Solicitor: No.
The Justice: Oh, so he lost all of his rights without even knowing it.

And then the justice groaned uncontrollably, and I was feeling quite calm. [Vivian laughed.]

Despite her focus and concentration, a colleague describes her as "never losing hold of the larger picture and enjoyment of the process. In the heat of battle she brings a joy and appreciation of the funny and ridiculous into the courtroom. She can be wickedly funny and plain old wicked." From Justice Marshall's groans in the Supreme Court to her earliest days in municipal court, Vivian depicts the humor of her courtroom dramas. Other women defenders distance themselves from victims or clients. Apparently Vivian's most effective form of emotion work is to distance herself from the criminal justice system by pointing out its absurdities.

> VG: My very first play in the press was also an educational experience. "A bad day for the Boo Hoo," the morning paper said. We at the courthouse knew what was coming. Charlie Brown had done it again. It seems that Charlie, better known as the wandering priest of the Berkeley Boo Hoo, had informed the police that he carried LSD in the religious jewelry he wore around his neck. Find it they did. Charlie presented quite a picture in the Berkeley courtroom. His testimony, to say the least, was erratic. He claimed that his spiritual guides had directed him to take certain drugs, like peyote. He testified he was told to take so many peyote buttons and a drop of acid for a trip. And he did, according to his admission.
>
> The deputy prosecutor conducted his examination of the defendant. It went like this.
>
> Prosecutor: Who are these guys?
> Charlie: They are here to advise me.
> Prosecutor: Are they in this courtroom now?
> Charlie: Yes.
> Prosecutor: Where?
> Charlie: Around the fire there [as he gestured around the courtroom].
> Prosecutor: What are they saying?
> Vivian: Objection, objection, hearsay.

According to Vivian, the judge could hardly contain himself, and she learned an important lesson: "Almost never put your client on the stand."

Being in private practice certainly meant that Vivian had some control over which cases she took. However, it does not mean that she avoided cases that pitted her identity against her client's. Her "ultimate" lesson came in the form of a death-penalty case.

> VG: It was a robbery-murder. Four men had robbed a motel and then engaged in a freeway chase with the police. The chases ended when the robbers' car crashed, and one of the suspects and one of the cops faced off and killed each other. Two suspects fled the scene, my client, of course, stayed to be arrested.

Vivian's defendant was convicted of killing a police officer in the line of duty. During the penalty phase of the trial, when the jury was to decide the fate of her client, he was accused of assaulting another prisoner. The timing could not have been worse. The circumstances were also difficult considering Vivian's identity as a Jew:

> VG: In came a witness to testify that he was an Orthodox Jew. He donned his skullcap in the jail and was at prayer after a meal when he was attacked violently by my client. A doctor confirmed that the man had lost the sight in his left eye as a result of the beating. The prosecutor called my client a "neo-Nazi." Two jailers confirmed that the attack was unprovoked. My client had to be pulled off the victim. I found myself in my first very, very heavy case arguing that, as a Jew, I was insulted by the prosecutor's argument. And the jury voted for life.

Vivian did not speak directly about the emotional conflict she felt as she made this argument, although she said that it was this case that taught her the duty and obligations of criminal defense work. Like so many other women defenders, Vivian sees her profession as a helping one. The emotions and stress of her job somehow dissipate when she receives a letter from a former client whose life she has helped to change. Such letters come from ex-addicts, who write to tell her that they have become productive members of society and are proud to say she represented them; from prisoners, who say that in their society her name is a "household word"; and from the woman who hired Vivian to represent her for killing her abusive husband.

In the early 1980s Vivian went to see this woman in jail. She had shot her physicist husband. The woman liked Vivian as a person but worried whether she "could handle a male-dominated courtroom." Women who killed their husbands after enduring years of physical abuse had been successfully represented. This case, though, was different. It was emotional abuse, and Vivian wanted to argue the case. She convinced the defendant that she was the best attorney for the job.

> VG: I wanted to take on emotional battering. [Gloria's] case is just that. She hired me and we achieved an incredible result. She and her husband had been married for thirty years. They had been happy until the last three years, when he began making bizarre sexual demands, pursued other women, and became dissatisfied with his job.
>
> The facts were bad. In July of 1980, the day of the argument, [Gloria] shot [her husband] six times with a .38 revolver. He staggered out into their driveway to call for help. She went back into her bedroom, reloaded six rounds, went outside, and emptied her gun into him. At her court trial she was found guilty of voluntary manslaughter. She was sentenced to two years in prison. She served about eleven months.

Vivian received a letter from Gloria just a few months before our meeting. It began, "I thought it was time for me to let you know that it is due to you that my life and my children's lives have followed a continuous straightening course." The woman described her daughter's graduation from college, her son's engineering business, and her continuing employment in civil service. At the time Vivian received the letter she was appearing in the same courtroom where she tried Gloria's case. Coincidentally the court clerk approached her and asked about Gloria. Vivian was able to report the good news: the clerk told her Gloria's case was the only time that she cried during a sentencing proceeding.

With all of the venues to which Vivian's career has taken her—from traffic court to the U.S. Supreme Court—there is no doubt that she paved the way for future generations of women defenders. In her reflections she described the barriers that women continue to face in the criminal court setting. She did not, however, comment on being chosen because of her gender to defend men's acts of violence against other women. As Sally Tan said, that strategy evolved in public defenders offices over time, and perhaps Vivian was spared by leaving public defense work in 1969. Perhaps she avoided it through pricing strategies. Perhaps she did not. Regardless, when Vivian reflects on her career she does not describe cases of sexual assault upon women as her most difficult. Rather, her most difficult cases questioned her identity as a woman who was "too aggressive," a Jew defending the hate crime against one of her own, and finally as a defense lawyer. The last of these happened when she was called as an expert witness on a case where a lawyer was attempting to get a new trial.

Vivian found herself on the witness stand testifying that one of the "most revered" defense attorneys in her lifetime was incompetent.

> VG: The case was known as "Dear Diary" in the media. It involved a fourteen-year-old girl who was charged in juvenile court with the suffocation death of her sister. She had, "confessed" in her diary. The first defense team had ignored critical medical evidence pointing to the very real possibility that the father was responsible for the death of the younger girl. The original defense had also ignored the psychology of young girls who can fib in diaries for many reasons. I testified at the motion hearing, and [the lawyer trying to get the new trial] won. I joined him at the retrial as co-counsel. This innocent young girl won an acquittal. The lesson was that even the great can fail, and they must be watched, and tested, and challenged.

Vivian's video-taped speech was presented to an association of women defense attorneys as she received their most prestigious award for a lifetime of service to their profession. It may read as ideological; it may also read as adamant, as it was presented to women to help fortify their professional identities. And it served that purpose. Vivian firmly believes in the meritorious nature of her profession and directs those (like the incompetent renowned defense attorney) who are "burnt out, [to] get out." She recognizes that the profession breeds bitterness, depression, and fatigue, whose byproduct is mediocrity—but somehow Vivian bypassed the cynicism that some might predict, especially as she now practices in California's current sentencing climate.

> VG: With criminal law's present confrontations and heinous penalties—and gutless judges—it's imperative that those who do this work practice at the highest level and maintain intensity and the

commitment to pursue excellence. I am proud to say that many of my best friends are criminal defense lawyers. They are devoted to the concept of justice and relentless in this quest.

Vivian said that in the '60s and '70s women defense attorneys had to be better and tougher, and they had to show that they were tougher. She likes to think that somehow her generation of women rose above the prejudice and barriers of the criminal justice system. Ultimately it is the ideology of the profession that helped them persevere: "We had a Constitution to defend, and that was our principal role." In the words of Clarence Darrow,[8] a man Vivian greatly admired, it is serving "that subtle indefinable quality that men call justice and of which nothing is really known."[9]

EMOTIONAL
TRIALS

6 Concluding Remarks

It's the state against this person. And to protect individual civil rights you need a vigorous advocate. But the state has all the resources of our state and federal law enforcement at its disposal. And the defendant just has you.
—Trudy Kaufman

IN examining the work of women defense attorneys, I have identified key themes: the conceptual overlaps between ideology and emotion, and the connection of ideological work and emotion work to the identity formation, transformation, and reinforcement that comprise moral careers. None is more important than how these women do their jobs.

The women defenders I interviewed let me glimpse how their emotion work incorporates an ideological component. For the majority, feminism becomes an ideological bridge between their everyday life situations as women and the feelings demanded of them in their work as criminal defense attorneys. The emotion work they evidenced in their stories is not only internal, but part of their external justification, or defense, of their work that can even be accomplished through their feminist ideologies. Fourteen of the nineteen women I interviewed told me they were feminists. Twelve of the fourteen said that feminism is consistent with criminal defense work, though this is the one place Rose Carr came close to losing her coherence (see p. 126). Annette Petroff gives an illustration of feminism as a bridge in her description of her feminist ideals in chapter one. She sees the defense of men who commit violence against women as separate from feminism; at the same time, the ideals of feminism justify her role.

> AP: Defending people who commit crimes against women . . . I don't think it damages in any way feminism or its goals. . . . I think if anything it's supportive of it. Because if everyone doesn't get treated with the same constitutional protections, then it's defeating the role of feminism. It's to make it so that everyone's on equal footing.

By definition, ideology is two-sided, incorporating the situational perspective of individuals and the total group outlook.[1] Ideologies are flexible, as are the ways individuals use their groups' ideologies to make sense of the contradictions they experience in everyday life. The individual may use the flexibility of an ideology as the "symbolic outlet" for emotional conflict.[2] Feminism can be a justification for women defenders' roles in a system that may seem to outsiders to be at odds with their values as women. As Sally responded when I asked if doing defense work was at odds with feminism:

> ST: No, absolutely not. . . . My job is to make sure that . . . every arm of government better play by the rules. . . . And that's important for women, too. Because women are also in the groups that have been discriminated against throughout history.

Emily Locatelli and Darla Wilson see a conflict. Darla's concern in domestic violence cases—a significant portion of her assignment—is not that women are being treated equally: "I really have to consciously not be concerned with the victims in the case. It's not my job. . . . We joke about sort of having to prostitute ourselves as public defenders."

According to Emily, the conflict contributed to her decision to leave public defense work: "It certainly was why I would no longer represent clients in [rape] cases." Interestingly, Darla and Emily are two of the three women who self-identify as lesbians.

Each of the women I interviewed described cases that included sexual violence against women. Recognizing a conflict between defense work and feminism seems to make cases involving crimes of violence against women and children the most difficult to handle: these cases would be less difficult for women who do not see the conflict.

Only two women told stories of difficult cases that did not involve men brutalizing women or children. Taking a horrible case to trial is just one of many events in these women's ongoing work lives, which they describe as continually stressful. Their stress includes managing a self that is constantly in flux and challenged by the very nature of their private and public worlds. In a career built around wins and losses, these women defenders learn that "a defensible picture of self can be seen as something that can be constructed, lost, and rebuilt with great speed and equanimity."[3] I argue that women defenders deftly manage the selves they present to others and their perceived and felt emotions through their ideologies.

ON THE NATURE OF EMOTION WORK

Emotion work is directly related to Marx's theory of alienation. That is, human beings pay a piece of their emotional selves when they work for others, hence Darla Wilson's "joke" of defenders having to prostitute themselves.[4] In studying emotion work on the job, there is a built-in assumption about considering the negative aspects of the subject's disconnection from her or his "true" nature. The negative aspects of doing emotion work at the levels of both body and mind are evident in these women's stories, especially in early stage careers. For example, Becky McBride loses excessive amounts of weight during trial. Darla fights with herself when defending the man who molested his three stepchildren. In her first year as a defense attorney, Sally Tan was devastated by the suicide of her client in a way that she would not be today. Emily Locatelli is haunted by the outcome of a "successful" case in which her client's acquittal led to the rapes of two other women. Even Becky admits that a defense attorney many times does not present her "real" self:

> BM: You might be really nice to some judge that you can't stand, or kind of yucking it up with a DA that you think is a complete idiot, or sort of presenting something to a jury that is really just an act. There are so many times when I'm not sincere in my job. And there are times when I feel kind of gross about that, sort of in a feminist way—the way that I interact with judges, a lot of times, and this goes back to your other question about how sometimes being a public defender might be in conflict with feminist ideals.

> The way I feel is in direct contrast because I will do quite a bit to further my client's cause, even if, for instance, there's a judge who might respond to you if you present youself as the young female who needs guidance from him. I would play that role. And then you walk away and you feel like I just perpetuated all the more stereotypes and sexism, but it worked. So sometimes you wear a hat just for what works, not because it's who you really are or what you believe in. And there are a lot of times when you don't feel very good about it.

Becky offers an excellent description of the downside to emotional labor when the self is alienated at work to the benefit of the work role—most often associated with women in the early stages of their careers.

Considering the implications of this work on the lives of women defenders, I believe it important to further the notion that emotion work may also be enabling at both societal and individual levels:[5] an inevitable component of their career positions them within the criminal justice system to bring about social change; and there are positive consequences at the level of the individual woman whose professional culture refines the practice of performing emotion work through ideological thought. Sociologists tend, when considering emotion work, to look primarily at the displays of emotions demanded of an occupation. My study is qualitatively different. It points to the use of ideology in combating not only the public emotions demanded of the profession, but also the emotional hardship intrinsic to everyday defense work.

Rather than seeing her heightened emotional state in court as a weakness, Fran Jones learned that women defenders' public display of emotions in court might be a powerful strategy in competition. As a woman defense attorney who understands "the game," she feels she has the advantage in court. Fran gives a classic example of how the woman defender does gender: "I can go into a judge's chambers, or I can go in front of a jury, and I can make arguments that are based on passion and compassion and win those, but a man could never do it. I think it's a gift that we have."

The women defenders in this study who began their practice prior to the mid-1980s never incorporated the gendered strategy of crying in court. They understood the legal culture to be at odds with such a gendered emotional display. Most, if not all, of these women defenders incorporated culturally dominant forms of masculine language.[6] The examples are numerous. Emily Locatelli was right up there with the men in her office "smoking and joking" after hearing their "war stories." Gina Rossi and Kay Owens use the phrases, "We live to fight again. We live to fight another day." Meg Lowe's ability to survive a horrendous case was her "test of fire." Even Fran Jones, who is not ashamed to cry in court and entered criminal law in the late '80s, speaks of her emotions in terms of an advantage in "the game."

ON THE IDEOLOGICAL WORK OF LAWYERS

The women defenders in this study appear less ambivalent and cynical than elite lawyers in previous studies.[7] Becky McBride adamantly distances herself from victims and her clients. She avoids any identification with victims and will go so far as to cast aspersions on their characters as women. She asserts to herself that she is not her clients' mother, sister, or wife. Becky will not "let herself go" to a place that might suggest anything other than her lawyer self. Fran Jones feels strongly about what she does: "when you are in trial it's you against the world." For Annette Petroff, "If you're choosing what cases you can defend and which ones you can't based on what the charges are, or what you think about the person, you're too emotionally involved. It has to be all or nothing." Gina Rossi holds dear the values she places on work and what she describes as a working-class acceptance of one's job: "If you can't do it, you shouldn't be doing it." Meg Lowe's passing of her "test of fire" appears to be the opposite of attachment.

The women defenders' rigid adherence to their profession's ideologies may, however, also be evidence of their ambivalence and need for emotion work: a person holds on tighter to a belief when combating the suppressed side of her or his mixed feelings.[8] Becky McBride claims not to have feelings for the rape victim; at the same time she is disturbed by the disdain she feels for this woman. This sort of ambivalence evidenced through rigidity might be described as a characteristic of emotion work.[9] Sally Tan's and Rose Carr's emphatic statements are examples of the suppression of emotion associated with ambivalence, as is Rose's statement that she has done nothing to feel ashamed of: "I've never demeaned a sexual assault victim, ever. And I've had numerous acquittals." When rigid determination surrounds ideology, we see another convergence of emotion work and ideological work.

Sally Tan, for example, is certain of her role in protecting individual rights. That certitude makes it easier for her to focus on her job. Focus does not mean concentration on the technical aspects of her work, as it does for attorneys who lose the idealism they entered law school with and pursue elite positions.[10] Holding ever more firmly to her legal ideals is much more effective in countering her personal feelings about a defendant or the negative particulars of a case. She makes room for the technical aspects after she finds focus. Gina Rossi says, "Even though you don't embrace the act you don't hate the person that does the act. It's an intellectual stance."

ON THE CAREER PATH OF WOMEN DEFENDERS

I argue that the women in my study represent different phases in the moral careers of women defenders. All careers have a natural progression and history.[11] I am not referring here only to professional or employment trajectories. Careers in this sense are segments of life that correspond to the similar phases that members pass through as they adopt the identity of their group. For example, careers could as easily be those of Olympic athletes as women defenders and drug addicts. We can imagine each member of a group would go through similar experiences on her or his road to becoming an Olympic athlete, a woman defender, or a drug addict. Like ideology's two faces—the formalized practices of social institutions and individual subjectivity—moral careers are two-sided: one side is tied to what they hold closest in terms of self-perception and how they feel. The other side is connected to their official status and institutional ideals.[12] However different they may be as individuals, over time, members of a social category undergo similar sequences of change in their selves and their framework for judging themselves and others vis-à-vis membership in that category. Careers are "moral" only in the sense that they are norms of a group at a particular time.[13] They lack the judgmental quality that is normally associated with the word; they may be both respectful and shameful. I identified three stages in the moral careers of women defenders that reflect their evolving self conceptions and ideological beliefs. Developing parallel to the specific phases are distinct strategies of emotion work.

Four of the five women defenders who are relatively new to the profession focus on disregard for, or distancing themselves from, the victim, even to the point of vilification. For example, Becky McBride suggests the victim of domestic violence was responsible for putting herself in such a position and that she "reflects poorly on women." Fran Jones showed disregard through her utilitarian approach to victims: how I handle each victim depends on what I can get out of it. If I think a woman is lying, if this is a crack addict who had sex with my client to get drugs and didn't get enough, I'm going to rip her, there's no mercy." Emily Locatelli was unable to distance herself from the victims in her cases and ultimately chose to leave criminal defense work. Annette Petroff, who has never been the responsible attorney on a case, experiences minimal conflict in her work and thus does less emotion work. Furthermore, the content of death-penalty work is highly ideological, and all the victims in the cases Annette worked on were deceased.

All seven women in their midcareers tended toward empathic identification with the defendant. Meg Lowe shows this strategy when she states that the defendant is someone "who's been kicked around and hurt." Iris Egan believes that, "all of these people have terrible histories. They've seen their father kill their mother, or they've been abused as children, or they've been sexually abused. I feel we've let them down. Society's let them down, and now I'm doing my job in this part of the process." Gina Rossi chooses to focus on the defendant because "the jury is sympathizing with the victim; nobody is sympathizing with you and the guy sitting next to you." Lily Tate feels to work with "the poorest of the poor is a virtue in itself." All offer vivid examples of empathic identification with the defendant.

Components of distancing self from the victim and seeing the defendant as a victim are present in the emotion work of the seasoned women defenders. However, all seven of the seasoned women defenders focus on their role in a higher system. Rose Carr is a public defender to serve the "greater good." Olivia George views herself as a protector of the Constitution. And Sally Tan's job as part of "the last bastion of the group trying to protect individual rights" is to make sure that the government does not get out of hand. Perhaps the most eloquent statement comes from Vivian Gold's reflections on her work:

> VG: I believe that I've chosen the most honorable of professions. You judge a society by how it treats its worst. And constitutional rights are meaningless unless they apply to the worst in society. We deal every day with the very fabric of life—with sex, with greed, with fear, with weakness, with regret. We are teachers. We teach toler-

ance, openness, variety in thought. We're always in the minority. We're always in the role of the opposition. This keeps our minds alert. This keeps us tough.

The same sentiment comes through when she looks back on a Hell's Angels racketeering trial. Vivian says that because the Hell's Angels are such a despised group she felt it her obligation as the defense lawyer "to stand before the jury and tell them that even though you might hate this group their rights are precious." Her closing words to the jury in that trial were:

> VG: And I say to you, and I say loud and clear, everybody has a right to a fair trial, and everybody gets the same rules. Whether you're Black or white. Whether you're a Hell's Angel, or an Earth Angel, rules are not adjusted for defendants. Nothing excuses any kind of violation of the oath up there on that stand. That is our system. It is the light that never fails.

Finally, Vivian invokes Clarence Darrow's words (who, she notes, died the same year she was born):

> Strange as it may seem, I grew to like to defend men and women charged with crime. It soon came to be something more than winning or losing a case. I sought to learn why one man goes one way and another takes an entirely different road. I became vitally interested in the causes of human conduct. This meant more than the quibbling with lawyers and juries. . . . It is dealing with life, with its hopes and fears, its aspirations and despairs. With me it was going to the foundation of motive and conduct and adjustments for human beings, instead of blindly talking of hatred and vengeance, and that subtle, indefinable quality that men call "justice" and of which nothing is really known.[14]

Moral careers include those decisive events that we might think of as turning points when a person's worldview changes.[15] When a person is connected to an institution, as the woman defender is to law, turning points may take the form of regularized challenges—moves from juvenile court to adult court, from municipal court to superior court, from misdemeanors to felonies, or from burglary to homicide.

The transition from early to midcareer defender is illustrated by the impending move of Becky McBride to the homicide team and the promotion that put Fran Jones in a position to supervise a death-penalty case. Gina Rossi's assignment to the complex litigation team in her ninth year of practice is another example. Their challenges are not all regularized by the institution, though they happen in the institutional setting of the criminal justice system.

For the woman defense attorney, undergoing the shift in identity that accompanies the move from mid- to seasoned career, the self-imposed challenge may be the handling of a particularly repugnant case. Midcareer transitions and transformations result from situations in which usual emotion work strategies are no longer sufficient to allow her to cope. These are the cases a woman defender is not assigned because of her life circumstances and cases she believes she cannot handle because of her competing identities and beliefs. Such cases hold the key to the development of her moral career. This was most strikingly illustrated by Meg Lowe's story. She consciously took on the challenge the administrators presented her in assigning her the case of the brutal rape of a fifteen-year-old girl. Meg's identity as a defense lawyer was transformed. She now believes she can handle any case handed to her by the administration. Rose Carr pinpointed another midcareer transition when she described handling cases involving children on her return from maternity leave. In both cases she said, "I can't do this," only to find that she could handle difficult cases that pitted her lawyer role against her new identity as a mother. Similarly, Kay Owens's emancipation at midcareer came about through surviving the type of case she thought would destroy or break her. Conceiving of herself as a social worker was crucial for this woman defender.

> KO: Almost all of it is social work for me. . . . There's a class of PDs that are as much or more so social workers than lawyers. They just use the law as the means to address the problems. That's their power in the relationship—they're the lawyer. And that's clearly why I wanted to be a lawyer. I wanted to be able to do something. And being a lawyer, you can do something. You're respected. You have a position that you take. You have some power in the system to help these people.

Like Kay, a significant number of women in government legal service view their work from a good-works perspective, believing they can make a difference in the institution and people's lives.[16] In my study, these include Kay Owens, Lily Tate, Holly Porter, and Jesse Madrigal, all midcareer women. Good works may manifest as a religious calling, as for Kay and Lily. The attorney may also see herself as a social worker, as Kay and Holly do. But an overlapping perspective is more problematic with respect to a woman's longevity in the profession—the caretaker perspective held by Kay and Jesse. The caretaker is less idealistic than her colleagues who rely on constitutional law to justify their work; she finds her work much more emotionally painful than her counterparts. She is the one who talks most about her days as a defense attorney being numbered. That Kay finds liberation in her survival is, thus, significant.

Women who have experienced midcareer transformations consciously take on the ideological cloak of their profession. When they realize that they can take on the challenge—whether self-imposed or presented by administrators—their professional ideals are fortified, as are their abilities to manage emotions through those same ideals.

I believe that is where we see most clearly how ideology spans the "emotional gap between things as they are and as one would have them be."[17] Through their transformation in identities and accompanying ideals, we see how women defenders change their beliefs to become consistent with what they are trying to feel.

The seasoned women defenders feel, and they manage what they feel. They also reason, and they reason about how they feel. They consciously use reason and ideals to combat feelings of wishing to be more consistent with their social group. Failure could lead to stigmatization by the group, as was the case with Emily Locatelli. Success, on the other hand, enables the woman to do her job. Not only is the seasoned woman defender's identity reinforced, but with time she identifies with the criminal defense institution and its ideals.

Though I did not have the luxury of following women criminal defense attorneys through the course of twenty-year careers, their reflections in this book show consistent themes, representing distinctive connections between emotions and ideals over time. The narratives indicate that women defense attorneys get better at managing their emotions through professional ideals as their self-images become more consistent with, and defend, the moral values of their profession. These women's accounts also indicate that negotiating between ideologies and emotions is a sophisticated form of emotion work. Moral work may be the most effective form of emotion management for the woman in this profession, and sustained performance of emotional labor that transforms self-identity and work role might be psychologically healthy for her and the larger criminal justice system. Bearing in mind the complex relationship between gender identity, emotion work inherent to the profession, gendered power relations, and the moral division of labor, the woman defense attorney is fully positioned to challenge the status quo of the criminal justice system.

Appendix

Ambivalent Identities: Men of Color Who Prosecute "Their Own"

PHASE I. IDENTITY FORMATION—EARLY-CAREER PROSECUTORS

Being a prosecutor educated me that there are some people who, for whatever reasons, have to be separated from the rest of us. I was not of that philosophy when I started. I felt that everyone must have been a victim of some kind of social, personal, or mental problem. And I learned that even if they were, there is still a need to separate them from the rest of us.
—Darryl Franks, three and a half years a prosecutor

Every once in a while it is interesting, because a witness or defendant says your name in court: it's somebody you went to high school with.
—Carter Vernon, five years a prosecutor

PHASE II. IDENTITY TRANSFORMATION—MIDCAREER PROSECUTORS

It's not a matter of race; it's a matter of social responsibility and protection.
—Louis Marks, eleven years a prosecutor

Somebody has to do the job. If not me, who?
—Martin Tong, twelve years a prosecutor

The people in the community didn't realize they were being treated equally, it was just equally unfair. I want to be in a position to make sure that when those kinds of crimes take place, that those victims were treated just as well as somebody who might be of the dominant culture.
—Ned Williams, thirteen years a prosecutor

PHASE III. IDENTITY REINFORCEMENT—SEASONED PROSECUTORS

They'll send some crack addict to prison for shoplifting a videotape, but this office will not stand up to whites who steal hundreds of thousands of dollars and laugh about it.
—Ray Bryant, twenty years a prosecutor

I feel that I'm doing more to help my people than I would if I was a doctor or a defense attorney. When you think about it, being a prosecutor is a position of power. I remember once telling someone, all your attorney can do for you is what I allow him or her to do. I can dismiss your case right this second, so I have more control over your life than he does. Think about how much power that gives me. The important thing is to make sure the people that have that power are not abusing it. I like to tell my victims, hopefully I'll be successful in bringing you some level of justice, but also putting your mind at ease that this is a society you want to live in.
—Stan Clifford, twenty-three years a prosecutor

When I was in the '60s there were a lot of issues, the Black Panthers, racist whites coming in and occupying the Black community. It's still happening today. We are apparently prosecuting some white officers now. I say, "Well, if you want white cops to stop kicking your butts, maybe you ought to be prosecutors." The joke around here is that justice is just that: just us.
—Turner Anderson, twenty-six years a prosecutor

The data collected from the larger study of women criminal defense attorneys led me to explore the overlaps between ideology and emotion in another criminal justice occupation where personal identity might clash with professional role. To offer a comparative perspective, I entered the world of district attorneys, strictly as an interviewer and observer. As with the women defenders, I was interested in men of color prosecutors and how their professional ideals were fortified so they could feel what they tried to feel. In this appendix I show how defense and prosecution cultures are motivated by very different ideals. Institutional notions of job duty ultimately mediate the emotional stress of men working in this environment when their professional roles contradict their personal identities as men of color and not their politics of race. This section discusses the similarities and differences between men of color prosecutors and women defenders in minimizing conflict and will show how the management of emotion through work ideals for the prosecutors follows a career trajectory that parallels that of the defense attorneys.

I assume when laypeople think of a criminal lawyer, they think of a defense attorney, and further, that most Americans think that this person is somehow less than ethical. Just to get an idea of what the "normal" person thinks about attorneys, I went to the Internet and did a Web search for lawyer jokes. Voilà, I was directed to 816 Web sites. Needless to say, not all of the lawyer jokes I found on these sites were limited to criminal attorneys—personal injury lawyers and corporate attorneys had their fair share of jokes on sites such as pondscumandlawyers.com. But when jokes had to do with criminal law, the majority dealt with defense attorneys or their clients. For example:

> *While summing up the state's case against the alleged despicable conduct of the defendant, the prosecutor addressed the jury, "Ladies and gentlemen—all I can say is that if Moses had known the defendant, there would have been two or three more Commandments."*

> *What is a criminal lawyer? Redundant.*

> *An attorney addressing the jury and speaking of his client, who recently killed his parents: "Dear ladies and gentlemen, please take mercy and release this poor orphan."*[1]

Rarely do the jokes have to do with prosecutors. There are some, though, for example:

> *In questioning potential jurors for an upcoming trial, the judge inquired, "Is there any reason why any of you cannot see this trial through to its conclusion?" A lone juror spoke up. "I can't!" stated the woman, "Why, just looking at the woman, I'm convinced she's guilty!" "Madam," said the judge, "that's the prosecutor."*

In 1997 Ellis Cose edited a book entitled *The Darden Dilemma: Twelve Black Writers on Justice, Race, and Conflicting Loyalties.*[2] This "jury of twelve"[3] analyzed Christopher Darden's role as a prosecutor in the O. J. Simpson trial. In fact, we could say that Darden was not portrayed simply as a prosecutor in the trial; he was vilified as the prosecutor of one of his own. In the first paragraph of his introduction Cose writes:

> Before the O. J. Simpson trial, black prosecutors were all but invisible, toiling, for the most part, in various degrees of obscurity. Christopher Darden's front-and-center role in the so-called trial of the century brought them out of the shadows, but it did much more. The endless media coverage and Darden's subsequent bestselling book created a

compelling and indelible portrait of the black prosecutor as a tortured soul—as a conflicted laborer in a perfidious place where celebrity, crime, and conflicting racial perceptions collide.[4]

I asked women defenders, "How can you possibly defend a man who has committed a sexual assault on another woman, especially if you have feminist sensibilities?" in the direct aftermath of Simpson's civil trial. Darden, in the limelight, was in a similar position to the women, that is, he was taking on a role that some criticized as symbolic prosecution. In his own words:

> I was a black prosecutor, nothing more. None of these armchair lawyers paid attention to the content of what I had said, only the pigmentation of my skin, the breadth of my nose, the thickness of my lips. "Yes, he's black all right. That must be why he's up there." Everything in this case was sifted through a filter of bigoted expectations, like the pressure Jackie Robinson faced when he broke the color barrier in baseball. "Pretty good hitter for a darkie."
>
> Beneath the court case that everyone else saw, Cochran and I fought another battle, over the expectations and responsibilities of being a black man in America. He took shots at me . . . I listened with clinched jaw. Later, I began to fire back to show there were responsibilities as a human being that were just as important as the responsibilities of being an African American.[5]

As with the women defenders, there were connotations of conflicting personal and public identities—racial rather than gendered. Black prosecutors face a critique from their communities for standing up, representing the state, and pointing the finger at another African American man. Darden presents himself as suffering from "inner turmoil": "Was I going to be seen as a brother putting another brother in jail?"[6] And he countered that dilemma by identifying the duality of his role as an African American man working within the system. "Perhaps I was naive, but I convinced myself that African Americans had to be represented in all segments of the law if we were ever to believe that the system was ours too."[7]

As I delved further into the stories of women defense attorneys, I became interested in comparing their conflicts with the ideological and emotional dilemmas of men of color who are prosecutors. In the summer of

2001 I interviewed male district attorneys who self-identify as men of color. Once again I utilized a snowball sample. By way of contacts in trial courts, again in central and northern California, I was introduced to and interviewed eight men. Again, I was searching for patterns in the interviews based on the logic of grounded theory.[8]

The men I interviewed ranged in age from thirty-one to fifty-three years (their mean age was forty-six). All identified as heterosexual, all but one was married, and four had children. As it turned out, they had been deputy district attorneys on average fourteen years (ranging from five to twenty-six years)—about the same as the women defense attorneys I interviewed. Their self-reported number of felony trials averaged about thirty—roughly three-quarters of the women defenders'. (The implication here might be that the women were overworked.) All of these men were deputy district attorneys at one point or another. Only two have since left the career, both to become judges—one in municipal court, the other in superior court.

Once more I divided the men into three groups, according to their number of work years, strictly as a heuristic device to further understand their moral work: Carter Vernon and Darryl Franks fell into the early-career category (one to ten years); Louis Marks, Martin Tong, and Ned Williams into midcareer (eleven to fifteen years); and Ray Bryant, Stan Clifford, and Turner Anderson into the seasoned category (sixteen-plus years). While Martin Tong is Asian American, all of the rest are African Americans. While I will discuss all eight of these men in what follows, I will focus on the stories of four men—Carter, Louis, Stan, and Ray—to exemplify the different stages in the prosecutor's career and the general experiences of the men I interviewed.

Again, my approach was inductive. However, based on experience with the women defense attorneys, I had expected to find that these men's stories would also reflect distinct strategies of emotion work that corresponded to their years in practice, shifting identities, and their ideological frameworks for judging themselves and others. This is not entirely what I found. At first I thought the difference was tied to gender and how much these men would open up. But these were not men who were reluctant to be interviewed, nor did they try to be overly macho with me.

Louis Marks actually cried in front of me when he described the politics of his office. Ned Williams, who has been a judge for six years now, told me that when he was a trial attorney, he became severely emotionally upset before court:

NW: Actually, my emotions I pretty much was able to keep in check. But I had dry heaves in the morning. I mean, you would never know that when I came in and prosecuted a case. I knew that was nothing more than the stress of knowing that it was my responsibility to make sure that somebody who did something to somebody else got convicted of that, so when I was in trial that would happen, and I weighed a lot less back then also.

Identifying with the victim did not make Ned sick before trial. The burden he felt resulted from knowing that if a defendant "walked, somebody else might get hurt as a result of something I didn't do." I asked Ned if he ever had such a case that he thought about later. He told me there was one, and it was a case with an African American defendant.

NW: I don't remember a lot of names, but I remember this guy's name, [Eric Ponsa]. Eric got in a fight with some guy, and the jury acquitted him. Eric ended up killing a cab driver later—it was cold-blooded murder and robbery. He shot him three times in the head.

Carter Vernon, who has been a deputy district attorney for only five years, told me about a debate he had with a friend, another African American man, who went to work at a public defender's office after law school. They would start talking about the criminal justice system, and his friend would say, "Well, that's okay for you, but I could never do that kind of thing." Carter would reply, "You are trying to help the Black community. This Black guy that you're pouring out your heart for is victimizing that very same community that you say you are trying to help." This seems to be a lesson those in Carter's position learned early in their careers. Time after time the prosecutors I interviewed did not have any problem justifying their roles in the system. It was as if the "Darden Dilemma" had been imagined by the media and a public thirsty for drama. But there was so much more.

What separates these men of color prosecutors from their women counterparts on the defense side does not go back to the formation of their gender identity and politics in college (as it did for the seasoned women defenders), but to their childhoods. The two factors that I saw reappear over and over in the men's stories that were not present in the women's were religion and parental discipline. Only one of these men, Carter, whose story begins below, was not exposed to religion as a child, and he is the only one who is not religious as an adult. Louis Marks, who exemplifies the midcareer prosecutor, said that his parents were "typical southern disciplinarians. If the laws today were around when I was a kid, my father would still be in prison."

PHASE I. IDENTITY FORMATION (ONE TO TEN YEARS)— EARLY-CAREER PROSECUTORS

I first saw Carter Vernon on the nightly news. He was prosecuting a road-rage case that reached national attention. I telephoned him soon thereafter and said that I had just completed a study of women defense attorneys and that I would like to interview him about conflicts he might experience at work as an African American man. He agreed. When we met, Carter told me how his job is different from that of the women I interviewed. First, prosecutors do not form the same emotional attachment to defendants:

> CV: The Constitution pretty much prevents us from talking to them, so we don't have to start on a one-to-one basis. All we know is this person committed this crime. We get a background history, but we don't have to talk to them about their kids, or watering their lawn, or anything like that. We don't form that sort of emotional attachment to them as a person. A good defense attorney, who has a guy going away to prison for a long time—you know he'll be upset. He did rape, or kill, or murder, but the defense attorney will say, "Yeah, I know, but he's a nice guy." Well, I'm sure when he is not out there stealing or stabbing somebody, he is a nice guy, but we punish him for that act.

At thirty-one, Carter is the youngest of all of the criminal attorneys—both prosecutors and defense attorneys—that I interviewed. Like many, he is a product of one of the University of California's law schools, and he graduated in 1995. Originally his intention was to join the FBI. Carter thought that his application to that federal agency would look better if he added a line on his resume that said he had interned in district attorneys offices while in law school. He realized, however, that he liked being a prosecutor and chose not to follow up with the FBI even though he made it to a second interview.

In practice only five years, Carter has already been the prosecutor in about thirty felony trials. At his interview with the district attorney's office Carter was not asked about cases he could not prosecute. Rather, he encountered ethical questions that would determine "what kind of person I am." For example, "If you saw an attorney doing something wrong, what would you do? Who would you tell? Or would you just keep it a secret?" Carter said that he would tell, and he got the job.

Carter's family had no negative feelings toward careers in law enforcement, not even "soft antagonism," in his words. His uncle is a police officer, as is his cousin, and his mother's cousin is in the FBI. Even his friends expected he would be involved in enforcing the law: "They would have been surprised or disappointed if I'd gone over to the defense side." Carter described himself and his friends as conservative and his parents as Democrats who are "far more conservative than they think they are. Actually, African Americans [in my parents'] generation have more conservative family values even though publicly they are very liberal. When it comes to their own families, they are pretty darn conservative."

While his family was part of the first migration of African Americans to cities in the north, he sees no "huge leaps" in its economic history. Carter's grandfather worked in the auto plants for forty years, and his father worked for the phone company for over thirty years before retiring. Back in the 1970s Carter's mother became a keypunch operator for a computer company and has done some sort of data processing for over twenty years. His family's working-class ethic calls for each generation being a little bit better off economically than the last. And their history has shaped Carter's approach toward his job.

> CV: Every generation has come to build on the last taking it a step further. I don't come at the whole process thinking, "As an African American male the entire system, the country, has been against my people for 400 or 500 years, and there is nothing I can do about it. If I am out of work and I commit a crime, it is not my fault." It is a very small percentage of people in any community that are going to be out there committing crimes and making it worse for everybody else. It is a small group. I wish we could just identify

them all at once, cut them out, and remove them. But we have to wait until they do something, which is unfortunate.

These remarks seem drastic when compared to those of the women defenders. However, not nearly as extreme as those of Ray Bryant, a twenty-year prosecutor:

> RB: I know a psychopath when I read the file on one. And psychopaths need to be killed. They need to be executed or disposed of. I don't believe in putting people in prison for life. I believe in getting rid of them. But you know our society usually doesn't work that way. Certainly, I believe in preventing them from procreating, and if they somehow have procreated, they should never be allowed to see or raise their children.

While Carter's words were not nearly as excessive, his expressed desire to identify and cut criminals out of society is indeed severe. His attitude that historical racism need not result in crime echoes through the stories of men of color who are prosecutors. So do the descriptions of their upbringings.

> CV: There were definitely consequences for your actions. I joke with my father that if the laws regarding children were in place then, he would still be in prison. There was definitely a feeling that sparing the rod would spoil the child. So there were definitely things that were expected of us—certain behavior, no talking back. You always had to be on your best behavior, and there were consequences for acting up or stepping out of line.

Despite his view of criminals and their need for punishment, Carter feels there are those times when he as an African American provides a different perspective to his supervisors. I asked him to describe such a case.

> CV: A bunch of homeless kids, most of them were African Americans, robbed this guy. They did everything you could possibly do wrong—robbed him, kidnapped him, took him from various spots to various spots, told him to take money out of the ATM, "Do this, do that." Essentially that is kidnapping for robbery. The pun-

ishment is life with the possibility of parole. They were nineteen [years old], homeless, and this guy was flashing money around.

You know, if I was in it just to get a conviction or just try a case, there is no chance that I would have lost. I could have done that. And they would be forced to spend pretty much the rest of their lives in prison for what they did. I like to think that I can look at it [differently]. They did something stupid, and they are spending a long time in prison. Nine years for one guy, and six and seven for the others. I mean, it is not really a slap on the wrist. But as opposed to the alternative, I think it was probably the right thing to do.

If they weren't African Americans, I might have just looked at these kids and said, "These are dangerous punks, they are out there, they are scary, these guys need to go away for absolutely the rest of their lives." I like to think that, coming from my perspective, I can give them one shot. It is going to be a hefty shot, and if they come out worse for it, that is their faults, not mine. It is not like I wouldn't prosecute. I mean, I can't think of any sort of category or crime that I wouldn't prosecute based on being an African American or something like that.

Friends have said to Carter, "The defendants are our people—friends to you. How can you do that? How can you do that? How do you prosecute Black people?" Given my original research focus with women defenders, I was delighted Carter brought this up. It is not surprising that he did. This is something Carter deals with frequently outside of work and beyond his conservative circle of friends. In his words, it is his profession's ideology that helps him distance himself from the criminal defendants—most of whom share Carter's "master status" as an African male.[9] In addition, his racial identity allows him to identify with the victim, an advantage on his side of the courtroom. In a sense, his identity works both ways. (Cases for women defenders where their identity as women worked two ways were limited to individual cases, such as Vivian Gold defending the woman who murdered her abusive husband.)

CV: My job is to protect the people. For the most part, when an African American commits a crime, it is against another African American. When a Hispanic person commits a crime, it is against another

Hispanic. When a Vietnamese person commits a crime, it is against another Vietnamese. The minorities out there are committing crimes against other minorities. I guess they think the cops are going to come after them more severely or the punishment will be more harsh if they go out and attack the elderly white guy. People do it against their own for some reason.

So my going in on the defense side, to protect this African American who is out there committing crimes and make sure that he gets some sort of benefit from me representing him. . . . I look at it like I am just sending him back out on the street to victimize more African Americans. A small percentage of people are victimizing individuals, and putting this person back out on the street would just send him back to rob my grandmother again, because that is who he is going to pick.

This loyalty to community reminds me of the way Holly Porter, the only African American woman defense attorney in this book, approached her work. It rings throughout the Black prosecutors' stories, and throughout the words of Martin Tong, the Asian American prosecutor, also early in his career.

Martin specializes in prosecuting gang-related crimes. He confirms for me that most of the people he prosecutes are young men of color—in his county, primarily Latinos. When I asked about any "tugs and pulls" he might feel when prosecuting these young men because of his own identity as a man of color, he said there is no conflict:

MT: I don't think that it's that difficult for me. I believe in community causes. I believe in the system. And I actually go and speak to schools in the community. I truly believe this. The reasons that some of these neighborhoods are so gang-entrenched is they know that their neighbors will not speak up. They know. We have a huge population of illegal residents in [south county] and they work in the fields all day. They get their paychecks on Friday, and then go to the local store to buy themselves a six-pack of beer, a bag of chips, or whatever. They cash their checks at the store, and there are gang members who know this. They wait for them along the path and rob them because they know that illegal residents are very unlikely to testify. And I try to tell them, if you will participate in the system, this will stop. And I truly believe that. They are starting to trust us, individuals like myself, prosecutors. When they see these [gang members] actually incarcerated, they see that it works.

Like Carter and Martin's, all of the prosecutors' primary self-identities were tied to the larger ideal of community, which translates into a strong identification with the victim, a member of that same community. While mandatory sentences cause greater emotional conflict for the defense attorneys who identify with the defendants, those same determinant sentences create conflict for deputy district attorneys who identify with the victim. However, their conflict moves in the opposite direction. Much like the women defenders, who find it difficult to deliver the "bad news" of sentences to their clients, the district attorneys are sometimes challenged by having to inform victims and their families that the system does not interpret their loss in a way that they believe suits the crime.

CV: You always feel bad if you are talking to a victim, if you have to settle a case for something less [than is fair], or you just have to dismiss it. And you absolutely believe that what the victim said, happened—a crime was committed. But you have to say, "I just can't prove it." Generally it is when a crime is borderline. It happened with a vehicular manslaughter that I had. The defendant was, depending on who you ask, the girlfriend, not the girlfriend, [someone who was] using the victim. They are both in the car; she is driving. They are both drunk. She hits a wall and kills him. [His] family is obviously outraged, because they don't like her. As far as they are concerned, she was the mistress who broke up this guy's happy home, then kind of toyed with him. I say, "You know, I understand that but . . ." Before I can even finish they say, "But she was drunk." And I say, "So was your brother. So was your son." I had to prove that besides being drunk, she did something else. That she violated the law in some other way when this happened. Unfortunately, it was one or two o'clock in the morning [on a remote mountainous highway]. Nobody else was there. We had no idea when the accident happened or what happened out there. So we wound up settling for a misdemeanor [meaning the defendant would spend no more than 365 days in a county jail]. It was really kind of tough because I had to talk to the family. The mother was actually in Iran. We were talking on the phone when I tried to explain it to her. I was talking to the brother, who was in Brazil. They don't understand the American legal system. They feel if you are drunk that is enough [to be guilty]. Essentially they leave the system feeling like their brother's and son's life is only worth a year.

Carter said that sometimes he gets overly wrapped up with the victims who have had horrible things happen to them. He implies the question, "Can there ever truly be justice?" After these cases he feels that the process has been overly focused on "essentially what is convenient for the defendant," to the neglect of what is good for the victim. The most emotional case he ever tried fits into this category.

CV: I had a case where a couple was on a motorcycle. They hadn't done anything wrong. The defendant was at 0.08 [blood alcohol level], right on the border [of the legal limit in California], weaving in and out of traffic, and hit them. [The husband's] leg was severed at the scene. The wife's leg was kind of spun around, suffering major compound fractures. There was never any question that the guy was guilty. The question was that the guy had no prior history—nothing. He was a twenty-five-year-old guy who got a new car and was doing something stupid. I wanted him to go to prison as an example. I know that he was right at the border. That is why the border is 0.08, because this is what happens. He lost control of his car, but he wound up not going to prison.

We went to the sentencing hearing. They put on his family to say what a nice guy he is, and we put on the victims' family to say they can't go back to work, they can't do this, they are dismembered and disabled. The judge eventually decided to keep him local [that is, in county jail versus state prison], and do some other non-jail alternatives.

I honestly felt bad for those people. We were essentially saying your leg was worth no jail time. The defendant was Black and the victims were white. And I felt bad for them. It was just awful. There wasn't anything else I could have done. We don't want to destroy the defendant's life. You look at the victims and think,

"There is nothing we can do that will bring back your leg. So now what do we do about him? How do we help him?" And the victims are saying, "Well, what about us? We weren't doing anything." They are sort of disregarded at that point. It is kind of hard. There are things the judge takes into account. I don't know that I would want the job. I don't know what to tell [the couple]. Essentially this twenty-five-year-old guy is facing seven years in prison. When you put that number on it, it is insulting to the victims. But it is the only thing that we can do. The other way is civil court. But how can you assign a dollar value to a leg? What is it, "Give me $600,000 for my leg?"

You know, they were just driving along at 35 miles an hour, and basically somebody ran over them. They didn't have time to get out of the way. It wasn't as if they were speeding and crashed. It wasn't a rainy night. It was the middle of the day. They didn't do anything wrong, and for that their entire lives are completely . . . I don't want to say shattered because, you know, I would feel bad and they would try to make me feel better. No, I'm supposed to be making them feel better. But it completely changed their lives. They can't do their jobs. Their house had stairs. And they were young. So they are going to have to go on for forty or fifty years more this way because on that day they decided to go for a ride, somebody else altered their lives.

Carter's saying "The defendant was Black and the victims were white. And I felt bad for them" could be read as a betrayal of race or as a socioeconomic aberration. He sees it as the latter, and based on the defendant's status. Carter said that there is a focus on seeing African Americans as being punished more—that is, until we look at the class situation of the defendant. The man who ran over the couple on the motorcycle was African American; he was also upper middle class. In Carter's mind, if the defendant had not testified in court that he had been "socially drinking," an acceptable middle-class phrase for "I was partying," the outcome might have been entirely different.

This is certainly an in-depth look at a case from a prosecutor's view. And the emotionality Carter feels is evident in his expression. Carter said that he is still dealing with his emotions. Actually, this particular case makes him believe there should be a first-strike for serious crimes that does not require that defendants have prior violations.

> CV: I don't understand the apprehension about "three strikes." Why should you get the first two? The first two have to be violent or serious felonies. Why should you get to stab somebody more than once . . . or twice? You get the third and, you know, I say, "I'm sorry."
>
> When I was doing misdemeanors, the defense attorneys talked about immigration concerns. You can't have this guy plead to the theft because that will hurt his immigration chances. And I don't view that as my concern. Why do I want him here if he is stealing, anyway? What would happen to him in his or her native country if he was caught stealing? Find me a country where it is okay to steal and I'll cut this person some slack.

I felt compelled to ask Carter, "If the public has this fear about large Black men, what about you in public? How do you respond when people have a fear of you?" In his response, he justified the role of law enforcement in policing his own life: "I'm getting past that. I am getting past the age. I've been stopped. You have the perception that it's because of your race, but you know what? I am also doing something wrong at the time. I have never been pulled over when I was doing nothing." Carter told me that if I saw him on the weekend, I would not recognize him. He wears nylon sweats, wraps a kerchief over his shaved head, and drives around in his sports car listening to his eclectic music, which, he said, defines his self. He actually finds it amusing that women will get out of his way as he makes his way down the street: "I know who I am and what I am. If a woman wants to walk further away or get out of an elevator because I'm coming in, that's cool. I'm going up, and she's waiting." He said that a person can think about it and dwell on it. Or he could imagine that this is a woman who was attacked at another time, and "she would have done that if I was a white guy walking alone. Unfortunately, because of history, you are always left with a question mark." To dwell on that, he said "would be to stagnate."

The closest thing Carter could come up with to a pivotal case was the high-profile road-rage case:

CV: I was on CNN, on the news in Europe and Australia. There was a DA in the office on vacation in Italy and found out what the verdict was from the paper. We were front-page in *USA Today.* So obviously that was important to win. It is better to be known as the bad guy than the guy who lost the case.

Still, Carter told me that his job is not to win. His job is to figure out what happened, and this may entail his distancing himself from the victim: "I am not an advocate in the sense that I am representing my victim. I am supposed to be representing the State of California." Even so, it hurts to lose, thus Carter's decision to never again try cases at Christmas time—a mistake he made this year—when juries are too sympathetic. Carter found out later that most of the attorneys in his office know to ask for continuances around the holidays. They just never told him that strategy. He has also never been told by a district attorney with more experience that there would come a day when a case would make or break him. Stan Clifford said that over twenty years ago: "I was told by one of my mentors in the office, 'There'll come a point in time, a particular case when, once it is over, you'll know you've arrived as a trial attorney.'"

Darryl Franks, the only other man I interviewed who would be classified as "early career," knew that he wanted to be more than a trial lawyer. His career ambition was to be a judge, and Darryl knew he needed both civil and criminal trial experience. His first two years out of law school Darryl worked at a neighborhood legal assistance clinic representing indigent clients on civil matters. He said it was "getting civil experience and also doing something that I could feel good about morally and socially." Darryl recognized early on that his politics were not completely consistent with prosecutorial law: "I knew the time would come for me to move on to something else."

Darryl sought out prosecution as a way to get criminal trial experience, but, he said, it taught him something else. He was a "product" of the University of California system in the '60s and a politically and religiously liberal household. As he described it, his parents were Democrats (although at one time while his father was in the South he registered Republican, "because that was the party of Lincoln"). As a child, Darryl went to church on Sundays but he "was raised in a household where you determined who your God is."

Becoming a prosecutor "educated" Darryl. He told me why he chose prosecution over defense.

> DF: I was born and raised in Oakland [a Black community]. And I knew there was no way I could be a part of the criminal justice system in [that county]. So I applied [to a white county] so I wouldn't be sending classmates to jail. If I was going to make mistakes that early in my career, I would rather not make mistakes hurting legal-aid clients or criminal defendants. I was more than willing to make them from a prosecution standpoint.

Darryl said in the first few months at the district attorney's office he did not know that he would need to separate himself from the rest of the prosecutors by defining himself, rather than having the job define him.

> DF: I decided at some point in that work to carry myself as an attorney who happened to be a district attorney. I think I was a rare prosecutor, who didn't only associate with prosecutors. I had friends who were criminal defense lawyers, and I ended up making friends who were judges, who really assisted in training me to become a lawyer who happened to be a district attorney.

Ultimately Darryl felt he needed to lessen the gap between his role as a public prosecutor and his identity as an African American man: "When I was a prosecutor, I attended a prisoner's self-help group. It was a group that brings clothes and books to people who were in jail. I realized in terms of balance, 'Okay, I'm doing this on one end, at least I can do this on the other.'" That was just one of the ways Darryl, in his words, "rationalized the job." He feels lucky to have been a practicing attorney for only six years before he was appointed to a superior court judgeship, his true career aspiration. However, he still feels tension now between passing judgment and his identity as an African American man. These days he rationalizes his position by sitting on the board of a socially responsible church, which welcomes congregants from all races, ethnicities, and sexualities. Darryl obviously knew that he would move on; only time will tell for Carter Vernon.

PHASE II. IDENTITY TRANSFORMATION—
MIDCAREER PROSECUTORS (ELEVEN TO FIFTEEN YEARS)

Louis Marks believes that his job as a deputy district attorney is to teach. Much like Vivian Gold, the seasoned woman defender who believes that her job is to "teach tolerance and variety in thought" to jurors, Louis believes his job is to teach district attorneys that their perceptions of race and class distort the value they place on the lives of individual human beings. As he sees it, prosecutors will "give a break" to the wealthy and powerful when they are accused of a crime, while minorities and the poor are always punished. They will use class and race biases to lessen defendants' responsibilities for their crimes—and ultimately the sanctions. Louis asked me:

> LM: Why is that? My job is to treat people equally and fairly. I'm not going to treat them any worse because they come from a different environment. From my perspective, because they are from a white, high-income family, where they have received all the advantages of life, they have less reason to commit a crime, as opposed to someone from a disadvantaged background.

Louis has been a prosecutor for eleven years and supervises a misdemeanor calendar—what he calls "the meat and potatoes of the office." He does not seek high-profile cases and never will. He sees prosecuting minor crimes as the place where he can make a difference in his community. In his words, this particular calendar allows him to "find the pulse of the community." The juvenile calendar is another. Louis works in one of California's medium size counties. While there is an even mix of women and men attorneys working in his office, he is one of three people of color—all men. He is the only African American, and there are no Latinos—the population you see most often in his county's jail. Louis works in an affluent, predominantly white, politically liberal county—a place with an "ostrich approach to everything. We bury our heads in the sand and wait until a problem is called an epidemic. Then we'll deal with it." As he sees it, the people in power wear blinders when it comes to certain crimes. Louis remembers four years before, when he was in the courtroom at juvenile hall, trying to let the probation officers there know of a growing use of heroin by minors— "kids who were eleven, twelve, and thirteen years old." His information came from community activists working in "the tracks" who told him that youths from all ethnicities and socioeconomic backgrounds were going into that Latino neighborhood to buy and smoke black tar heroin. Louis says he felt like the proverbial Chicken Little, crying, "The sky is falling, the sky is falling." And the response he got from the people in power was, "Heroin was the scourge of the '50s and '60s, when people were injecting it: this isn't happening in our community." After some young people died, the community decided there was a problem to be dealt with. That is the way Louis sees things happening.

> LM: We talk about how this is a progressive community and how open-minded we are. It's open-minded to certain things. We blind ourselves to others because we don't want to offend someone. We don't want to offend someone by looking in [the tracks], because we might look racist saying that population has a high use of heroin or drugs or sniffing glue, and we don't want to do a thing about it because we want to be touchy feely and find some other way. The minorities in this community—those of us who work with people there—are begging for help. And the people in power won't help until after a crisis that involves whites. And that is the drug scene in this community as far as I have seen. We excuse the drug dealers because they are Latinos or Black. Our politics are that there are too many Blacks and Latinos in jail or too many people being sent to prison of a certain race or color. So we say, "Let's give Johnny a break even though he is out there pushing drugs, until a twelve-year-old white kid ODs. Then we march all of our resources out to try and make a change."

Louis "hates" the politics of his progressive town in general, and the district attorney's office in particular—something that public defenders in California rarely have to put up with. As an elected official, the district attorney brings to his or her office a political view. Louis believes that politics do not belong in the criminal justice system, and they are the element of his job he embraces the least. He tells me, district attorneys "talk the talk but don't walk the walk." Because judgeships in his county so often go to former district attorneys, Louis has had three different bosses in the last three years—a white man, a Latino, and a white woman. As he saw it, their gender and race hardly mattered when it came to the power they wielded.

In fact, his most stressful years were spent working as a deputy under the Latino district attorney.

> LM: I guess the old adage holds: "absolute power corrupts absolutely." And I think that goes across the board. People in the seat of power don't check themselves and look at themselves daily. They buy in themselves all of the things that we are out there complaining about. And during that particular administration there were a number of things that happened that were totally outrageous in my mind. For instance, if a citizen wrote a letter critical of [the DA], investigators in this office called those people on the phone [and investigated their lives]. There were situations where people's personal information was leaked to the press that could not have happened unless somebody in this office had done it. I stood up and said that these things were wrong; I said what everyone else in this office felt. Since I stood up, I was attacked left and right.
>
> Here's an example, a colleague and I were given the same assignment. Neither one of us completed it because of our [heavy] workload. [At the moment Louis is personally prosecuting sixty to seventy cases, and overseeing another 150.] I was given a letter of reprimand saying that I was incompetent because I didn't complete the assignment. My colleague got a letter that she shared with me—it said, "I understand that you are busy." I finished the assignment, turned it in, and wrote a letter saying that I was disappointed because the letter of reprimand obviously showed deferential treatment. I pointed out that my colleague did not get the same letter and had yet to finish the assignment. I was then given another letter that said I was totally incompetent. I guess that you can tell from my voice that it really upsets me, even now.

At this point in the interview Louis's eyes were filling with tears, and his voice quivered. He said that he could list many more situations but the one that bothered him most was when he had heart problems: "I told my supervisor, and he laughed at me."

> LM: I grew up in a segregated South, and I have been in situations where I have been tear-gassed, and I have been in situations where I have been arrested. And I've been in situations where I've been

called every name in the book. Where people refused to sit next to me, give me service. Never in my life have I ever been as depressed as I was under the roof of that administration.

I guarantee you that if you talk to anyone in this office that was here during that time, they would tell you it was not a pretty sight. One tends to believe just because one is a minority, or comes from a progressive background, or wears a certain hat and a certain type of suit that they are in some way immune from abuse of power. We as a society tend to look at people based on their type or what uniform they wear. We make a judgment based on that [visible] endowment. We are lazy. We refuse to go beyond that title, or that hat, or suit to find out what the person is about. And I think that is the biggest mistake that we make. And that is the thing that I try to teach people to look at. Look beyond what is obvious.

This happens every day in Louis's work. He said it happened when he was just out of law school and a legal-aid worker. One day a woman came into the office and the first thing that she told him was, "I am not going to court with a Black man." His response was to smile and say, "I'm all you got." He went on to help her with her legal problem, and he hopes that left her with a different perspective of African American men. Louis said that the natural reaction would have been to get angry, but that he has a societal responsibility to react tactfully: "Rather than being offended and indignant, we should use those opportunities to teach."

Like each of the prosecutors I interviewed, Louis came from a background where children were taught there are consequences for their behaviors, "regardless of who you are, what you are. We came from a family that believed in discipline and social responsibility." His relatives said that it was "a great thing" that Louis chose a career as a prosecutor, which does not mean that his family has been immune from its share of run-ins with the criminal justice system. His Latina wife has family members who are in prison, and Louis has cousins who "are currently going through the system."

LM: When my family members had their problems, we were the first ones to say, "Hey, they should take some responsibility for their actions." So when you look at how many Latinos are going through the system here, I can't give you a statement of how I feel, because I don't know whether these people are here because of their own actions or because they are being unjustly singled out. Why I became a prosecutor is to bring a different perspective.

Teaching and bringing a different perspective is a clear mechanism of emotion work for Louis. His ideology is present in his job duty: "My job is not so much to punish people, but to make people accept their responsibilities for their actions. My job is to protect the public, and the public I am protecting is not those who can afford to live in [the heights]." Unlike the women defenders, Louis did not need to adjust his ideologies to fit the emotion work demanded of his job. His ideologies came from his experience as an African American man living in minority communities. Louis grew up in the South and has lived in largely African American communities in the San Francisco Bay Area (although that is not where he currently lives).

LM: The people I am protecting are the people who sleep right next door to the people who are being prosecuted. I have lived in communities where we as minorities had to lock our doors and bar our windows, not because we were afraid that the whites or Anglos from on the hill were going to come down and rob and kill us but because we were afraid that our own neighbors would do the same. So when you ask, "How do I feel about that?" I feel that, regardless of our economic background, regardless of our situation, it's not an excuse for us who are minorities to harm other minorities.

Regardless of who you are, where you come from, I cannot arbitrarily say, "I'm going to cut you some slack." Because there are a large number of Latinos [in the system] won't keep me from charging them when they are out there beating up on their wives that are Latinas. I'm not going to excuse it when they are out there raping people who are Latinas. So we have to look beyond ethnicity, and look at what they were doing, and what they are being charged with.

Certainly there is some social distancing from defendants occurring in these statements. One could say it is based on ethnicity—Louis is African American and he is speaking of Latinos. However, this is the community he married into and where he will bring up his children. (Louis's wife is about to give birth to their first child.) Social distancing seems most obvious in the differences in his behaviors and the defendant's.

While Louis finds the politics of his office to be the most stressful aspect of his work, he still finds the content of particular crimes emotionally draining. Unlike Carter Vernon, who distances himself from victims by representing "The People of the State of California" in court, Louis finds certain cases overly difficult because he gets too emotionally involved with his representation of the victim. He said, "I cannot prosecute child molests. I would be so angered that it would affect my ability to do the job properly, to represent the victims in those particular crimes. Because I would be so angry it would affect my judgment."

There is nothing in Louis's background that says he should have difficulty prosecuting sexual assaults on children. Rather, that variety of crime conflicts with his prosecutor self, the teacher. Prosecution is about punishment for Louis, but it is also about getting people to change their behavior. What he has witnessed in the criminal justice system supports the notion that pedophilia, like domestic violence, is a difficult pattern to change. He recognizes that in both categories of crimes he would, in his words, "demonize" the perpetrator.

LM: I had a situation this past week. A woman came in to ask me about domestic violence. She was a Latina, a nineteen-year-old, very attractive, had two kids and I found interviewing her that this was the second time [her boyfriend beat her up] in less than a year. The first time her nose was broken. Second time he choked her and bloodied her face. I used the opportunity not to say "just say no" but to sit with her and say, "I understand what you are going through and let's talk about this a bit. Let's talk about what's to be taught in this case. Let's talk about what this does to you, and what it does to society." And then I pointed out to her [if the behavior continues], "This makes you a victim forever for a number of reasons that you may not have even thought about. One, if this case is dismissed, the next time it comes up, we have to tell the defense that. They are going to use that, and I will tell you how they are going to use that. They will say, 'You made a false claim the last time. It wasn't the prosecutor that made the false claim. So you are making a false claim now.' Number two, while he is going through the system, your boyfriend will tell you that he will do everything including bringing the stars down from the sky because the case is hanging over his head. And then after that is over, there is less incentive for him to do that. And he'll likely beat you again, and that happens all the time." And I told her what I tell all victims in that situation, "The purpose is not so much to put him in jail; the purpose is to stop the activity." Obviously there's a pattern here. The first case was dismissed because she left town. A year later [after she returned] it came up again. I had to say, "This is a pattern; it's not going to stop. He may tell you now that it will." It is not all just punishment. I need to make sure she has counseling.

Another prosecutor who identifies the content of domestic violence as more emotionally demanding than other cases is Ned Williams. Ned was a prosecuting attorney for thirteen years, someone who is "forty-four going on sixty-six." This is the man who revealed that before a trial he could be found in a stall of the men's restroom, vomiting. He does not remember being "more stressed out" than when he worked on a death-penalty case. However, the possible death sentence was not what bothered him. In this case, sentencing guidelines serve as a rationalization for what may seem to some to be the most extreme punishment. It was the crime and the recognition that it was up to him to "make sure that the jury arrived at a decision based on the facts." Again it was domestic violence, and the facts as told by Ned are as follows:

> NW: The guy had his pregnant wife killed, so the child was killed too. It was a double murder. He had his buddy kill her. He was cheating on her. I couldn't believe this situation. I mean these guys . . . It was the worst crime scene I've ever seen. Okay I did it. [I handled it. The husband] tried to make it look like a suicide, went out in the garage with a shotgun, set it up so his stepdaughter, who was in the third grade at the time, would come home it find her. It was real hard.

He ended this statement not with the Constitution, but his job's duty: "My job was to make sure the jury did the right thing according to whatever the advised sentence was going to be." In other cases Ned has used his duty to include his perspective on race relations.

> NW: I dismissed a case back east because a short time after my cops brought the victim [in to view a lineup, he identifies] two guys that just happened to fit the general description. . . . So I was talking to him, trying to figure what about these particular guys was characteristic of the people who perpetrated the case. He couldn't tell me. I kept asking him was it something about their face, distinguishing characteristics, clothes, anything. Nothing was matching up. Finally he says, "You know, they were Black and all Black guys look alike." I often wondered if somebody else had that case, would that conversation ever have been disclosed. Or how would that have gone? Fair is just a concept involving doing the right thing under the circumstances.

Ned is no longer vomiting in the men's bathroom stall before a trial. Now he wears a judge's robe and has taken up the game of golf to relieve his stress.

In both of these men's midcareer stories—especially those involving domestic violence—they risk sympathizing with victims much like the women defenders at their midcareer points risk overly identifying with defendants. However, for the woman defender, identification with the defendant relieves emotional stress by allowing her to distance herself from the victim. Meg Lowe's form of emotion work is to see the defendant as a victim of society. When defending the man who raped the fifteen-year-old girl in the orchard, she was unsuccessful in this sort of emotion work, and she ended up with an ulcer. One could argue Louis Marks is in a similar position, though on the opposite side of the courtroom, adding to his need for emotion work. He wants to "demonize" the pedophile or girlfriend beater and has his own set of medical problems. In both situations these attorneys have ailments that might be caused by factors other than their work. However, each attributes their illness to their work. Meg left the felony team after the sexual-assault trial led to her ulcer, and Louis has his heart problems, which he ties to emotional involvement in certain cases and the political context of his work.

PHASE III. IDENTITY REINFORCEMENT—
SEASONED PROSECUTORS

Like most of the African American district attorneys I interviewed, Stan Clifford is impeccably dressed. We met after court on a Friday afternoon when his office was slowing down for the weekend. Stan effectively convinced me that he was learning to take things in stride. He had just returned to prosecution after a triple-bypass surgery. Like Louis Marks, Stan believes his work contributed to his heart problems.[10] He said, "I don't take things as serious as I once did. They're still serious issues, and I still treat them as though they're important. At one time I would jump up and rant and rave."

Just under the knot of Stan's tie is a gold charm that has become his trademark. It was a gift from a college girlfriend given two weeks before she was killed by a drunk driver. Stan has worn it ever since. While that event certainly influenced his choice to become a prosecutor Stan was driven more by idealism in his early days than by some need for revenge. In my interviews with the prosecutors, rarely did they bring in the Constitution and its ideals to justify their work. I will argue that most of the prosecutors did not experience a conflict between their personal politics as men of color with their professional identities as prosecutors. Stan told me that Constitutional beliefs were more important to him in law school but that when he started working in the profession the ideals that drove him began to shift. When he started as a prosecutor twenty-three years ago he began "paying much more attention to how people victimize others."

> SC: I'm one of those old fashioned guys who believe that our Constitution says the burden is on the petitioner, "The People," to prove a case beyond a reasonable doubt, and that if you fail to do so, a person is entitled to walk free. So long as I go in and do my job, I feel justified, and I feel that I've obtained a just result. The only question then is what the sentence should be. The sentence should be commensurate with the crime.

Stan said he has been called a "traitor, a turncoat, and a 'Tom.'" Those aspersions on his character as an African American normally come from the relatives of African American defendants who challenge what they see as a conflict in identities. Stan's classic response is, "You know, you may not realize it, but you're a hell of a lot better off now with me in the system than you would be with me out of the system." And that usually shuts them up. People rarely say that to him these days. It happened more in his early career, about sixty jury trials ago. As he sees it, people victimize others, as does the criminal justice system, "and I think I play a large part in alleviating some of that victimization."

Clearly victimization goes both ways for Stan. The perpetrator victimizes as does the system of justice. He said, "If I don't have a good-faith belief that the person charged should be prosecuted or that the person charged is responsible for the crime, whether or not the crime occurred, I don't prosecute. I have the authority to dismiss the charges, and I've done so in murder cases, and lesser cases." Stan's statement indicates identification with defendants of color. Throughout the interview, he implies that African Americans in his largely Black county are victimized by the system, and he is in the position to alleviate some of that. The decision making that goes into whether to file and what charges to file is stressful.

Just weeks before, another prosecutor, Turner Anderson, told me that by the next morning he had to make a decision that would affect a young man and his family forever. A murder was committed during the course of a robbery. No gun was used. And the victim was killed by someone other than this young man, but he had been present. Turner said that the call whether to file murder charges or not was weighing heavily on him. The youth's mother would likely come back at him and say, "But he wasn't involved in the killing. He didn't know the killing was going to take place. It didn't happen at my son's hand."

A case that weighed even more heavily upon Turner involved a woman police officer with two kids, ages six and four. The six-year-old found her hidden revolver while she was at work then shot his four-year-old brother. The brother lived, but there was a statute that allowed Turner the discretion to prosecute the woman because she was the owner of the gun; she was also the parent, and the perpetrator was her child. He decided against prosecuting the woman. Turner's decision was challenged in the news, and he needed to justify it publicly. He finally asked a reporter, "What would have happened if the four-year-old had died? The mother would be burying one son and being sent to prison. Who would raise the other child?"

Unlike most of the prosecutors Turner does not find sexual-assault or domestic-violence cases to be the more draining aspects of his work. He told me that he has never lost a sexual-assault case. At the same time he lets me know that, as the prosecutor, he is very careful in what rape cases he will file, "It is not about men raping women and getting away with it. As a prosecutor, I want to know what the truth is." Imagine he is talking to a rape victim. Turner will say to her, "You said he did this to you. You said he stuck it in, but you gave it to him. You consented. So the issue is consent, not penetration." She will respond, "He must've done something to me. I don't remember telling him it was okay." I asked Turner if he felt that he was walking a fine line of demeaning the victim. His response was, "You're not just dealing with sexual assault. You're dealing with the whole politics of rape. I've told people that if I had to prosecute those cases for a living, then I would probably not be the best person because of my attitude."

At the other end of the prosecutorial spectrum is Stan. He finds cases of sexual abuse against women and children to be the most emotionally taxing. I related to Stan what Turner said just weeks before. He responded that not all prosecutors are "enlightened" in the area of assaults on women. Stan said that he understood the emotions involved in this type of crime, though not from any direct experience. For example, his wife was never raped. But he still has a lot of sympathy for victims of rape. He told me that one case that "tried" him was the sexual assault of a white woman committed by an African American man.

> SC: When she saw me her immediate response was, "Oh no!" Over a course of time I was able to convince her that, despite her experience being raped by a Black man, the case was going to be prosecuted to the full extent of the law and that the person responsible would come to justice. I gained her confidence. She went from a person calling me a "nigger" to a person feeling as though the system worked.

Stan did not describe this case as pivotal, though it would certainly meet the criteria for serious cases where identities conflict. He has had some gruesome cases, which we might imagine fit the category of transformative.

One involved a paraplegic who was tortured, murdered, and robbed by his attendants. "The person was stabbed forty-eight times, had their throat slit from ear to ear, and was set on fire. And he was confined to a wheelchair, so it was a particularly brutal case. Both parties responsible were convicted of first-degree murder, and they're still serving time." He did not describe this particular case as a turning point either. That case came nine years in, when he was assigned to the office's homicide team.

SC: It was a massacre case involving a person who was using an assault weapon indiscriminately killing people. So there was a lot of pressure on the office to get a good result. I felt extremely successful in the way the case was tried and the result that was obtained. I was tested as a trial attorney because I had to bring skills to bear that I never had to before. And I did a good job. After that case I felt confident to be able to try any case that was thrown my way.

As he proceeded, Stan offered me a glimpse at his straightforward job duty that is complementary to those of the seasoned women defenders: "I really believe that certain types of crime demand certain types of punishment. That is what you seek. Nothing more." Like Sally Tan and Rose Carr, Stan makes short emphatic statements about the obligations of a prosecutor. Turner Anderson made a similar emphatic statement: "Justice is just that: just us." In neither the men's or women's cases is sense of duty guided by a Constitutional ideal. In each case there is a problem-focused coping style reminiscent of criminal attorneys who have at one point or another undergone a career transformation in their work that allows them to focus on the demands of their job through their fortified identity as trial attorneys who can take any case that is given to them.[11] In Stan's case it is bolstered by his father's ethic toward life, which goes beyond the courtroom: "The most important thing is your integrity. And only you can give that away."

According to Ray Bryant, also an African American who has worked in a district attorney's office for over twenty years, the Constitution is something public defenders manipulate more often than prosecutors. Ray sees the Constitution in the hands of defense attorneys as a document that "basically means people get to do whatever they want, regardless of who it hurts. There's no balancing and there's no obligation to consider the rights of [victims]. I mean, the Constitution hurts sometimes. I don't mind enforcing it, but I don't think the government necessarily has to allow human sacrifice at the same time."

As the son of a physician, Ray comes from a "family that had social standing within Black society back east." Ray's upper-class bias surfaces throughout the interview. He remembers being in the first grade of a Catholic school during the civil rights movement. His school experience seems to have had an equal effect on his identity formation as the civil rights movement. He said, "I was the son of a doctor, literally sitting next to children of butchers, service people, whatever." At school he learned not to "act out" because the nuns "did not hesitate to get physical if someone provoked them in the slightest." And beyond that, he would have had to contend with his parents. Ray learned at an early age that deviating from the norm would be punished—something, "defendants don't learn."

Throughout the interview Ray actively distinguished himself from African American defendants. One way was by repeatedly pointing out their class differences. His family had social standing; the defendants were from the "welfare class." When we walked to lunch at a diner across the street from the courthouse he criticized the largely Black male passersby for trying to make themselves "even more different than white folks" by braiding or knotting their hair. I suggest that creating this social distance between Black defendants and himself makes prosecuting men of color easier for Ray. However, the majority of his cases stem from white-collar crimes, and the defendants are typically white men. In those instances Ray uses race differences to separate himself from defendants and, I would argue, to bolster his role in the system.

> RB: This is a bureaucracy, and I am here to complain, to push, to nag when necessary, to call the newspapers on occasion, which I've done with great frequency. I can have an effect on this bureaucracy from the inside [that] I would not have as a defense attorney. People can't even get their phone calls returned from the police department. I file felony warrants on cases based on a victim writing a police report no one else would. I not only do it, I laugh while I'm doing it. Usually whites get away with [white-collar crime], and the white DA's won't touch them. The white police won't touch them. I have to get these criminal cases investigated. I've had victims hire private investigators. I've filed victims' letters. I have horse-traded to get the cops to do even basic things because a white police officer detaining and interrogating a fifty-year-old white male with a coat and tie makes them physically nervous.

Entertaining the idea of becoming a doctor, like his father, was what made Ray nervous as a young man. The family home was next door to his dad's office.

RB: I knew what being a doctor was all about, and I didn't feel like dealing with blood, the cutting, the bureaucracy, and the lab work business. It was like living next door to a mortuary, a mortuary in the sense that you have to deal with people. So I didn't want to be a doctor, so [in my family] that left one option, [a lawyer]. You know, silly me, I should have gone into computers.

Ray offered a telling comment on distancing himself from the people he comes into contact with on a daily basis: "I deal with people, but I don't have to deal with people like doctors do. I don't have to get invasive." Avoiding invasive relationships with victims becomes another form of social distancing, as it did for Vernon Carter.

While Ray's parents were happy he chose to become an attorney, they did not like the idea of him becoming a prosecutor.

RB: My parents are "colored," they have the "colored" mentality from the '50s or something. In fact they had both feet firmly planted in 1955. They were very happy. There was a segregated society: they were on top of the Black society. The whites left them alone. It's heaven. You know, they had everything they needed. The money was rolling in. And their feeling about this law thing was that I was supposed to be a defense attorney and help people. And I do more good as a DA than I could, in my opinion, as a defense attorney.

There have never been more than three African Americans in Ray's office, which now boasts eighty-eight prosecutors. Currently he and a woman are the sole Black lawyers in the office. These numbers reflect the demographics of California's attorneys.[12]

Ray prefers filing cases where the victims are elderly minorities who have been "trolled" for money. These elderly are not people normally served by the district attorney's office, "because they don't have a powerful friend who can call the prosecutor."

RB: It's an old game. You sell promissory notes to these stupid victims. Then you put the money in a corporation, pay yourself your bonuses, payroll, or whatever, and then you bankrupt it and walk away from it. And you can do it over and over and over. It's absolutely felonious, and it's hardly ever prosecuted. Keep it under a million and the feds don't get involved. It can go on forever.

I found out about it when a little old lady walked into my office who'd given them $25,000. I issued arrest warrants for the president of the corporation, who was an engineer, who was sort of the cat's paw and the secretary-treasurer, who was the 100 percent stockholder and mastermind. I'd never met them. The victims had never met them. They'd never set foot in [my county]. I had them dragged here in chains, and you should have seen the look on their faces when they saw it was me. They said, "This isn't illegal; this isn't a crime; this is a civil case; we'll have you disbarred; we'll get you for doing this." They said this in court.

And I set high bail. And we had a bunch of jury trials, and I convicted everybody. They got probation because white folks don't get prison for being serial criminals who rip off elderly people. They get probation because they're white, and they'll send [Blacks] to prison for shoplifting. I've done twenty-four of these cases. They usually have private attorneys. They hire out-of-towners who come in here. They get "hometowned." They try to take me on in my town, my judges, and we just go to it, and I win. They get probation. The office says it's a waste of time because they're getting probation. They're marked. The stockbroker who did that particular case lost his state and federal licenses forever. The other guy was in and out of jail. I mean these prosecutions last years. Some of these cases have taken three to five years.

While Ray finds amusement in this aspect of his job, he still is very bothered by the race disparities that he sees in court on a daily basis.

RB: I've been in the courtroom waiting for my case to be called. And I see what I call "Ken and Barbie"—"Otis and Latifah" differences. Otis and Latifah [are Black and] make a mess of their situation and get twenty years. Ken and Barbie . . . I've seen white folks come in here with seven or eight burglaries. Should be mandatory state prison. They walk out with probation while Otis and Latifah will get to prison for shoplifting.

Ray's most upsetting recollection of this kind of disparity was his first felony insurance fraud case. A Black couple who worked at Safeway had committed fraud on their car insurance company. He was the prosecutor and was trying to get a better outcome on a plea bargain than the public defender was willing to give. Then another case was heard in the same courtroom. The son of a local car dealer was convicted of seven burglaries, and he got "straight probation." The only other Black prosecutor was in the courtroom at the same time. He and Ray were so angry they had to leave the courtroom.

> RB: We were getting upset because this was really irrational. We knew well what was going on. I turned, and there was the defense attorney for the [Black couple]. I amazed him and settled for misdemeanor pleas. He said, "Why the hell did you settle for misdemeanors?" And I said, "Did you see what went on in there? I don't have to get approval from the administration." When I see these Ken and Barbie–Otis and Latifah differences I try to keep a sense of balance.

This was Ray's pivotal case. He learned that within the organization he had the power to balance a system that weighs in heavily on the side of whites. He went on to rationalize his proactive role in evening out these differences by adding, "Most of my defendants are white anyway."

Still, the last reflection that Ray offered on his work was that there is a fine line between the actors in the courtroom—between "cops and robbers." I would argue that much of his emotion work is directed toward turning that line into a social barrier that separates him from the victims—and even further from the defendants.

Like most of the prosecutors, Ray relies on the belief formed in childhood that there are consequences for "acting out," whether you are a parochial school boy or the son of the car dealer burglarizing homes. Unlike the women defenders who wrestled with the contradictions between feminism and their work, most of these prosecutors did not have a political ideology conflicting with their public roles that required moral work or moral justification. The sole interview that evidenced an ultimate clash between competing situational identities was based on a political ideology that conflicted with a public role.

The first time Darryl Franks registered to vote, it was as a member of the Peace and Freedom Party. Darryl's rationale for choosing a third party was that "George Wallace [who unsuccessfully ran for president at the time] was a Democrat and Ronald Reagan [who was California's governor] was a Republican. I was not going to be a part of either party." Darryl knew that he could never be a career prosecutor: "It just didn't fit with my political philosophy. I was going to be part of a system putting people in jail, especially poor people, minority people. And given the way I felt at that time, I had personal concerns about being a part of that process." However, trial practice was needed to become a judge, and judgeships in his county often go to prosecutors, and only rarely to criminal defense attorneys. Darryl's father advised, "If you don't take the job, somebody else will." So he took the job in the county where he would not be sending his classmates to jail, and, in his words, he "defined himself as an attorney that happened to be a district attorney." Identity formation as a prosecutor in Darryl's early years was, thus, impossible, and he continued in his pursuit of a judgeship. Had his identity taken form, as it did for Vernon Carter (also early in his career), who aspired to join the FBI, I would likely have interviewed Darryl in a district attorney's office. It was, however, an improbable outcome given his politics.

I asked Darryl if there were any crimes that he wouldn't prosecute. His responded, "I just never got to that point when I was a prosecutor that they handed me a death-penalty case. I would have had to do a lot of soul-searching." So Darryl was never put in the midcareer position of taking on a pivotal case. We can only imagine the sorts of emotion work, ideological work, and ultimately moral work that are required of Darryl as a judge. Unfortunately, he and I made an agreement at the beginning of his interview that we would not discuss his inner life as a judge.

Unlike Darryl's, the emotional conflicts for the majority of prosecutors I interviewed arose primarily from competing situational identities rather than ideological conflict between their political and professional selves. Competing situational identities that are not heavily value-laden will likely endure in an ambivalent relationship. Ambivalent selves, as Erving Goffman would say, rest somewhere within the cracks of the institution.[13] For prosecutors who are men of color, their ambivalence can at once be a source of strength and confusion.[14] Still, each of the prosecutors was ideally positioned as a tempered radical.

Carter Vernon said that he was in a no-lose situation in prosecuting the young African American homeless men on kidnapping for robbery. Instead of winning the case at trial and seeing these young men put away for virtually the rest of their lives, he plea bargained the cases to less than nine years each. His supervisors were offered a new perspective—and the young men one last chance. Likewise, Louis Marks teaches. He taught the white legal-aid client that she could trust rather than fear a Black attorney. Louis educated the young Latina about the long-term nature of domestic violence. And he showed his superiors that how they perceive race and class may warp the worth they place on individual lives. Stan Clifford uses his discretion in prosecuting cases as a way to alleviate the criminal justice system's victimization of African American men. Ray Bryant believes that he does more good as a prosecutor than he could as a public defender. As a district attorney he gleefully files cases against white men in business suits that would make white officers of the court uncomfortable. And after seeing the son of a local white businessman get probation for multiple burglaries, he offered the Black grocery clerks misdemeanors on car insurance fraud.

The men in each of these cases attempt to even out the power differences in the criminal justice system. Whether they are termed tempered radicals, or outsiders within—as people whose core identities threaten the system at the same time they are threatened by it—they are well positioned to help bring about change in a system that weighs heavily against men of color.

Notes

CHAPTER 1

1. Susan Ehrlich Martin and Nancy C. Jurik, *Doing Justice, Doing Gender: Women in Law and Criminal Justice Occupations* (Thousand Oaks, Calif.: Sage Publications, 1996).

2. American Bar Association, "A Snapshot of Women in the Law in the Year 2000," www.abanet.org (2002).

3. Deborah L. Rhode, *Professional Responsibility: Ethics by the Pervasive Method* (Boston: Little, Brown, 1994), 222.

4. Harriet Beecher Stowe, *Uncle Tom's Cabin* (New York: MacMillan, 1994).

5. See Everett Hughes's 1948 lecture, "Good People and Dirty Work," in *The Sociological Eye: Selected Papers* (New Brunswick, N.J.: Transaction Press, 1971). Hughes identifies the type of work performed by "pariahs who do the dirty work of society . . . acting as agents for the rest of us" (ibid., 93). "In any occupation, people perform a variety of tasks, some of them approaching more closely the ideal or symbolic work of the profession than others. Some tasks are considered nuisances and impositions, or even dirty work—physically, socially or morally beneath the dignity of the profession" (ibid., 401). Hughes's strongest example is members of the Nazi S.S. performing the epitome of social dirty work—the extermination of people(s).

6. Ibid., 402.

7. Cynthia Fuchs Epstein, *Women in Law* (Urbana: University of Illinois Press, 1993), 114. The stereotype is that "women should bring a special understanding, compassion, or knowledge of society" to violent and brutal cases. Ibid., 123.

8. Ibid., 106.

9. Bennett M. Berger, *The Survival of a Counterculture: Ideological Work and Everyday Life Among Rural Communards* (Berkeley: University of California Press, 1981).

10. Arlie Russell Hochschild, *The Managed Heart: Commercialization of Human Feeling* (Berkeley: University of California Press, 1983).

11. Erving Goffman links the term "moral career" to "early social anthropological work on ceremonies of status transition, and . . . classic social psychological descriptions of those spectacular changes in one's view of self that can accompany participation in social movements and sects." See Goffman, *Asylums* (Chicago: Aldine Publishing, 1961), 128, n. 1.

12. The conflict between what is internal to an individual and what is external has been described in cognitive psychology as "cognitive dissonance" (Leon Festinger, A

Theory of Cognitive Dissonance [Evanston, Ill.: Row, Peterson, 1957]) and, more recently, attempts to minimize such conflict have been described in sociology as ideological work or emotion work. "Cognitive psychology recognizes a disparity between what is 'out there' and its internal representation" (Edward E. Sampson, "Cognitive Psychology as Ideology," *American Psychologist* 36 [1981]: 730–743). In both the cognitive psychological and sociological approaches individuals try to reduce the dissonance they experience to protect their self-images. My approach is social-interactionist: people construct justifications for the possible contradictions between their personal beliefs and their professional role in interaction with their selves and with others to protect their images of self for themselves and others.

13. Joey Sprague and Mary K. Zimmerman, "Overcoming Dualisms: A Feminist Agenda for Sociological Methodology," in *Theory on Gender/Feminism on Theory*, ed. Paula England (New York: A. de Gruyter, 1993), 255–280.

14. See Donileen R. Loseke and Spencer E. Cahill, "The Social Construction of Deviance: Experts on Battered Women," *Social Problems* 31 (1984): 296–310, and Howard S. Becker, "Practitioners of Vice and Crime," in *Sociological Methods: A Sourcebook*, ed. Norman K. Denzin (New York: McGraw-Hill, 1978).

15. Susan Ehrlich Martin, "Police Force or Police Service? Gender and Emotional Labor," *Annals of the American Academy of Political and Social Science* 561 (1999): 111–126.

16. Lillian B. Rubin's reflections on field work in *Families on the Fault Line* (New York: Harper Perennial, 1995) influenced this paragraph.

17. Sprague and Zimmerman, "Overcoming Dualisms," 273.

18. While I have no statistics on race or ethnicity for women who practice criminal defense law in California, a 2001 California State Bar demographic survey found that Asians account for 6 percent of participants, Latinos 3.7 percent, African Americans 2.4 percent, Native Americans .5 percent (California Bar Association, "Bar Demographics Are Shifting Slowly," www.calbar.ca.gov [2001]).

19. Barney G. Glaser and Anselm L. Strauss, *The Discovery of Grounded Theory: Strategies for Qualitative Research* (New York: Aldine de Gruyter, 1967), 61.

20. Sprague and Zimmerman, "Overcoming Dualisms."

21. Symbolic interactionism is the primary theory of sociological social psychology. The first three premises of symbolic interactionism are: (1) people act on the basis of meanings (i.e., meanings that may be provided by culture in the form of symbols or conventions), (2) those meanings are not fixed or predetermined but arise out of social interactions (the negotiation of meaning is constantly shifting between participants; thus actions continually adjust to shifting meanings emerging from interaction), and (3) people's actions are filtered through their interpretations of the situation. See George Herbert Mead, *On Social Psychology* (Chicago: University of Chicago Press, 1956) and Herbert Blumer, *Symbolic Interactionism: Perspective and Method* (Berkeley: University of California Press, 1969).

22. Anselm L. Strauss and Juliet Corbin, *Basics of Qualitative Research: Grounded Theory Procedures and Techniques* (Newbury Park, Calif.: Sage Publications, 1990), 42–43.

23. Glaser and Strauss, *The Discovery of Grounded Theory*. I designed a list of inter-

view questions that would allow the interviews to be as conversational in character as possible. Besides a few demographic questions I asked at the beginning of the interview, questions were open-ended, allowing the women to develop answers that often turned into long stories. I revised the questions before each interview to cover themes that might have emerged in the previous interview. When I started my research, I divided my interview questions into four larger categories: (1) demographics, (2) early career, (3) career, and (4) ideological work. I changed the fourth category to ideological work/emotion work soon after the study began.

24. Norman K. Denzin, *Symbolic Interactionism and Cultural Studies: The Politics of Interpretation* (Oxford: Blackwell, 1992), 74.

25. See Maria Mies, *Patriarchy and Accumulation on a World Scale: Women in the International Division of Labour* (London: Zed Books, 1991), and Donna Haraway, *Simians, Cyborgs, and Women: The Reinvention of Nature* (New York: Routledge, 1991).

26. Sprague and Zimmerman, "Overcoming Dualisms," 240.

27. Cynthia Siemsen, "Negotiating Ideals: Women in the Line of Criminal Defense Duty," unpublished paper presented at the ninety-third American Sociological Association meeting (San Francisco, Calif., August 21–25, 1998). Findings for a study to test my hypothesis that when sociologists examine questions of ideology they tend to study men, and when they explore emotion they tend to study women revealed clear gender-aligned assumptions. Of all articles found in the Sociological Abstracts database using ideological work as their theoretical frame, only 12.5 percent focused on women. Likewise, of the articles exploring emotion work, only 10 percent focused on men.

28. Jennifer L. Pierce, *Gender Trials: Emotional Lives in Contemporary Law Firms* (Berkeley: University of California Press, 1995). Women represented only 6 percent of United States law school students in 1968. By 1983 this figure increased to 31 percent of enrollments (Epstein, *Women in Law*, 21). These figures can be compared to 47 percent in 1999 (American Bar Association, "A Snapshot of Women in the Law in the Year 2000"). Only 4 percent of practicing attorneys were women in the 1960s (U.S. Department of Labor, Bureau of Labor Statistics, cited in Epstein, *Women in Law*) contrasted with just below 29 percent in 1999 (U.S. Department of Labor, Bureau of Labor Statistics, cited in American Bar Association, "A Snapshot of Women in the Law in the Year 2000").

29. Gary LaFree, "Too Much Democracy or Too Much Crime," *Law and Social Inquiry* 27 (2002): 875–902. "The three-strikes law passed by the U.S. Congress in 1994 had an impact on the criminal sentences of 35 offenders in its first four and a half years, [*sic*] the California law passed the same year affected the criminal sentences of more than 40,000 offenders during the same period" (ibid., 886).

30. Franklin E. Zimring, Gordon Hawkins, and Sam Kamin, *Punishment and Democracy: Three Strikes and You're Out in California* (New York: Oxford University Press, 2001).

31. In November 2002, the U.S. Supreme Court heard oral arguments in the cases of Andrade and Ewing to decide the constitutionality of California's TSL. On March 5, 2003, the high court voted five to four that California's Proposition 184 does not violate a person's constitutional protection from cruel and unusual punishment under the Eighth

Amendment. See *Lockyer v. Andrade*, 000 U.S. 01-1127 (2003); and *Ewing v. California*, 123 S.Ct. 1179 (2003).

CHAPTER 2

1. If that were the case, I would begin with a generation of philosophers who directly connected ideas to the senses. For example, the seventeenth-century philosopher John Locke argued that there is a unidirectional flow that turns sensations into beliefs: "All ideas come from the sense, or are the product of sensations." Quoted in Michael Billig, *Ideology and Social Psychology* (Oxford: Basil Blackwell, 1982), 12.

2. Karl Mannheim, *Ideology and Utopia: An Introduction to the Sociology of Knowledge* (1936; reprint, New York: Harcourt Brace Jovanovich, 1985), 80.

3. Clifford Geertz, *The Interpretation of Cultures: Selected Essays* (New York: Basic Books, 1973), 205.

4. Ibid., 207 (emphasis added).

5. Geertz points out that ideology is most important exactly when our extrinsic sources of information ("institutionalized guides for behavior, thought, or feeling") fail to respond to cultural, social, or psychological stresses. Carol Gilligan would say this is a man's view: in moral reasoning, or moral dilemmas, women put relationships and consequences of actions for others first. See *In a Different Voice* (Cambridge: Harvard University Press, 1982). I would argue that women may put consequences of action for others first, but they also may use ideology in the service of resolving moral dilemmas.

6. Bennett Berger, *The Survival of a Counterculture: Ideological Work and Everyday Life Among Rural Communards* (Berkeley: University of California Press, 1981).

7. Ibid., 16.

8. Ibid., 17.

9. Berger uses the term "feeling work," referring to Arlie Russell Hochschild's "Emotion Work, Feeling Rules, and Social Structure" *American Journal of Sociology* 85 (1979): 551–575, only in a footnote (Berger, *Survival of a Counterculture*, 143, n. 16).

10. Berger, *Survival of a Counterculture*, 5.

11. Bennett Berger, *An Essay on Culture: Symbolic Structure and Social Structure* (Berkeley: University of California Press, 1995), 82.

12. Michael Billig et al., *Ideological Dilemmas: A Social Psychology of Everyday Thinking* (London: Sage Publications, 1988).

13. Ibid., 32.

14. Raymond Williams, *The Long Revolution* (New York: Columbia University Press, 1961), 55.

15. Ibid.

16. Roger Cotterrell, *The Politics of Jurisprudence: A Critical Introduction to Legal Philosophy* (Philadelphia: University of Pennsylvania Press, 1992), 210.

17. Ibid., 211.

18. According to David Kairys: (1) Law is predictable and available to those who have the skill to understand it; (2) the facts of a case emerge through objective hearings that ascertain the truth; (3) case outcomes are the result of "routine application of the law to facts"; and (4) a competent judge will reach the right decision. See *The Politics of Law: A Progressive Critique* (New York: Pantheon Books, 1990), 1.

19. Max Weber, *Economy and Society*, ed. Guenther Roth and Claus Wittich (Berkeley: University of California Press, 1978).

20. Kairys, *Politics of Law*.

21. Heather Ruth Wishik, "To Question Everything: The Inquiries of Feminist Jurisprudence," in *Feminist Legal Theory: Foundations*, ed. D. Kelly Weisberg (Philadelphia: Temple University Press, 1993), 22.

22. Ibid.

23. Catharine A. MacKinnon, "Feminism, Marxism, Method, and the State: Toward Feminist Jurisprudence," and "Feminism, Marxism, Method, and the State: An Agenda for Theory," in *Feminist Legal Theory: Foundations*, ed. D. Kelly Weisberg (Philadelphia: Temple University Press, 1993), 427–436, 437–453, see especially 436.

24. Catharine A. MacKinnon, *Toward a Feminist Theory of the State* (Cambridge: Harvard University Press, 1989), 249.

25. MacKinnon, "Feminism, Marxism, Method, and the State: Toward Feminist Jurisprudence," 433.

26. Hochschild, "Emotion Work, Feeling Rules, and Social Structure," 551.

27. Ibid., 561. She implies that individuals engage in *joint* emotion work, as Kathryn J. Lively asserts in "Reciprocal Emotion Management," *Work and Occupations* 27 (2000): 32–66.

28. Hochschild, "Emotion Work, Feeling Rules, and Social Structure," 561.

29. Mannheim, *Ideology and Utopia*, 80.

30. See also Candace Clark, "Emotions and Micropolitics in Everyday Life: Some Patterns and Paradoxes of Place," in *Research Agendas in the Sociology of Emotions*, ed. Theodore D. Kemper (Albany, N.Y.: SUNY Press, 1990).

31. Ibid., 567.

32. Robert Granfield, *Making Elite Lawyers* (New York: Routledge, 1992) and Robert Granfield and Thomas Koenig, "The Fate of Elite Idealism: Accommodation and Ideological Work at Harvard Law School" *Social Problems* 39 (1992): 315–331.

33. Debra E. Meyerson and Maureen A. Scully, "Tempered Radicalism and the Politics of Ambivalence and Change," *Organization Science* 6 (1995): 586.

34. Erving Goffman, *Strategic Interaction* (Philadelphia: University of Pennsylvania Press, 1969), cited in Meyerson and Scully, "Tempered Radicalism."

35. See Gregory M. Matoesian, *Reproducing Rape: Domination through Talk in the Courtroom* (Chicago: University of Chicago Press, 1993).

36. See Cynthia Fuchs Epstein, *Women in Law* (Urbana: University of Illinois Press, 1993) and R.W. Connell, *Gender and Power* (Stanford: Stanford University Press, 1987).

37. Everett Hughes, "Dilemmas and Contradictions of Status," in *The Sociological Eye: Selected Papers* (New Brunswick, N.J.: Transaction Press, 1971), 149.

38. Meyerson and Scully, "Tempered Radicalism."

39. Patricia Hill Collins, "Learning from the Outsider Within: The Sociological Significance of Black Feminist Thought," *Social Problems* 33 (1986): 514–532.

40. Lani Guinier, Michelle Fine, and Jane Balin, *Becoming Gentlemen: Women, Law School, and Institutional Change* (Boston: Beacon Press, 1997), 75.

41. Jennifer L. Pierce, *Gender Trials: Emotional Lives in Contemporary Law Firms* (Berkeley: University of California Press, 1995), 180.

42. Susan Ehrlich Martin and Nancy C. Jurik, *Doing Justice, Doing Gender: Women in Law and Criminal Justice Occupations* (Thousand Oaks, Calif.: Sage Publications, 1996).

43. "Doing gender means creating differences between girls and boys and women and men, differences that are not natural, essential, or biological. Once the differences have been constructed, they are used to reinforce the 'essentialness' of gender." Candace West and Don Zimmerman, "Doing Gender," *Gender & Society* 1 (1987): 137.

44. Martin and Jurik, in *Doing Justice, Doing Gender*, citing Connell, *Gender and Power*, Iris M. Young, *Justice and the Politics of Difference* (Princeton: Princeton University Press, 1990), and James W. Messerschmidt, *Masculinities and Crime: Critique and Reconceptualization of Theory* (Lanham, Md.: Rowman and Littlefield, 1993).

45. Pierce, *Gender Trials*; Martin and Jurik, *Doing Justice, Doing Gender*; and Susan Ehrlich Martin, "Police Force or Police Service? Gender and Emotional Labor," *Annals of the American Academy of Political and Social Science* 561 (1999): 111–126.

46. Amy S. Wharton, "The Psychological Consequences of Emotional Labor," *Annals of the American Academy of Political and Social Science* 561 (1999): 162.

47. Erving Goffman, *Asylums* (Chicago: Aldine Publishing, 1961).

CHAPTER 3

1. A preliminary hearing, or examination, is a court trial held in felony cases. The judge decides whether the defendant should be "held to answer" on the charges based on evidence presented to her or him by the prosecutor and motions to suppress evidence presented by the defense attorney. See California Penal Codes, Sections 738, 872.

2. Erving Goffman argues that the self is actually the product of its social presentations. Depending upon the requirements of the situation, a person will strategically perform for others. See Goffman, *The Presentation of Self in Everyday Life* (Garden City, N.Y.: Doubleday, 1959).

3. I thank Claire Renzetti for this insight.

4. Using a theatrical metaphor, Goffman suggests that, like a stage, our social spaces are divided into front and back regions. In the front region (such as the courtroom), individuals perform for others to maintain their self-proclaimed identities according to the rules that guide social interaction. The back region is where contradictions in individual selves may emerge. Goffman, *The Presentation of Self in Everyday Life*.

5. "Three strikes" refers to California Penal Code, Section 667, which calls for sentencing "enhancement for prior felony conviction of serious or violent offense, including possible life imprisonment upon third conviction." See discussion in chapter one, pp. 18–20.

6. "People get violated" is a reference to a probation violation that is a felony conviction distinct from their original conviction.

7. The client's "exposure" refers to the possible sentence he will receive if convicted.

8. I thank Candace West for this insight.

CHAPTER 4

1. Erving Goffman, *Asylums* (Chicago: Aldine Publishing, 1961).

2. Ibid., 165.

3. Karl Marx, *The Marx-Engels Reader*, ed. Robert Tucker (New York: Norton, 1978).

4. Arlie Russell Hochschild, *The Managed Heart: Commercialization of Human Feeling* (Berkeley: University of California Press, 1983).

5. Gina's description of the floorperson's nature to sympathize with the victim is revealing. She is doing gender when pointing to the woman's sympathetic nature toward the victim.

6. Erving Goffman, *Interaction Ritual: Essays on Face-to-Face Behavior* (New York: Pantheon Books, 1967).

7. Erving Goffman, *The Goffman Reader*, eds. Charles Lemert and Ann Branaman (Malden, Mass.: Blackwell Publishers, 1997), 122.

8. Pierre Bourdieu, *Outline of a Theory of Practice* (Cambridge: Cambridge University Press, 1977).

9. Harold Garfinkel, *Studies in Ethnomethodology* (New York: Prentice Hall, 1967).

10. Bourdieu, *Outline of a Theory of Practice*.

11. Without explicitly referring to critical legal studies, Kay is describing what scholars in that tradition suggest is the one constant to law—that it is politics practiced by the participants in the system. See David Kairys, *The Politics of Law: A Progressive Critique* (New York: Pantheon Books, 1990).

CHAPTER 5

1. See Kathryn Lively, "Reciprocal Emotion Management" *Work and Occupations* 27 (1999): 32–66.

2. A preliminary hearing, or examination, is a court trial held in felony cases. The judge decides whether the defendant should be "held to answer" on the charges based on evidence presented to her or him by the prosecutor and motions to suppress evidence presented by the defense attorney. California Penal Code, Sections 738, 872.

3. Under California law, the girlfriend was required to testify. (California Evidence Code, Section 972[f].) The reasoning is that the statutory rape preceded the marriage, and even though she became the defendant's wife, the victim-girlfriend was aware her husband-to-be was charged with the crime before the wedding.

4. Personally Sally's story is painful for me to tell. In the last year I heard of a former client taking a gun to his head. As a consultant I was in the position to choose what cases to work on. I would not work on rape cases where I believed the client was guilty. In my mind, as I write, this young man would still be alive if not for a wrongful accusation.

5. I remembered my own work, the moment I realized the human being behind a crime. It was also in a jail cell and involved a young woman accused of cutting up one person while on methamphetamines and torturing another. Two people were dead. When I met the defendant her head was shaved, she had a skull interwoven with barbed wire and roses tattooed on her arm; she was shackled and dressed in a red (not orange) jail jumpsuit, the color indicating she was in for something serious. She said "hello" in a high-pitched, childlike voice, and I shook her hand and thought, "It's odd that I'm not bothered that the hand I'm touching may have been involved in murders." Instead I was concentrating on her as a human being. We were meeting so that I could learn more about her life. In just a few days her defense attorney and I would meet with the district

attorney and tell him why, based on her history, she should not face the death penalty. In doing so I realized the importance of the work.

6. Gary LaFree, "Too Much Democracy or Too Much Crime?" *Law and Social Inquiry* 27 (2002): 880.

7. Cynthia Fuchs Epstein, *Women in Law* (Urbana: University of Illinois Press, 1993).

8. Like the attorneys in this book, Clarence Darrow was at times despised for his role defending unpopular people and their political ideologies. Darrow's career included defending the Socialist Eugene Debs (in 1900, for union organization) and John Scopes (in 1925, for teaching Darwin's theory of evolution). See Clarence Darrow, *The Story of My Life* (New York: Charles Scribner's Sons, 1932).

9. Darrow, *Story of My Life*, 76.

CHAPTER 6

1. Karl Mannheim, *Ideology and Utopia: An Introduction to the Sociology of Knowledge* (New York: Harcourt Brace Jovanovich, 1985).

2. Clifford Geertz, *The Interpretation of Cultures: Selected Essays* (New York: Basic Books, 1973).

3. Erving Goffman, *Asylums* (Chicago: Aldine Publishing, 1961), 165.

4. Arlie Russell Hochschild, *The Managed Heart: The Commercialization of Human Feeling* (Berkeley: University of California Press, 1983), 3.

5. Amy S. Wharton, "The Psychological Consequences of Emotional Labor" *Annals of the American Academy of Political and Social Science* 561 (1999): 158–176.

6. See Gregory M. Matoesian, *Reproducing Rape: Domination through Talk in the Courtroom* (Chicago: University of Chicago Press, 1993).

7. Robert Granfield, *Making Elite Lawyers* (New York: Routledge, 1992).

8. Debra E. Meyerson and Maureen A. Scully, "Tempered Radicalism and the Politics of Ambivalence and Change," *Organization Science* 6 (1995): 585–600.

9. Hochschild, *The Managed Heart*.

10. Granfield, *Making Elite Lawyers*.

11. Goffman, *Asylums*.

12. Ibid., 127.

13. Group life, or society, is "a source of life *sui generis*," existing in its own right yet constraining human activity (Emile Durkheim, *The Division of Labor in Society* [New York: Free Press, 1984], lii). In terms of subjectivity and identity, group life gives the individual "the best part of himself, all that gives him a distinct character and a special place among other beings, his intellectual and moral culture" (Emile Durkheim, *The Elementary Forms of Religious Life* [New York: Free Press, 1995], 388). The frameworks of ideas and conceptual categories given to the individual allow thought and constrain behavior. Through social constraints people are fulfilled.

Durkheim argues that without social constraints, people would be "incapacitated by the 'void' of infinite possibility" (*Moral Education* [New York: Free Press, 1961], 25). Knowledge of social constraints (in Hochschild's terms, feeling rules) and appropriate accompanying expressions of emotions implies membership and identity with the group:

The emotional state in which the group finds itself reflects the circumstances it is then going through. . . . The society exerts moral pressure on its members, and they bring their feelings into harmony with the situation. . . . When the individual feels firmly attached to the society to which he belongs, he feels morally bound to share in its grief and its joy. To abandon it would be to break the ties that bind him to the collectivity, to give up wanting collectivity, and to contradict himself (Durkheim, *Elementary Forms of Religious Life* [New York: Free Press, 1995], 403).

14. Clarence Darrow, *The Story of My Life* (New York: Charles Scribner's Sons, 1932), 75–76.

15. Goffman, *Asylums*, 168.

16. Cynthia Fuchs Epstein, *Women in Law* (Urbana: University of Illinois Press, 1993).

17. Geertz, *Interpretation of Cultures*, 205.

APPENDIX

1. These jokes come from http://www.re-quest.net/g2g/humor.

2. Ellis Cose, ed., *The Darden Dilemma: Twelve Black Writers on Justice, Race, and Conflicting Loyalties* (New York: Harper Perennial, 1997).

3. Ibid.

4. Ibid., vii.

5. Christopher Darden, quoted ibid., vii–viii.

6. Ibid., viii.

7. Ibid.

8. Barney G. Glaser and Anselm L. Strauss, *The Discovery of Grounded Theory: Strategies for Qualitative Research* (New York: Aldine de Gruyter, 1967).

9. "Master status" refers to how others perceive a person's primary identification. For the development of this concept see Everett Hughes's essays, "Dilemmas and Contradictions of Status" and "Social Change and Status Protest: An Essay on the Marginal Man," in *The Sociological Eye: Selected Papers* (New Brunswick, N.J.: Transaction Press, 1971), and Elijah Anderson, *Streetwise* (Chicago: University of Chicago Press, 1990).

10. See Mark D. Hayward et al., "The Significance of Socioeconomic Status in Explaining the Racial Gap in Chronic Health Conditions," *American Sociological Review* 65 (2000): 910–930, for a discussion of the social conditions of disease.

11. See Carolyn M. Aldwin, *Stress, Coping, and Development: An Integrative Perspective* (New York: Guilford Press, 1994).

12. As indicated in chapter one, note 14, only 17 percent of California attorneys are non-white, in a state where the minority population is 53.7 percent. African Americans make up 6.4 percent of California's population, but only 2.4 percent of its bar. (A greater discrepancy is found in the state's Latino population, which is one-third of the state's population, while only 3.7 percent of California's attorneys are Latino.)

13. Erving Goffman, *Asylums* (Chicago: Aldine Publishing, 1961).

14. Debra E. Meyerson and Maureen A. Scully, "Tempered Radicalism and the Politics of Ambivalence and Change," *Organization Science* 6 (1995): 585–600.

Bibliography

Aldwin, Carolyn M. *Stress, Coping, and Development: An Integrative Perspective*. New York: Guilford Press, 1994.

American Bar Association, "A Snapshot of Women in the Law in the Year 2000," www. abanet.org. (2002).

Anderson, Elijah. *Streetwise*. Chicago: University of Chicago Press, 1990.

Becker, Howard S. "Practitioners of Vice and Crime." In *Sociological Methods: A Sourcebook*, edited by Norman K. Denzin. New York: McGraw-Hill, 1978.

Berger, Bennett M. *The Survival of a Counterculture: Ideological Work and Everyday Life Among Rural Communards*. Berkeley: University of California Press, 1981.

———. *An Essay on Culture: Symbolic Structure and Social Structure*. Berkeley: University of California Press, 1995.

Billig, Michael. *Ideology and Social Psychology*. Oxford: Basil Blackwell, 1982.

Billig, Michael, et al. *Ideological Dilemmas: A Social Psychology of Everyday Thinking*. London: Sage Publications, 1988.

Blumer, Herbert. *Symbolic Interactionism: Perspective and Method*. Berkeley: University of California Press, 1969.

Bourdieu, Pierre. *Outline of a Theory of Practice*. Cambridge: Cambridge University Press, 1977.

California Bar Association, "Bar Demographics Are Shifting Slowly," www.calbar.ca.gov (2001).

California, State of. *The Standard Penal Code with the Evidence Code and Selected Penal Provisions*. New York: Matthew Bender, 1998.

Clark, Candace. "Emotions and Micropolitics in Everyday Life: Some Patterns and Paradoxes of Place." In *Research Agendas in the Sociology of Emotions*, edited by Theodore D. Kemper. Albany, N.Y.: SUNY Press, 1990.

Collins, Patricia Hill. "Learning from the Outsider Within: The Sociological Significance of Black Feminist Thought." *Social Problems* 33 (1986): 514–532.

Connell, R. W. *Gender and Power*. Stanford: Stanford University Press, 1987.

Cose, Ellis, ed. *The Darden Dilemma: Twelve Black Writers on Justice, Race, and Conflicting Loyalties*. New York: Harper Perennial, 1997.

Cotterrell, Roger. *The Politics of Jurisprudence: A Critical Introduction to Legal Philosophy*. Philadelphia: University of Pennsylvania Press, 1992.

Darrow, Clarence. *The Story of My Life*. New York: Charles Scribner's Sons, 1932.

Denzin, Norman K. *Symbolic Interactionism and Cultural Studies: The Politics of Interpretation*. Oxford: Blackwell, 1992.

Durkheim, Emile. *Moral Education*. 1906. Reprint. New York: Free Press, 1961.

———. *The Division of Labor in Society*. 1893. Reprint. New York: Free Press, 1984.

———. *The Elementary Forms of Religious Life*. 1912. Reprint. New York: Free Press, 1995.

Epstein, Cynthia Fuchs. *Women in Law*. Urbana: University of Illinois Press, 1993.

Ewing v. California, 123 S.Ct. 1179 (2003).

Festinger, Leon. *A Theory of Cognitive Dissonance*. Evanston, Ill.: Row, Peterson, 1957.

Garfinkel, Harold. *Studies in Ethnomethodology*. New York: Prentice Hall, 1967.

Geertz, Clifford. *The Interpretation of Cultures: Selected Essays*. New York: Basic Books, 1973.

Gilligan, Carol. *In a Different Voice*. Cambridge: Harvard University Press, 1982.

Glaser, Barney G., and Anselm L. Strauss. *The Discovery of Grounded Theory: Strategies for Qualitative Research*. New York: Aldine de Gruyter, 1967.

Goffman, Erving. *The Presentation of Self in Everyday Life*. Garden City, N.Y.: Doubleday, 1959.

———. *Asylums*. Chicago: Aldine Publishing, 1961.

———. *Interaction Ritual: Essays on Face-to-Face Behavior*. New York: Pantheon Books, 1967.

———. *Strategic Interaction*. Philadelphia: University of Pennsylvania Press, 1969.

———. *Frame Analysis: An Essay on the Organization of Experience*. Boston: Northeastern University Press, 1974.

———. In *The Goffman Reader*, edited by Charles Lemert and Ann Branaman. Malden, Mass.: Blackwell Publishers, 1997.

Granfield, Robert. *Making Elite Lawyers*. New York: Routledge, 1992.

Granfield, Robert, and Thomas Koenig. "The Fate of Elite Idealism: Accommodation and Ideological Work at Harvard Law School." *Social Problems* 39 (1992): 315–331.

Guinier, Lani, Michelle Fine, and Jane Balin. *Becoming Gentlemen: Women, Law School, and Institutional Change*. Boston: Beacon Press, 1997.

Haraway, Donna. *Simians, Cyborgs, and Women: The Reinvention of Nature*. New York: Routledge, 1991.

Hayward, Mark, et al. "The Significance of Socioeconomic Status in Explaining the Racial Gap in Chronic Health Conditions." *American Sociological Review* 65 (2000): 910–930.

Hochschild, Arlie Russell. "Emotion Work, Feeling Rules, and Social Structure." *American Journal of Sociology* 85 (1979): 551–575.

———. *The Managed Heart: Commercialization of Human Feeling*. Berkeley: University of California Press, 1983.

Hughes, Everett. *The Sociological Eye: Selected Papers*. New Brunswick, N.J.: Transaction Press, 1971.

Kairys, David. *The Politics of Law: A Progressive Critique*. New York: Pantheon Books, 1990.

LaFree, Gary. "Too Much Democracy or Too Much Crime." *Law and Social Inquiry* 27 (2002): 875–902.

Lively, Kathryn J. "Reciprocal Emotion Management." *Work and Occupations* 27 (2000): 32–66.

Lockyer v. Andrade, 123 S.Ct. 1166 (2003).

Loseke, Donileen R., and Spencer E. Cahill. "The Social Construction of Deviance: Experts on Battered Women." *Social Problems* 31 (1984): 296–310.

MacKinnon, Catharine A. *Toward a Feminist Theory of the State*. Cambridge: Harvard University Press, 1989.

———. "Feminism, Marxism, Method, and the State: Toward Feminist Jurisprudence," and "Feminism, Marxism, Method, and the State: An Agenda for Theory." In *Feminist Legal Theory: Foundations*, edited by D. Kelly Weisberg, 427–453. Philadelphia: Temple University Press, 1993.

Marx, Karl. *The Marx-Engels Reader*, edited by Robert Tucker New York: Norton, 1978.

Matoesian, Gregory M. *Reproducing Rape: Domination through Talk in the Courtroom*. Chicago: University of Chicago Press, 1993.

Mannheim, Karl. *Ideology and Utopia: An Introduction to the Sociology of Knowledge*. New York: Harcourt Brace Jovanovich, 1985.

Martin, Susan Erhlich. "Police Force or Police Service? Gender and Emotional Labor." *Annals of the American Academy of Political and Social Science* 561 (1999): 111–126.

Martin, Susan Erhlich, and Nancy C. Jurik. *Doing Justice, Doing Gender: Women in Law and Criminal Justice Occupations*. Thousand Oaks, Calif.: Sage Publications, 1996.

Mead, George Herbert. *On Social Psychology*. Chicago: University of Chicago Press, 1956.

Messerschmidt, James W. *Masculinities and Crime: Critique and Reconceptualization of Theory*. Lanham, Md.: Rowman and Littlefield, 1993.

Meyerson, Debra E., and Maureen A. Scully. "Tempered Radicalism and the Politics of Ambivalence and Change." *Organization Science* 6 (1995): 585–600.

Mies, Maria. *Patriarchy and Accumulation on a World Scale: Women in the International Division of Labour*. London: Zed Books, 1991.

Pierce, Jennifer L. *Gender Trials: Emotional Lives in Contemporary Law Firms*. Berkeley: University of California Press, 1995.

Rhode, Deborah L. *Professional Responsibility: Ethics by the Pervasive Method*. Boston: Little, Brown, 1994.

Rubin, Lillian B. *Families on the Fault Line*. New York: Harper Perennial, 1995.

Sampson, Edward E. "Cognitive Psychology as Ideology." *American Psychologist* 36 (1981): 730–743.

Siemsen, Cynthia. "Negotiating Ideals: Women in the Line of Criminal Defense Duty." Unpublished paper presented at the ninety-third American Sociological Association meeting (San Francisco, Calif., August 21–25, 1998).

Sprague, Joey, and Mary K. Zimmerman. "Overcoming Dualisms: A Feminist Agenda for Sociological Methodology." In *Theory on Gender/Feminism on Theory*, edited by Paula England, 255–280. New York: Aldine de Gruyter, 1993.

Stowe, Harriet Beecher. *Uncle Tom's Cabin*. New York: MacMillan Publishing, 1994.

Strauss, Anselm L., and Juliet Corbin. *Basics of Qualitative Research: Grounded Theory Procedures and Techniques*. Newbury Park, Calif.: Sage Publications, 1990.

Sutton, Francis X., et al. *The American Business Creed*. Cambridge: Harvard University Press, 1956.

Weber, Max. *Economy and Society*, edited by Guenther Roth and Claus Wittich. Berkeley: University of California Press, 1978.

West, Candace, and Don Zimmerman. "Doing Gender." *Gender & Society* 1 (1987): 125–151.

Wharton, Amy S. "The Psychological Consequences of Emotional Labor." *Annals of the American Academy of Political and Social Science* 561 (1999): 158–176.

Williams, Raymond. *The Long Revolution.* New York: Columbia University Press, 1961.

Wishik, Heather Ruth. "To Question Everything: The Inquiries of Feminist Jurisprudence." In *Feminist Legal Theory: Foundations*, edited by D. Kelly Weisberg, 22–31. Philadelphia: Temple University Press, 1993.

Young, Iris M. *Justice and the Politics of Difference.* Princeton: Princeton University Press, 1990.

Zimring, Franklin E., Gordon Hawkins, and Sam Kamin. *Punishment and Democracy: Three Strikes and You're Out in California.* New York: Oxford University Press, 2001.

Index

African Americans: and community loyalty, 110–11, 117, 183–84; conservative family values of, 178, 180, 181, 193–94, 205
alienation, emotion work and, 163–64
Anderson, Turner, 174, 176, 199–200, 201
Andrade, Leandro, 20, 211–12n.31

Barker, Ralph Sonny, 151–52
battering, emotional, 155–56
Berger, Bennett, 10, 25, 27–29, 34, 212n.9
Billig, Michael, 29
Black Panther Party, 120
Bryant, Ray, 173, 176, 181; background of, and social distancing, 201–3; cases preferred by, 203–4; and Constitution, 201; pivotal case of, 205; and professional duty, 207; and racial disparities in sentencing, 204–5
burnout, 109, 157

California: breakdown of mental health system in, 100; three-strikes law in, 18–20, 150, 211–12n.31, 214n.5
California Penal Code, Section 667, 214n.5
California State Bar, 210n.18
California Supreme Court, 153
Carr, Rose, 118, 153; and assignment of cases, 122–23; background of, 15, 119–20; cases refused by, 121–22; and fairness, 125–27; and feminism/public defender dilemma, 161; identity transformation of, 169; ideological work of, 165–66; "impossible" cases, 123–25; motivation of, 120–21
character evidence, indirect, 124
child abuse, and emotional trials, 63, 123–24
child molestation, 76; attorneys as victims of, 81; and distancing of client from crime, 147–48; and emotional trials, 81–84; and women defense attorneys, 129–30

Child Protective Services, 76
children, cross-examination of, 133
civil rights movement, 137, 151
client/defendant: and attempts to minimize sentence, 56–58; and attorney identification with victim, 62; disagreeable, 131–32; distancing of, from crime, 147–48; gender and defense table seating arrangement, 73–74; identification with, 85, 104–6, 123, 129–33, 147–49, 150, 167; indigent vs. paying, 138–39; informing of sentence, 19–20; kindness toward, 108–9; men of color prosecutors and, 179, 182, 194–95; mentally ill, 98; notoriety of, 75; power over, 46–47; private practice and, 117; rights of, as career motivation, 142–43; sharing emotions with, 47–48; as societal victim, 74–75, 104–6, 148–49, 167, 197, 215–16n.5; suicide of, 145, 215n.4 (Ch.5); verbal harassment by, 48–49, 56–57, 83; women defenders refused by, 131–32
Clifford, Stan, 174, 176, 198–99, 200–201, 207
cognitive dissonance, 209–10n.12
community: loyalty to, as career motivation, 110–11, 117, 183–84; public defender culture as, 133–34, 137
compartmentalization, 7, 52–53, 72–73
Constitution: defense of, as rationalization, 135–36, 138, 142–43, 158; men of color prosecutors and, 198, 201. See also right to representation
convictions, erroneous, 132–33
Cose, Ellis, 175–76
Cranfield, Robert, 35
criminal justice system: criminal defense culture as subsidiary of, 17; cruelty of, 109; and emotional conflict, 146–47; faith in, as con-

criminal justice system *(cont.)*
flict resolution, 55–56; homophobia in, 52–53; ideology/identity/emotions in, 35–37; inequality in, 21–22, 119; men of color prosecutors and, 207; politics and, 99–100; race and, 86; racial/ethnic minorities in, 217n.9; seasoned women defenders and, 167–68; and societal membership, 41; and victimization, 199
criminal lawyers, public stereotypes of, 174–75
critical legal studies (CLS), 30–32, 212n.18, 215n.11
cross-examination: of children, 133; of victim, 61, 82, 83–84, 149–50
crying, in courtroom, 67–68, 105–6

Darden, Christopher, 175–76
Darden Dilemma, The (Cose), 175–76
Darrow, Clarence, 158, 168, 216n.8 (Ch.5)
date rape, 85, 136
Davis, Richard Allen, 18–19
death-penalty cases, 72, 75–76, 155
Debs, Eugene, 216n.8 (Ch.5)
defendant. *See* client/defendant
Denzin, Norm, 17
depression, 106; postpartum, 123
dirty work, 9, 209n.5
district attorney: attorney contempt for, 101–2; and cross-examination of victim, 82; as moral adversary, 100–101. *See also* men of color prosecutors
DNA evidence, and erroneous convictions, 133
domestic violence cases, 68, 85; and emotional trials, 114–15; men of color prosecutors and, 195–96, 199
drug dealers, refusal to defend, 115–16
dualisms, gendered, 17
Durkheim, Emile, 216–17n.13

Egan, Iris, 110, 115, 153, 167
emotion: display of, in courtroom, 67–70, 101, 105–6; ideology and, 6–7, 9–10, 25–26, 27; in justice system, 35–37; men of color prosecutors and, 176–77; and professional duty, 58–59; work ethic and, 88, 92
emotion management. *See* emotion work
emotion work: defendant as societal victim,

74–75; definition of, 10–11; distance from client, 46–49, 125; effects of, 163–65; gender and, 17, 211n.27; hierarchical nature of, 33; humor as, 154; identification with victim, 43–46, 83–84, 133, 141–42, 143; and identity transformations, 38; ideological work and, 21, 34, 165–66; ideology and, 32–35, 161–62; and "impossible" cases, 124; maintaining objectivity, 49–50, 76, 144; of men of color prosecutors, 189, 197; moral work as, 170–71; private practice and, 115; and right to representation, 58; seasoned women defenders and, 146; sentencing, 50, 96–97. *See also* specific attorney
emotional conflict: gender/sexual orientation and, 59, 64–65; identity and, 209–10n.12; justice system and, 41, 146–47; men of color prosecutors and, 177, 183–84, 189, 198–99, 206–7; right to representation and, 63; and unfair sentences, 121. *See also* feminism vs. public defender role, moral dilemma of
emotional trials: and identity transformations, 169; "impossible" cases, 102–4, 123–25; of men of color prosecutors, 185–87, 200–201; physical effects of, 42–43, 163; private practice and, 113. *See also* specific attorney
Epstein, Cynthia Fuchs, 9, 209n.7
equality: feminism and, 6–7, 161–62; ideology and, 21–22; seasoned women defenders and, 119; and socioeconomic status, 89–90
ethnography, ideological dilemmas of, 28–29
evocation, 33
Ewing, Gary, 20, 211–12n.31
extortion cases, and emotional trials, 149–50

fairness: vs. letting guilty go free, 126–27, 134–35; in sentencing, 67–69, 96–97, 100–101, 121, 124–25
feeling rules: hierarchical nature of, 33; ideology and, 34; women defenders and, 11
feeling work, 28, 212n.9
feminism: and equality, 6–7, 161–62; as rationalization of conflict, 20–21
feminism vs. public defender role, moral dilemma of: and compartmentalization, 52; Constitution and, 135–36; emotion work and, 125–26, 161–63; and interview ques-